HORIZONS IN FEMINIST THEOLOGY

HORIZONS IN FEMINIST THEOLOGY

IDENTITY, TRADITION, AND NORMS

Edited by
Rebecca S. Chopp
and
Sheila Greeve Davaney

FORTRESS PRESS
MINNEAPOLIS

HORIZONS IN FEMINIST THEOLOGY
Identity, Tradition, and Norms

Cover design: Patricia Boman
Interior design: The HK Scriptorium

Library of Congress Cataloging-in-Publication Data

Horizons in feminist theology : identity, tradition, and norms /
    edited by Rebecca S. Chopp and Sheila Greeve Davaney.
        p.   cm.
    Papers from the Conference on Feminist Theology and the Role of
Theory, held in 1994 at the Iliff School of Theology, Denver, Colo.
    Includes bibliographical references.
    ISBN 0-8006-2996-5 (alk. paper)
    1. Feminist theology—Congresses. I. Chopp, Rebecca S., 1952–
. II. Davaney, Sheila Greeve, 1949– .   III. Conference on Feminist Theology
and the Role of Theory (1994: Iliff School of Theology)
BT83.55.H66   1997
230'.082—dc21   97-26135
                                                                              CIP

The paper used in this publication meets the minimum requirements of American National Standard for Information Sciences—Permanence of Paper for Printed Library Materials, ANSI Z329.48-1984.

Manufactured in the U.S.A.   AF 1-2996
01   00   99   98   97   1   2   3   4   5   6   7   8   9   10

Contents

Contributors   vii

1   Introduction
    Sheila Greeve Davaney   1

2   Identity, Feminist Theory, and Theology
    Linell Elizabeth Cady   17

3   Women's Experience between
    a Rock and a Hard Place:
    Feminist, Womanist, and *Mujerista* Theologies
    in North America
    Serene Jones   33

4   Seeking and Sucking:
    On Relation and Essence in Feminist Theology
    Catherine Keller   54

5   The Self between Feminist Theory and Theology
    Thandeka   79

6   Contesting the Gendered Subject:
    A Feminist Account of the *Imago Dei*
    Mary McClintock Fulkerson   99

7   THE BODY POLITIC VS. LESBIAN BODIES:
    Publics, Counterpublics, and the Uses of Norms
    Janet R. Jakobsen   116

8   BAD WOMEN:
    The Limits of Theory and Theology
    Paula M. Cooey   137

9   BECOMING AN AMERICAN JEWISH FEMINIST
    Laura Levitt   154

10 A HISTORY OF OUR OWN:
    What Would a Feminist History of Theology Look Like?
    Sheila Briggs   165

11 SOCIAL THEORY CONCERNING
    THE "NEW SOCIAL MOVEMENTS" AND
    THE PRACTICE OF FEMINIST THEOLOGY
    Kathryn Tanner   179

12 CONTINUING THE STORY, BUT DEPARTING THE TEXT:
    A Historicist Interpretation of Feminist Norms
    in Theology
    Sheila Greeve Davaney   198

13 THEORIZING FEMINIST THEOLOGY
    Rebecca S. Chopp   215

NOTES   232

INDEX   260

Contributors

Sheila Briggs teaches at the University of Southern California. She is the author of a number of articles and audio recordings on feminist theology and feminist history.

Linell Elizabeth Cady teaches modern Western thought at Arizona State University, where she has served as chair of the Religious Studies Department. She is author of *Religion, Theology, and American Public Life*.

Rebecca S. Chopp is Academic Dean and Professor of Theology at Candler School of Theology, Emory University. She is author of *The Power to Speak: Feminism, Language, God* and *The Praxis of Suffering: An Interpretation of Liberation and Political Theologies*. She is coeditor, with Mark McClain Taylor, of *Reconstructing Christian Theology*.

Paula M. Cooey teaches modern religious thought and theology at Trinity University, San Antonio. She is author of *Family, Freedom, and Faith: Building Community Today* and *Religious Imagination and the Body: A Feminist Analysis*. She is coeditor, with J. B. McDaniel and William R. Eaken, of *After Patriarchy: Feminist Transformation of the World Religions*, and coeditor, with Sharon A. Farmer and Mary Ellen Ross, of *Embodied Love: Sensuality and Relationship as Feminist Values*.

Sheila Greeve Davaney teaches theology at Iliff School of Theology. She is author of *Divine Power: A Study of Karl Barth and Charles Hartshorne* and is coeditor, with Dwight N. Hopkins, of *Changing Conversations: Religious Reflection and Cultural Analysis.* She is also editor of *Theology at the End of Modernity* and *Feminism and Process Thought.*

MARY MCCLINTOCK FULKERSON teaches theology at the Divinity School, Duke University. She is author of *Changing the Subject: Women's Discourse and Feminist Theology.*

JANET R. JAKOBSEN teaches ethics at the University of Arizona.

SERENE JONES teaches theology at the Divinity School, Yale University. She is author of *Calvin and the Rhetoric of Piety* and coeditor, with Rita Nakashima Brock and Claudia Camp, of *Setting the Table: Women in Theological Conversation.*

CATHERINE KELLER teaches theology at the Drew Theological School and Drew University. She is author of *From a Broken Web: Separation, Sexism, and Self* and *Apocalypse Now and Then: A Feminist Guide to the End of the World.*

LAURA LEVITT teaches at Temple University. She is author of *Jews and Feminism: The Ambivalent Search for Home* and is coeditor, with Miriam Peskowitz, of *Judaism since Gender* (forthcoming).

KATHRYN TANNER teaches theology at the Divinity School, University of Chicago. She is author of *God and Creation in Christian Theology: Tyranny or Empowerment?* and *The Politics of God: Christian Theologies and Social Justice.*

THANDEKA has taught at the University of San Francisco and Williams College. She is author of *The Embodied Self: Friedrich Schleiermacher's Solution to Kant's Problem of the Empirical Self.*

CHAPTER I

INTRODUCTION

Sheila Greeve Davaney

IN THE FALL of 1994 a group of scholars came together at the Iliff School of Theology in Denver to discuss recent developments in feminist theory and their relation to and role in feminist theological reflection. The idea for the conference grew out of a chance conversation between the eventual conveners of the meeting, myself and Rebecca Chopp, at the annual meeting of the American Academy of Religion the previous year. During that conversation we each remarked about our own interest in theoretical issues and our desire to find a location to pursue in depth questions that were emerging under the interdisciplinary rubric of feminist theory. We were particularly concerned with how feminist theologians and thinkers in related fields in the study of religion were appropriating, challenging, and contributing to the central debates that have been taking place among women in other disciplinary locales.

From that conversation plans for the "Conference on Feminist Theology and the Role of Theory" emerged. Linell Cady, of Arizona State University, and Paula Cooey, of Trinity University, joined the steering committee that designed and directed the meeting. The overriding concern that shaped the work of the committee was the strong sense that feminist theology has embarked on a new stage of development, one characterized by increasing diversity in theoretical perspectives. While women engaged in theology have begun to attend to the diversity of race, cultural and social location, and sexual identity, that we are locating ourselves in a number of different theoretical locales out of which we are developing our constructive theological proposals has yet to receive sustained attention. Thus this conference sought to focus attention on the debates within feminist theory and feminist theologians' relation to them.

This weekend-long exchange of views was, therefore, not intended as an all-embracing conference on feminist theology. Many important issues were left unattended. Moreover, many women who are engaged in other kinds of creative theological work were not among the participants. Instead, this meeting had the specific purpose of bringing together a collection of women who, while quite different in many respects, shared an interest in theory. The participants delivered papers, debated, and criticized one another. Out of this intense process the present volume took shape.[1]

Why focus on theory at this time in feminist theology's history? Why is this an important topic to pursue at this particular juncture? The role theory should play in feminist thought has been a contested issue for a number of years. Many feminists, along with other contemporary scholars, have raised questions about theory's "totalizing" tendencies, the ease with which it moves to general claims, its mirroring of male theories, and its abstract quality. Moreover, theoretical debates, with their methodological overtones, seemed to many to distract us from the pressing work of substantive proposals and constructive agendas. Hence, feminist thought, including feminist theology, has often exhibited an indifference to theoretical issues or even an antitheoretical tone or orientation.

While feminists have at times eschewed "grand" theories, for many years fundamental theoretical assumptions have been shared by many, though certainly not all, feminists. When assumptions are accepted and functioning well they are rarely the object of debate; they are taken for granted and not seen as one set of possibilities among competing ones. Other issues come to the fore and focus the work of thinkers in particular disciplines. As long as feminist thinkers worked with assumptions about women's nature, experience, ways of knowing and being that were broadly compelling both within particular intellectual disciplines and across them, then the drive for theoretical clarity was muted. Thus not only did many feminists question theoretical tendencies but, at the same time, the very theoretical assumptions and frameworks that in fact shaped our work went unacknowledged and unexamined because they were not viewed as problematic.

In recent years much of this has changed. Many feminists, including the contributors to this volume, have been exploring theoretical issues and rehabilitating the category of theory in general. These thinkers concur with the widespread disaffection toward ahistorical claims to truth or theoretical posturing that asserts universal validity. But we have come to recognize that our positions nonetheless bear operative assumptions and that these assumptions reflect, contribute to, and are often embedded within wider theoretical frameworks. The refusal to engage in theoretical reflection does not make these implicit and explicit theories and premises disappear with some magical sleight of hand; it only allows them to continue operating without critical scrutiny. For the feminist thinkers represented in this volume, a turn to theory is not a covert return to the grand theories of old but a commitment to a critical analysis that seeks to make clear the often implicit and unacknowledged presuppositions that shape our feminist proposals.

This commitment to critical analysis is also propelled by the recognition that underlying premises and theoretical frameworks are not neutral descriptions or valueless suppositions. Rather they harbor normative implications; they commend one way of proceeding rather than another; they body forth some values over others; they set certain agendas and deny the legitimacy of differing ones. As Rebecca Chopp states in her conclusion to this volume, "The importance of theory consists of its staging the problems and possibilities of politics, culture, and subjectivity." And as Kathryn Tanner's article, "Social Theory concerning the 'New Social Movements' and the Practice of Feminist Theology," notes, "These theories amount, therefore, to a specific recommendation from among alternative existing practices. . . ." Trafficking with theory is thus not, for the contributors to this volume, an exercise in abstract thinking, disengaged from the real concerns of feminist work, but the self-conscious attempt to confront and take responsibility for the assumptions we hold and the repercussions that flow from them.

In all this a new way of viewing theory has been emerging. Theoretical reflections and the frameworks within and through which they are articulated no longer appear as grand schemes with universalistic pretensions. Instead, theory has come to be interpreted as a heuristic device that clarifies presuppositions, gives a better grasp of the issues involved in feminist debates, locates feminist thought in relation to other theoretical proposals, and explores the repercussions of varying feminist frameworks. Theories and the assumptions that underlie them are thus contingent hypotheses, constructed not found, that need to be tested and continually revised.

As stated above, when there is more or less general agreement (there is never total agreement in any context and there certainly was never unanimity within feminist contexts) on assumptions and frameworks, then these often do not command our attention. Today there is less and less agreement as once-assumed categories have become problematic and been contested across the feminist landscape. Indeed even the term *feminist* has been repudiated by many women and replaced by terms and categorizations that individuals and groups assert reflect their particular reality more accurately.[2] North American women of color, women from the Two-Thirds World, lesbians, working-class women, and women of varied religious heritages are only some examples of those who have rebelled against the premises and the classificatory systems that once seemed so obvious to those women in the vanguard of feminist thought. What many thought was once an at least loosely unified feminist political movement and intellectual perspective has now emerged as multiple, contending, and not easily reconciled views and commitments. It is this fragmentation of feminism that has provided the central impulse for the turn to theory and the critical evaluation of our frameworks and assumptions.

But if the fragmentation of feminist thought and political solidarity has moved many women to theoretical considerations, this renewal of interest in theory has not lessened our differences nor reconstituted a once again unified movement. Instead it has intensified the issues before us, especially as it has centered attention on those assumptions and theoretical underpinnings that held the most widespread credence in earlier feminist thought. In particular, the tendency of many feminists, including many feminist theologians, to refer to *woman* or *women* as unified, inclusive concepts and, predicated on those notions, to appeal to women's experience as the source and norm of feminist thought has come under severe challenge. Moreover, what once looked like an adequate response to criticisms of these concepts and categories, an additive or cumulative strategy whereby more and more women and their experiences were appended to or folded into these categories, is now also being called into question as another tactic that may intend an inclusive feminism but fails to account for radical differences in power, experience, and commitments among women. At many locales on the feminist spectrum, therefore, the very notions of woman and women's experience have now been called into question and, with them, the whole edifice of feminist commitments and strategies. Feminist theorists across contemporary intellectual disciplines are engaging these issues, articulating various versions of such theoretical developments, and constructing new feminist positions predicated on altered assumptions about female subjectivity and identity, historical situatedness and particularity, and the possibility and modified nature of normative claims and commitments.

This volume examines these theoretical changes and their impact on and within feminist theology. The articles are located at the juncture of feminist theory, broadly conceived, and feminist theology. The authors engage not only earlier feminist theological efforts but feminist theory as it is taking shape in other intellectual disciplines such as philosophy, the social sciences, cultural studies, and history. They thus seek to situate feminist theology within the context of ongoing feminist theological reflection and the larger theological debate today but also, significantly, to locate these theological discussions within the parameters of feminist theory.

The relation of feminist theological reflection to feminist theory as it is being articulated in other disciplines is an important but not fully resolved issue. There is little doubt that feminists in other academic fields entered the theoretical fray earlier than feminist theologians. There is now a large and rich body of work, across numerous disciplines, focused on the very issues that are beginning to preoccupy feminist theologians in greater numbers.[3] Thus there is a sense in which, at this juncture, the work of feminist theologians is parasitic of the ideas, debates, and critical work already carried out by scholars in other fields. These articles do, indeed, reflect this fact. They refer to, appropriate for their own purposes, and depend on arguments developed in other contexts. But the thinkers represented in this volume do not intend to merely borrow others' theoretical positions. They not only engage theoretical perspectives developed elsewhere but contend with the issues concerning the status and function of theory itself and offer constructive proposals of their own to the debate. By doing so the authors seek to be informed by discussions in other disciplinary locales, but also to bring feminist theology into those conversations as a partner and constructive contributor.

Bringing feminist theological reflection into these debates is no easy matter, however. This is so not only because feminist theologians have, for the most part, been reticent to engage in theoretical discussions of the type that have characterized other disciplines. It is also the case that theology and the study of religion in general have at best been ignored and at worst repudiated as legitimate disciplines in much of the academy, including among scholars interested in feminist issues. Adding to this dismissal of scholars of religion, especially theologians, by many in the academy is the prevailing lack of interest in religion as a significant topic for analysis. Feminist theory replicates the indifference found in the broader academy.

A perusal of the works in feminist theory will quickly demonstrate that the topic of religion and scholarly work on religion, including feminist theology, are generally absent. This absence is the norm not only for fields such as philosophy, whose relation with religious and theological studies has been long, complex, and increasingly tension-filled, but also for new areas of scholarship such as cultural studies. The latter includes an enormous expanse of human practice in its scholarly reach, especially in terms of popular culture. Yet somehow religion escapes the attention of much of the field, including consideration by feminists. The authors in this volume seek, therefore, not only to fill a lacuna within feminist theology, but also to challenge our colleagues in feminist theory in other disciplines to see religion as an important subject for study and to acknowledge us as scholars with particular expertise in an area of great importance for interpreting the condition of women, and as full partners in contemporary feminist discussions.

In part, then, this volume is an attempt to turn the attention of other feminist theorists to the arena of religion and the concrete reality of religious persons' lives. The absence of these dimensions of women's reality often seems the result and perpetuation of a blindness and elitism within feminist theory itself that, while eschewing claims to objectivity, dismisses religious belief and practices as outmoded and subjective, and reflection about them as nonacademic. Paula Cooey focuses on this gap in feminist theorizing by accentuating the importance of including religion within the scope of feminist theory, arguing that religious teachings and practice play a vital role, for good or ill, in the production of culture. To neglect the arena of religious beliefs and practices misses a significant means through which culture and, with it, female identities and experiences are constructed. If feminist theorists are really to engage women's concrete existence, then religious beliefs and practices, too, must be analyzed, and not only negatively as atavistic and inherently oppressive male creations, but also as they in fact exist for numerous women as sites of life-giving and transformative meaning and action.

This call to include religion in the purview of feminist theory certainly does not rule out critical reflection on religious beliefs and practices. Nor does it privilege or protect feminist theological claims from the scrutiny of other theorists. Certainly feminist scholars of religion, including theologians, have done our share of critical analysis of religion and theology, including the problems within our own feminist approaches. But this call does suggest that if feminist scholars in religious and theological studies can benefit from the work in other disciplines, then these, too, need to include religious beliefs and practices as significant domains of analysis. Moreover, it also contends that the most fruitful exchanges among feminist scholars do not rule out ahead of time mutually enhancing conversation but are open, on all sides, to the insights and challenges particular disciplines and perspectives bring to the table.

While the thinkers writing for this volume share the conviction that both theology and its subject matter, religious beliefs and practices, should not be ignored by feminist theorists in other fields, they exhibit no unity concerning what positions are most compelling, either in terms of issues common to feminist theoretical discussions across the disciplines, such as the nature of subjectivity, or in relation to matters particularly pertinent to religious or theological studies. The articles found here reflect varying and distinctive locations on the theological spectrum; their authors espouse different methodological and constructive agendas and are identified with a variety of different theological approaches. Moreover, on particular topics of concern to feminists these thinkers also cover a broad range of possible positions reflecting and contributing to the diversity of contending perspectives. Hence when feminist theologians seek to become partners in theoretical discussions they do so not of one voice but out of the same cacophony of possibilities that characterize other disciplinary locations.

These articles enter the theoretical debate at a number of different points. The conference out of which they came was organized around three issues—subjectivity, normative criteria, and the nature, status, and function of historical traditions. However, while thinkers primarily addressed one subject matter or another, certain concerns emerge over and over again in almost all of the articles.

In particular, the same question that has vexed feminist theorists in other disciplines emerges as central here as well, and that is how to rethink subjectivity or identity in the face of the dissolution of feminists' historical appeal to women's experience. As Sheila Briggs and Catherine Keller note in their articles, "Subjectivity is 'on trial.'" The articles by Linell Cady, "Identity, Feminist Theory, and Theology," and Sheila Davaney, "Continuing the Story, but Departing the Text," sketch how female identity and experience have functioned in feminist theology and theory until recently. Both articles detail the problematic nature of earlier claims; Davaney focuses on theology's long-held assumption of common experience shared by all women, and Cady analyzes the developments within modern and postmodern forms of feminist theories more broadly conceived, in which modern notions of unified selfhood are oddly mirrored in the postmodern dispersal of the self. Serene Jones's article, "Women's Experience between a Rock and a Hard Place: Feminist, Womanist, and *Mujerista* Theologies in North America," offers an ambitious and critical examination of current conflicting proposals among feminist theologians as they reconceive women's experience out of differing contemporary theoretical assumptions. All three articles press the constructive point that, not only have earlier understandings of subjectivity and its attendant notion of experience been rendered questionable by virtue of their now discounted universalism and hidden essentialism, but many of the options vying for allegiance on the current scene are equally problematic. Each moves toward an alternative that seeks to hold together the radical historical character of subjectivity and the possibility for individual agency and corporate solidarity.

Other authors, too, raise pressing concerns related to the issues of subjectivity and identity. Catherine Keller and Thandeka, each in her own way, criticize the widespread tendency among feminist theorists, including theologians, to focus and theoretically build their cases on the notions of difference and separation. If feminist thought was, it now seems, wrongheaded in its early assumptions of commonality and unity, its current singular attention on particularity and its relentless drive to divest itself of all essentialism or universalism have also resulted in theoretically problematic and practically deleterious results. Keller, in "Seeking and Sucking: On Relation and Essence in Feminist Theology," and Thandeka, in "The Self between Feminist Theory and Theology," argue that we need interpretive frameworks that make sense of particularity without eschewing our connectedness to one another and to a broader web of reality. For Keller, feminist theologians, eagerly appropriating theoretical positions that are *au courant* in other venues today, stand in danger of articulating a postmodern discourse of the carnivalesque in which pluralistic autonomy reigns and no one is responsible to anyone else. Keller urges us to attend more closely to the theoretical company we keep and to become accountable for the concrete repercussions of our theoretical choices. For her part she calls for the articulation of a social ontology that "supports practices of normative mutuality between subject and subject." Keller claims such a social ontology is not (though Jones's article claims it is) a return to an ahistorical foundationalism but a theoretical rendering of subjectivity that accounts for both connectedness and particularity, for relationality as well as "the fluidity characteristic of postmodern subjectivity." The alternative, Keller's position implies, is not the absence of ontology but one that assumes and reinscribes new forms of individualism and leaves us unaccountable to those outside our local context. Thus Keller urges us, especially as theologians, to overcome our theoretical reticence and to set forth interpretations of subjectivity and experience that enhance the possibility of more global accountability and contribute to what she terms an "ethical mutuality."

Keller also suggests that while we attend to how we are constituted by cultural and linguistic formations, we must also recognize that we negotiate our world nondiscursively, and that it is not only though speech and linguistic constructions that mutuality is mediated. Thandeka echoes both the concern for an ontology that is not predicated, often unknowingly, on separation and for the body as a site of knowledge, connectedness, and relationality. She asserts that our failure to take the latter into consideration leads us to such an extreme emphasis on difference that feminist solidarity becomes difficult to defend. Thus she calls for feminists to rethink the link between body, mind, and world and through a dynamic, nondualistic rearticulation of embodied selfhood to affirm unity and relationality at the core of human experience. Beginning our theoretical reflection on subjectivity with the body, understood as "site and sign of human knowledge," will enable us, Thandeka argues, to avoid a still-prevalent dualism that continues to infect our theoretical positions, though in postmodern guise.

Both these positions run counter to a number of developments in feminist theory, especially those connected with negative judgments concerning the possibility of ontological claims. Each assumes that we should acknowledge that we have working or functional ontologies and that we need to ask what our theories include or exclude, including such important elements as the body. And both are self-consciously aware of the fact that theories reflect and, in turn, support or hinder concrete practices of solidarity or separation. Thus each author unabashedly contends for her own version of a social and relational ontology that she believes will better support the broad web of interconnections of which we are a part and to which we are accountable.

If Thandeka and Keller ask, in part, what is excluded from our theory, other articles also raise the issue of exclusion in different ways. In "Contesting the Gendered Subject: A Feminist Account of the *Imago Dei*," Mary McClintock Fulkerson turns to the question of the destabilized subject and to the contention that this subject is always a product of an ongoing process of exclusion. She, like all the thinkers in this volume, argues that identity is not just the function of some positive or unchanging essence. Rather she, like others, contends that identity is wrought in the midst of multiple cultural and natural relations. However, finding post-structuralism more helpful than several other theorists represented here, she emphasizes the poststucturalist claim that identity is also the product of what, at any moment, is excluded, what is left outside, what is left unsaid. It is not only what is given in each moment that constitutes us but what is denied, who is rendered invisible or unacceptable. By turning to the excluded, Fulkerson does not think feminist theory and practice are lost in an endless swirl of difference in which women are now pitted against one another and all hope of solidarity is foregone. Instead, she utilizes the recognition that identity is always the result, not only of inclusion, but exclusion, to reinvigorate both feminist theology and theory as "social-change practices." Such recognition can, in particular, lead us to a critical practice of continually asking who and what are left out in any claim we espouse, any norm we set forth, any theological vision to which we commit ourselves. Hence the theoretical acknowledgment of exclusion can entail the critical practice of continual questioning. Fulkerson thus pushes us to theorize the gaps, what we have failed to say when we think we have said it all.

Janet Jakobsen is also interested in what our constructs of subjectivity and identity include in bestowing legitimacy on certain subjects, and what they exclude in rendering others invisible or demonizing them. Her article, "The Body Politic vs. Lesbian Bodies: Publics, Counterpublics, and the Uses of Norms," considers how lesbian bodies function in relation to a supposedly inclusive public realm. In particular, she examines the complex processes by which minority groups are constructed and the insidious manner in which groups, such as African Americans and lesbians, are then pitted against one another in the struggle to gain legitimacy. Jakobsen notes the obvious fact that these categories do not exclude one another and analyzes how such a denial is embedded in the construction of societal norms, which then encourage minority groups to distance themselves from other groups for fear of losing their acceptable status. Jakobsen further explores not only how dominant discourses operate between groups but also *within* communities to domesticate and control behaviors in the quest to gain entrance into the body politic. For Jakobsen the central task then for lesbian, feminist, and queer movements is to construct effective counterpublics challenging these mechanisms of containment and exclusion.

Paula Cooey argues, in her article, "Bad Women: The Limits of Theory and Theology," that one of the issues feminists have failed to theorize about adequately is the moral ambiguity of all subjectivity. She suggests that this absence relates to a continuing bifurcation in feminist theory, in which women are divided into categories of agents and victims. Women, when they perform according to our feminist dictates, are agents, capable of self-directing and creative action. Women, when they fail to live up to our expectations, are violent, or act destructively must, according to feminist versions of the world, be victims. They are not responsible agents acting out of their capacity for freedom but somehow have been stripped of their agency, and hence are not responsible for their behavior. The larger culture also splits women into groups of good women, who live up to societal expectations, and bad women, those who do not act according to the norms of the dominant society. In this case, however, the splitting does not render women victims if they do not live up to society's expectations but blames and damns these women. Moreover, these societal demarcations closely reflect other distinctions, such as class differences, that function in the covertly normative discourse of our society. Cooey argues strongly that feminist theory must avoid its own dualistic renderings of women if it hopes to counter society's division of women into those who are acceptable and those who are "bad." In particular, we must, she contends, listen with care to the very women we have excluded from our theories or have rendered in one-dimensional terms as victims or, at best, as survivors of victimization. Only from attention to these voices can we reconfigure our understandings of female subjects as morally ambiguous, capable of using our capacity for agency for both good and bad purposes, never totally free but likewise never shorn of all moral capacities. We must, she tells us, forego the easy path of claiming that women are exclusively victims or demons or morally good agents. When we interpret ourselves or others in such unambiguous terms we contribute, albeit unwittingly, to the cultural construction of woman as good or bad that then functions to keep *all* women in our place.

Cooey, Fulkerson, and Jakobsen all speak to what is left out of feminist theory and dominant discourses. Several other articles question not how to theorize the excluded but how to understand the manifold character of women's identities. Cady, Davaney, and Levitt all assert that women do not possess a nature common to all females nor an individual identity that is unified and stable, a self that has an unchanging core that then undergoes experiences. Cady proposes that in letting go of notions of a unified self we must also avoid simply mirroring its opposite, offering ideas of subjectivity or identity so dispersed that they lack even temporary coherence. Moreover, she suggests that such a view of the subject as utterly dispersed is closely linked to consumer capitalism in which our historical location and, with it, bonds of responsibility are erased. Instead, she argues for a historicized notion of the subject in which identity is "constituted by the subject's creative, agential negotiation of the intersecting currents and competing loyalties that run through her."

Davaney's article also articulates notions of historicized subjectivity. In this view, we are synthetic selves whose identities emerge out of the commingling of varied, contradictory, and always plural influences. Such composite selves are neither the unified essentialist selves of modernity nor the curiously similar disconnected subjects of much postmodern lore. Instead, historicized subjects are continually constituted by the creative interplay of inheritance, contexts, and agential negotiation that results in historically particular identities and experiences. In this approach antiessentialism does not imply antirelationalism, and contextuality and agency are not opposites but two interconnected dimensions of historical existence.

If Cady and Davaney offer theoretical portrayals of plural subjectivity, Laura Levitt's article, "Becoming an American Jewish Feminist," embodies this multiple, even fragmented identity in the most concrete terms. A Jewish woman in a liberal society that has granted her admission at the cost of downplaying her Jewishness, someone who has been raped and experienced the undoing of even the fragile momentary unity of a self, a white feminist aware of both her alienation from and embeddedness within her religious tradition and of her implication in the realities of racism and classism—as each and all of these Laura Levitt asks how she can re-create an identity out of the fragments, how she can find home. Levitt's article not only "performs" what it means to be a nonunified self, but she also indicates what direction women must go in re-creating home as both the reconstruction of individual identity and the remaking of community. We cannot, she makes abundantly clear, return to some safe haven, for there never was one. We can only piece together the bits and pieces of our histories, putting them to new uses in a continual process of renegotiating identity, community, and home. Such a home is the site, Levitt tells us, of "many conflicting desires." It is a place where "some things are lost while others are gained," a place of bitter legacies and fragile hopes. It is finally how and where we continually remake ourselves.

If one of the tasks before us is not the recovery of a stable, given identity but the creative negotiation of ever-changing ones, then the question of how we are to understand, utilize, and negotiate with those multiple traditions that form our historical inheritance becomes crucial. Kathryn Tanner and Sheila Briggs take up this issue from differing locations. In her article, "A History of Our Own: What Would a Feminist History of Theology Look Like?" Briggs enters the debates concerning feminist historiography. Importantly, she links the discussions about what it means to recover women's histories to the arguments about female subjectivity. What is it we seek to recover when gender appears as a construct and women shatter into an endless plurality? Briggs argues that feminist historians should not out of hand dismiss the categories of women or women's experience as analytical tools. Instead we must critically deploy them, recognizing their constructed and limited character. In particular, Briggs notes that the use of these analytical tools has resulted in, as she puts it, women "doing all the work of gender." Women become "the bearers and markers of gender difference" while men continue to function as the universal and unmarked human. Moreover, Briggs suggests that another limit often attends historiographical approaches focused on the history of women or women's experience; these approaches lead feminist historians, often helpfully, to search out women's presence in historical traditions, seeking to recover what has been ignored or lost. But Briggs admonishes us, saying that "the history of women is also the history of the exclusion of women." What is required, she asserts, is a feminist interpretive strategy that can function where women are not present and can utilize analytical tools to uncover how gender operates even when its supposed carriers are nowhere to be found. Thus a feminist history of theology would attend not only to where women are found in a religious tradition and to doctrinal statements directly concerned with women. It would turn as well to those places where women are not mentioned but where gender is constructed nonetheless. In all this Briggs urges feminist historians to develop theoretical models that not only aid the reclamation of a history in which women were always present but that also aid the nuanced analysis of our absence, though not the absence of gender, in the construction of social and personal reality.

In her article, "Social Theory concerning the 'New Social Movements' and the Practice of Feminist Theology," Kathryn Tanner also explores the terrain of religious traditions and their role in feminist reflection. Tanner sets forth her position by articulating a political theory of culture. Drawing on the work of Marxist and poststructuralist theorists, Tanner develops a view of culture as the site or domain of struggle over symbolic resources. Culture is not a stable deposit of agreed-upon meanings or values; rather it is a dynamic sphere or ongoing process in which competing meanings and values circulate, conflict, and seek to gain ascendancy. If human subjectivity and identity are not stable, as so many thinkers in this volume contend, neither is the cultural context within which such selves take shape.

Tanner asks about the implications of this political interpretation of culture for theology in general and especially for feminist theology. She argues that in this view religion and theology become subspecies of culture in general, and hence are part of the ongoing production of and struggle over cultural resources. As such, neither religious beliefs nor practices nor theological interpretations of them offer settled or exhaustive meanings, but rather temporary and contested ones. The task of the theologian thus centers on the elucidation of these cultural elements and, importantly, on the construal and reconfiguration of these symbolic resources for concrete purposes. That is, the theologian becomes, for Tanner, a player in an ongoing cultural struggle, not an isolated thinker dealing with timeless truth or even settled historical meanings.

Feminist theology takes, for Tanner, a particular posture. Feminists should not assume the givenness of the various religious traditions we have inherited. Instead we should see these historical lineages as inherently unstable sets of resources, lacking essences or fixed meanings that can be aligned with either oppressive orientations or feminist political agendas. Moreover, Tanner argues that these resources are most effectively commandeered when a group appears to be in continuity with those traditions rather than in critical disjunction. Thus Tanner argues for the "strategic importance for feminist theology of remaining traditional" and contends that "the more feminist theologians use for their own purposes the cultural elements that have been appropriated by patriarchal interests the greater the feminist claim on theological credibility, and the harder it is for the feminist agenda to be dismissed by those committed to the dominant patriarchal organization of theological discourse."

For Tanner, then, feminists interested in furthering cultural change should attend closely to the roles religion and its theological offspring play in the production of societal and cultural organization. Feminist theologians, in particular, should not give up the inheritance of our traditions but do battle for them as the resources for change they are. We should not do this because our traditions are inherently liberating but because they are unstable and thereby available for multiple uses, including feminist ones. The past thus takes on, in this view, not an intrinsically authoritative status but a strategically authorizing function that, when deployed, enhances the possibility for feminists to compete successfully in the production of cultural meanings and values.

While a number of articles indicate the important function of the past in the constitution of the present, there is virtually a unanimous rejection of the past as the site of normative criteria. The majority of articles stress that the present is the locus of our normative judgments, that we are responsible for the content and character of our criteria, and that finally we must evaluate the adequacy of our claims, not by whether they cohere with an authoritative past, but by how they contribute to or constrain the creation of more viable cultures, societies, and communities. Thus, not only do these articles stress that religious beliefs, practices, and theological claims are formed for practical purposes but that our evaluative criteria are also, as Rebecca Chopp notes in her conclusion, pragmatic in character. Even Tanner's strong emphasis on the importance of tradition flows not from an argument about the authority of the past or a desire to cohere with origins or sources, but out of a sense of how cultural struggles are waged and won.

Many of these articles focus on issues of interest across disciplinary perspectives. But a number also ask explicitly about the repercussions for theology in light of the shifts in notions of subjectivity, traditions, historical inquiry, and so forth. Linell Cady and Sheila Davaney each suggest that, parallel to historicized notions of human subjectivity and identity, historicized conceptions of theological inquiry should emerge. This not only means that theology must forego its traditional quest for certitude and absolute truth, but that the elevated status that has so often attended a religious tradition's past, especially its classics or sacred scriptures, must also be denied. Instead the two authors push, like Tanner, for theology to be interpreted as a critical cultural practice in which theologians join the struggle for cultural resources. Significantly, both Cady and Davaney propose that the manifold character of our historically wrought identities suggests that theology cannot concern itself any longer with singular traditions. As Levitt argues that home is built out of the interaction of numerous inheritances and former homes and Davaney that individual and communal identities emerge, not within the confines of one tradition, but at the juncture of many, Cady calls for a theology that does not "privilege a single language in the formation of identity and the construction of a world" but rather attends concretely to "the multiple traditions and forces that are operative in shaping the lives of those to whom or about whom one is writing." Thus for a number of the writers in this book, feminist theology will be less interested in correlating its claims with the supposed essence of a tradition or even in relating exclusively or primarily to one particular tradition. While they may, à la Tanner, attempt to appropriate the past for present uses, the stakes they are playing for are thoroughly of the present.

On each of the issues attended to in these articles—the importance of theoretical clarity, subjectivity, the desirability of an ontology that supports accountability, moral ambiguity, the construction of the public sphere, multiple and contradictory identities, the nature and status of the past, the struggle for cultural resources, the location of norms, the task of theology—the authors set forth constructive positions that engage one another and demand attention, not only from other scholars in religious or theological studies, but also from thinkers in different academic fields. They do so, however, not in one voice; these articles do not exhibit a singular version of feminist theology nor a uniform theoretical stance. Indeed, their theoretical explorations raise profound questions about such a project. Moreover, these articles are not all written in the same register or style; some are very concrete, while others tend toward the abstract; some invoke the personal while others range more broadly. In both their theoretical and their stylistic diversity they assert the value and right of feminists to speak in different voices.

In many ways, this volume is one example of the coming of age of a new generation of feminist theologians. Deeply indebted to earlier work, sometimes in profound agreement with earlier claims but often at odds with what has gone before, it sets forth new directions for feminist theologies and suggests new alliances not only within theology but, significantly, with feminists theorizing in other fields. Perhaps most significant, it proclaims to us that, as there is no common women's experience or nature, neither is there a single feminist viewpoint nor one acceptable feminist mode of expression. In that proclamation these articles embody the most important element in concert—a commitment to feminist theology as always emergent, self-consciously critical, and thereby eminently revisable.

CHAPTER 2

Identity, Feminist Theory, and Theology

Linell Elizabeth Cady

TRACKING THE TRANSFORMATIONS within feminist theory in the past few decades is both interesting and useful. It not only reveals a great deal about the controversies within and surrounding the feminist movement, but it provides a good vantage point for viewing the ongoing contestation between modernism and postmodernism within theoretical debates and the larger culture. Perhaps most important, however, the argumentative battles within recent feminist theory have helped produce an alternative to the modernist and postmodernist visions that is, in my judgment, very compelling. Insofar as this alternative lacks a common label, its presence fades into the prior oppositional encounter between modernism and postmodernism. This nascent vision rests on a reconceptualized notion of identity, with implications for interpretations of the self, collectivities, and rationality. This emerging alternate construal of identity raises some interesting questions about the nature of theological reflection.

My aims in this paper, then, are twofold: first, I will attempt to sketch out the contours of this embryonic vision, setting it against the backdrop of the more clearly defined modernist and postmodernist alternatives. Second, I want to consider what changes in theology might be needed to accommodate this emerging construal of personal and collective identity.

Feminist Construals of Identity

The emergence of a reconceptualized notion of identity can be most easily traced and identified by situating it against the backdrop of the modernist/postmodernist debates that have preoccupied much recent feminist theory. Although the contrast between modernism and postmodernism does not, significantly, illuminate the whole feminist terrain, it is useful in sorting out some of the major alternatives, particularly in regard to the notion of identity. Linda Alcoff's article, "Cultural Feminism versus Post-structuralism: The Identity Crisis in Feminist Theory," is particularly helpful in mapping much recent feminist theory on this issue. She argues that since the late 1970s there have been two primary responses in feminist theory to the question of women's identity, which she labels "cultural feminism" and "post-structuralist feminism." "Briefly put," she writes, "the cultural feminist response to Simone de Beauvoir's question, 'Are there women?' is to answer yes and to define women by their activities and attributes in the present culture. The poststructuralist response is to answer no and attack the category and the concept of woman through problematizing subjectivity."[1] In other words, cultural feminism embraces an essentialist definition of women, seeking to identify and revalue the nature and attributes of women that have been erased or denigrated within a patriarchal social order. The poststructuralist alternative has centered its attack on feminist essentialisms, contending that such positions fail to expose the way in which subjectivity and gender are themselves constructed. This failure, they argue, leads to the reinscription of the very structures and categories that are oppressive to women. Hence their efforts to resist the aura of permanence or givenness in reference to the subject and to gender require a deconstructive strategy.

I want to borrow and build on Alcoff's very instructive analysis of these two construals of identity that dominate feminist theory. Before looking more closely at the cultural and poststructuralist options, which I shall relabel essentialism and postmodernism, it is worthwhile to consider another variation on modernism that is typically called the liberal feminist alternative. After exploring these various constructions of the subject, we will be in a better position to trace the outlines of an emerging alternative that is indebted to though not locatable in either camp. It is this alternative, I would argue, that holds the most promise for resolving some of the conundrums that have emerged within feminism and feminist theory.

Liberal Feminism

It is important to consider the liberal feminist position even if it does not dominate current literature on feminist theory. It is the earliest version of feminism that emerged in the second wave of modern feminism, a feminism that appropriated, but gave a twist to, classical liberal theory. As such it was a decisive option against which much feminist theory developed, as feminists sought to articulate theories rooted within their own experience and struggle. In tracing the indigenization of feminist theory, it helps to see to what it was opposed. But there are other, more compelling reasons to consider liberal feminism. Remembering it as the earliest version of feminism obscures the fact that it remains the most culturally diffused version, the one that commands the greatest respect and allegiance from men and women alike. This point is, of course, due to the fact that liberal feminism is rooted in the modernist ideology of classical liberalism, the primary language of American culture. It expresses its dominant vision and values, and hence a feminism grafted onto this worldview will, not surprisingly, be more widely received.

The assumptions and strategies that underlie liberal feminism can best be illuminated by considering classical liberal theory more generally. Classical liberalism is a vision of self, society, and rationality that was forged against the backdrop of the religious wars of the sixteenth and seventeenth centuries. It was a vision driven by both irenic and emancipatory aims. The religious wars spurred efforts to develop a "neutral" secular language that could articulate the nature of society and the individual without recourse to sectarian religious beliefs. It is now clear that this secular language was anything but neutral; nonetheless its original posture as a neutral, objective alternative to the purported parochialism of the warring religious factions lent it a power that it still retains.

The primary accent in the liberal vision falls on the individual abstracted from the relations through time and space that in any way limit or define him or her. The freedom and autonomy of the individual self are inviolate. Society, according to classical liberalism, is a collection of autonomous individuals who possess idiosyncratic values and goals. It is not based on a shared vision of the good nor is it the product of any intrinsic connections among individuals. On the contrary, individuals "choose" to enter into a social contract for purposes of order and protection. As Iris Young explains, in this modernist ideology "the authentic self is autonomous, unified, free, and self-made, standing apart from history and affiliations, choosing its life plan entirely for itself."[2]

This vision of self and society rests on a sharp bifurcation between the private and public spheres. The drive to envision a cosmopolitan public that is free from the divisiveness of particular attachments and distinctions lies behind the sharp differentiation between that which is public and that which is private.[3] The public realm is constituted by individuals who are thought to share a common rational capacity that, if only theoretically and eventually, can yield consensus. The distinguishing marks of the person which identify him or her as a particular individual of a certain race, gender, class, or religion are in principle irrelevant within the public realm as well as for the exercise of our rational capacities.

Liberal feminism gains its leverage by underscoring the contradictions between liberal theory and the actual social order. The freedom, autonomy, and equality accorded individuals in the liberal vision are not socially embodied, thereby allowing liberal feminism to function as a critique of certain forms of social oppression. The feminist movement and the civil rights movement have both used this theory to expose and challenge the legal and political oppression of women and African Americans, as evidenced, for example, in the struggles for integration, androgyny, equal opportunity, and equal pay. Liberal feminism is rooted in the insight that the abstract individual and the cosmopolitan public of liberal theory were neither as abstract nor as inclusive as they postured.[4] Nevertheless, rather than undermine the framework of this theory, liberal feminism revises it in the interests of advancing the equality of women.

Essentialist Feminism

At the risk of oversimplifying, I would say that essentialist feminism evolves out of an increasing recognition of the thoroughly gendered character of liberal theory. The abstracted individual of liberal theory was increasingly seen as not just superficially male, but fundamentally so. The privileging of the autonomous individual over social relations, independence over dependence, rationality over feelings, and the mind over the body was simultaneously privileging that which was stereotypically male rather than female. Hence the abstracted individual could not include women too, unless women were willing to model themselves on the male stereotype. The recognition of the depth of the exclusion contributed to the turn to a distinctively female nature and experience. But the articulation of women as a distinct class, oppressed in a particular way by virtue of membership in that class, was an important plank in the development of a distinctive feminist movement and politics. Judith Grant in her recent work *Fundamental Feminism* argues that this need led to the identification of the essentialist category *woman,* and to an embrace of experience as that which can validate the feminist intuition regarding the oppression of women.[5] She suggests that the categories of woman and experience have served ever since as the fundamental and defining categories of feminist theory, generating many of the theoretical riddles with which it has struggled.

The political and cultural ramifications of essentialist feminism clearly differ from those of liberal feminism. Rather than embracing androgyny and formal equality, essentialist feminism motivates the turn to a separatist female culture responsive to women's needs, characteristics, and values. Explicitly rejecting the veil of neutrality that surrounds the liberal construal of the subject, essentialist feminism tags it as "male" and seeks to articulate its "female" counterpart. Significant effort has been directed to charting, for example, a distinctively female moral development or women's ways of knowing.[6] This work clearly contributes to combating the fictitious neutrality in the myth of liberalism which helps to secure its hegemony. However, it does so by duplicating some of the moves by which liberalism achieves its supposed unity and universality. The female subject purportedly shares a common identity with other women and a common experience of oppression. Built into essentialist feminism is the propensity to secure unity through abstract homogeneity, a procedure that reflects the same ahistorical tendencies of the alternative it rejects. Feminist theory, as Grant notes, "was becoming captured by the patriarchal ideas it sought to oppose. . . . It had created a stereotypical Woman, a monolithic, abstract being defined only by her source of oppression."[7]

A great deal has been written about the limitations of this version of feminism. The earliest and most influential writings were by women of color who challenged the homogeneous construal of identity and experience on which it was based. The feminist subject was exposed as an abstraction from the identity and experiences of white, well-off, typically heterosexual women, no more universal than the supposed liberal individual. As bell hooks explains:

> Simplistic definition of women's liberation is a dismissal of race and class as factors that, in conjunction with sexism, determine the extent to which an individual will be discriminated against, exploited, or oppressed. Bourgeois white women interested in women's rights issues have been satisfied with simple definitions for obvious reasons. Rhetor-

ically placing themselves in the same social category as oppressed women, they were not anxious to call attention to race and class privilege.[8]

Hooks captures the problem well in her remark: "To the bourgeois 'feminist,' the million-dollar salary granted newscaster Barbara Walters represents a victory for women. To working-class women who make less than the minimum wage and receive few if any benefits, it means continued class exploitation."[9] This critique magnified for feminist theorists the sharp differences among women, and was instrumental in the shift from a focus on a monolithic woman to a more particular identity. The homogeneity of the feminist subject and the commonality of oppression were undercut by a historicizing turn to identity.

The rapid development of cross-cultural gender studies has further contributed to shaking the grounds of an essentialist feminism. As scholars have explored in detail the ways in which gender intersects with identity in cultures around the world, the ethnocentrism and imperialism of the essentialist feminist position have became more and more apparent. These challenges to "modernist" feminisms, however, were soon overshadowed by the emergence of postmodern feminist theory, setting up the reigning opposition, for which Alcoff uses other labels, between essentialist feminism and postmodern feminism.

Postmodern Feminism

It is intriguing to observe the way in which these two orientations mirror each other, with postmodernism accentuating the extreme that is most different from feminist modernisms. Hence in place of a unified subject, postmodernism speaks of the multiplicity, even fragmentation, within the subject. Identity is not homogeneous but destabilized, revealed as the site of a contestation of multiple, conflicting discourses. The accent on the multiplicity of conflicting discourses and practices that constitute the subject often tends toward the collapse of the subject into these social/cultural currents, making it difficult if not impossible to account for agency. So, too, the challenge to the epistemological status of the experience of the subject moves toward a radical skepticism regarding the ability to make normative judgments.

Scholars have begun to explore the link between an emerging postmodern identity and the spread of consumer capitalism and modern technologies in the past few decades. Kenneth Gergen, for example, argues that the dissolution of the self that marks postmodern identity is largely a "by-product of the century's technologies of social saturation."[10] Rather than living primarily within a local horizon, individuals are increasingly exposed to a much wider array of images, goods, symbols, and peoples that destabilize the self. The ensuing multiplicity within the self correlates with a perceived loss of norms with which to adjudicate the competing perspectives and values that now constitute the self. Sharing the assumption that a postmodernist identity is linked to the development of new discursive mediums in popular culture, Ann Kaplan uses the MTV video to analyze its form.

> What characterizes the postmodernist video is its refusal to take a clear position vis-a-vis its images, its habit of hedging along the line of not communicating a clear signified. In postmodernist videos . . . each element of a text is undercut by others: narrative is undercut by pastiche; signifying is undercut by images that do not line up in a coherent chain; the text is flattened out, creating a two-dimensional effect and the refusal of a clear position for the spectator within the filmic world. This leaves him/her decentered, perhaps confused, perhaps fixated on one particular image or image-series, but most likely unsatisfied and eager for the next video where perhaps closure will take place.[11]

Postmodernist tendencies within the culture, and the theory which takes account of them, accentuate the continual play of images in an everchanging present, resulting in a "disappearance of a sense of history."[12] The connections across time that sustain the identity of the individual and the group are under siege, as narrative gives way to pastiche. Identity is subject to fragmentation, and the political and normative voice is muted as the individual loses a sense of location from which to speak.

An Emerging Historicist Alternative

The postmodernist construal of identity is clearly responsive to social, cultural, and technological developments of the past few decades. It is just as obviously an exercise self-consciously carried out to end the long reign of the modernist paradigm, thereby accounting for its tendency to mirror the latter. The emerging feminist alternative, to which I alluded earlier, is seeking to appropriate the insights of the postmodern critique without embracing the ahistorical, apolitical, relativistic propensities that it harbors. It is an alternative that can be discerned in the writings of such theorists as Linda Alcoff, bell hooks, Jane Flax, Susan Bordo, Teresa de

Lauretis, and Minnie Pratt.[13] It is distinguished, in my view, by a commitment to a historicist perspective that seeks to situate the individual within a particular social and historical location. The specificity of discourses and practices is, in this approach, critical to an excavation of the subject which turns out to be multiple, though not necessarily fragmented. Reflecting this historicist sensibility, Judith Butler reflects on the limitations of the category woman:

> If one "is" a woman, that is surely not all one is; the term fails to be exhaustive, not because a pregendered "person" transcends the specific paraphernalia of its gender, but because gender is not always constituted coherently or consistently in different historical contexts, and because gender intersects with racial, class, ethnic, sexual, and regional modalities of discursively constituted identities. As a result, it becomes impossible to separate out "gender" from the political and cultural intersections in which it is invariably produced and maintained.[14]

However, recognizing this point does not necessarily lead to the conclusion that gender, or the category woman, is a fiction, a form of nominalism that Alcoff argues epitomizes the poststructuralist vision. Such a conclusion glosses over much too quickly the biological/cultural specificities that mark the individual as a particular person in a particular time and place. Alcoff rightly notes that "the rejection of subjectivity, unintentionally but nevertheless, colludes with [the] generic human thesis of classical liberal thought, that particularities of individuals are irrelevant and improper influences on knowledge."[15] A historicist construal of identity rejects the abstract, unified subject of modernism. But it does so without embracing its mirror opposite. It recognizes that identity is multiple, fluid, and shifting, but for all that, it is not fictitious, ephemeral, or limitless. Identity is still bounded, constituted over against that which is different. While it is multiple and tensive, perhaps even contradictory, all differences do not lie within its domain. Identity is constituted by the subject's creative, agential negotiation of the intersecting currents and competing loyalties that run through her.

A historicist lens is best equipped for exposing the overlap between personal and collective identities. In other words, it can highlight the traditions of thought and practice that the self has made its own to varying degrees. This locates the self within social groups which themselves have distinctive corporate identities, with distinguishing patterns of practice and thought. A historicist perspective makes clear that the self does not

IDENTITY, FEMINIST THEORY, AND THEOLOGY

precede social groups, or in any way stand isolated or insulated from them. On the contrary, membership in such groups constitutes personal identity in very basic ways. The ideology of modern liberalism in collaboration with the forces of consumer capitalism has conspired to obscure and weaken these collective bonds. As Cornel West puts it, "A culture and society centered on the market, preoccupied with consumption, erode structures of feeling, community, tradition."[16] Postmodernism can be seen as feeding into this same trajectory insofar as it pursues a deconstructive strategy that perpetually destabilizes the self. While this focus does capture an important insight into the provisional and shifting nature of identity, it fails to account for the equally important integrating moment in identity which renders it sufficiently stable and enduring to be differentiated from another. Neither the modernist nor the postmodernist construal of identity adequately illuminates the bonds through time that provide historical specificity and limitations to the self, and render fitting the ascription of corporate identities.

A historicist perspective also underscores the point that identity is not given; it is continually achieved in and through the specific ways in which the self negotiates the multiple, contesting currents and loyalties that constitute her. As B. Honig expresses it, the "multiple self is . . . the site of a struggle that is quieted, temporarily, each time the self acts and achieves an identity that is a performative production."[17] Hence identity is not the stable coherent base of actions; on the contrary, the multiple self "seeks its . . . episodic self-realization in action and in the identity that is its reward."[18] The multiplicity of the self can function as both a source of paralysis when feelings of ambivalence predominate, as well as the source of creativity when tensions, even conflicts, demand a performative resolution.

A historicist view of the self and a performative construal of identity help to combat the tendency to see either the self or the social groups to which it belongs as static, homogeneous, or epistemically privileged. At the heart of personal and collective identity is a perennial "rewriting" that is responsive to the changing historical and social contexts within which one is embodied. This rewriting includes, though is not limited to, the telling and retelling of personal and collective narratives which situate the individual and the group in a historical and social web. As George Lipsitz, who has written on the relationship between collective memory and identity, notes, "What we choose to remember about the past, where we begin and end our retrospective accounts, and who we include and exclude from them—these do a lot to determine how we live and what decisions we make in the present."[19] Such acts of memory are political and moral strategies that simultaneously weave personal and collective identity.

The negotiation of identity can be far more strenuous, of course, in practice than in theory, where one need not traffic with the pain, confusion, ambivalence, guilt, and regrets that attend its enactment. On the other hand, it is important to recognize that not all individuals experience this subjective vertigo to the same degree. As noted above, there is considerable evidence to suggest that this may well be a peculiarly, if not exclusively, modern affliction, reflecting the pluralism of modern societies which have effected what Peter Berger calls the transition from "fate to choice." Sociologist of religion Hans Mol argues similarly that it is only in highly advanced modern societies that "over-choice and consequent indeterminacy of a given focus of identity arise." It is only in such societies, he argues, that "the finding of an ever-changing identity becomes a major psychological enterprise."[20] Certainly even within modern pluralistic societies there is considerable variance in how much inner pluralism and disequilibrium any given individual is forced, able, or willing to tolerate. Indeed a major response to the increased pluralism and globalization of life in the late twentieth century has been a reassertion of tightly bounded personal and communal identities, what some have called tribalization. This makes clear that theorizing identity is not an ahistorical ontological exercise, nor a purely descriptive endeavor to explicate the nature of identity in a given time and place. Although adequate theory must take account of the enabling and constraining forces of what is the case, there is a clear normative dimension to the construction of identity that is fitting and appropriate to the times.

Implications for Theology

This brief sketch of shifts in feminist theory reveals that constructions of identity serve as cornerstones for more encompassing feminist theories. Not surprisingly, a similar relationship between the construal of the subject and a broader theoretical orientation obtains in theology. This reflects the paradigm-like character of these distinctive orientations, which are constituted by a complex of interlocking assumptions, ranging from the ontological to the epistemological. It is of particular importance for theology, in my judgment, to reflect on the form of theologizing that correlates with the historicist construction of identity that has begun to take shape in the writings of a number of feminist theorists. Does theological reflection assume a new form when identity is no longer understood in the abstract, essentialist mode characteristic of modernism? What shape does or should theology assume when it rests on a construction of identity that eschews both the modernist model for the subject and its mirror opposite, the fragmented deconstructed self of postmodernism?

George Lindbeck's theological typology in his book *The Nature of Doctrine: Religion and Theology in a Postliberal Age* provides a very helpful point of departure for exploring these questions. In this work he identifies and analyzes several theories of religion that embody strikingly different interpretations of the self, rationality, language, experience, and theology. The two theories that are particularly pertinent to the current discussion include, in Lindbeck's terminology, the "experiential-expressive" and the "cultural-linguistic"; the first reflects the modernist alternative and the second approximates the historicist alternative, as described above. Those who adopt an "experiential-expressive" approach, in his words, "locate ultimately significant contact with whatever is finally important to religion in the pre-reflective experiential depths of the self and regard the public or outer features of religion as expressive and evocative objectifications of internal experience."[21] There is an affirmation of a common religious experience available to the self apart from linguistic and cultural channels. Lindbeck compares this approach to a "cultural-linguistic" one, which construes religions as "comprehensive interpretive schemes." In his words, "like a culture or language, it is a communal phenomenon that shapes the subjectivities of individuals rather than being primarily a manifestation of those subjectivities" (33).

Lindbeck's influence has gone far beyond simply charting major theories of religion. His writings have been instrumental in moving theology beyond the modernist framework, and in establishing what he terms "postliberal theology" as the most widely embraced alternative to it. While other theologians have pursued the deconstructionist strategy in relationship to modernism, Lindbeck can be read, with some qualifications, as helping to forge a historicist alternative. This turn reflects a reorientation from religious experience to language and rhetoric. In other words, the move is from a largely ahistorical focus on individual religious experience to the social and discursive mediums that constitute that experience. This has refocused attention on the religious traditions and communities within which the individual is situated. The subject is no longer the abstract individual disembedded from local contexts, but a historical being whose identity, rationality, and sensibilities are constituted in and through temporal and social relations.

Although Lindbeck's move beyond modernism leads toward a historicist alternative, his postliberal theology does not fully reflect the historicist construction of identity that is emerging in feminist theory. There is considerable overlap, located in a common accent on the social and temporal embeddedness of the individual. Lindbeck, however, assimilates his historicist turn to a form of confessionalism by privileging a Christian grammar in the formation of self. He recognizes that contemporary life is marked by pluralism, by an ideology of the individual as functioning, even flourishing, apart from social collectives, and by the presumption that the eclectically choosing self is the prevailing norm. This situation makes it exceedingly difficult for religious communities to socialize individuals into the tradition, a process that is, Lindbeck suggests, akin to learning a language. It is also a key factor in the dominance of the experiential-expressive form of theology that is governed primarily by the quest for a satisfying "personal religious vision" (22). Despite this psychosocial context, or rather because of it, Lindbeck advocates a theology that locates itself squarely within the parameters of a textually based religious community. Such a theology is governed by allegiance to the intratextual, untranslatable specificity of its own scripturally based grammar (see 112–35). Hence Lindbeck writes: "What is important is that Christians allow their cultural conditions and highly diverse affections to be molded by the set of biblical stories that stretches from creation to eschaton and culminates in Jesus' passion and resurrection" (84). In other words, there is a "privileged interpretive direction from whatever counts as holy writ to everything else," which is tantamount to the theological "practice of absorbing the universe into the biblical world" (135–36).

Although Lindbeck's work is exceedingly illuminating about the theoretical limitations of theology conducted in a modernist key, his constructive alternative to it is also problematic in my judgment. He moves too quickly from a social and temporal construal of identity to the embrace of a single tradition as the cultural-linguistic medium that constitutes it. It is not that he denies the multiple sources of identity in contemporary life, but he refuses to make this empirical reality normative. In a real sense it constitutes the problem, and the solution is the turn to a particular community whose enduring grammar can socialize the self and secure a more harmonious, ordered life. In addition to these functional advantages of postliberal theology, it has the greatest capacity, according to Lindbeck, to preserve the "integrity of the faith" (134).

Lindbeck's postliberal alternative to modernism rests on the privileging of the Christian grammar, which alone sustains his leap from the pluralistic, eclectic context of contemporary life to the embrace of a particular community whose Sacred Scripture "defines being, truth, goodness, and beauty" (136). Although Lindbeck's constructive alternative reflects a historicist construal of the self, it is a historicism that has been married to a religious confessionalism. What form of theology would emerge if this bond were dissolved? If recent feminist theorists are correct in identifying the multiplicity within the self, then the critical problem is in negotiating the conflicting social and cultural trajectories that constitute the self. To choose a tradition in Lindbeckian fashion prematurely opts out of this negotiating process. It is to choose to become monolingual, after knowing how to speak multiple languages. Even if this is imaginable, it is not clear that it is desirable. Certainly a Christian feminist would resist the suggestion that the biblical text should always "trump" nonscriptural sensibilities or values. The reverse is also true, although perhaps it has been more difficult to concede, particularly when feminism positioned itself as the universal bearer of liberation rather than a particular tradition reflecting the interests of some, not all, women.[22] Again, the question is what form of theology is appropriate to a historicist orientation that refuses to privilege a single language in the formation of identity and the construction of a world.

In another context I have tried to identify a form of theology that accepts the historicist insight into the traditioned nature of life and thought without assimilating it to confessionalism.[23] The theologian, I suggested, is engaged in extending a tradition, seeking to articulate its most appropriate interpretation for a particular time and place. The process is akin to writing a chain novel; continuities are important but there is considerable creativity in writing the next chapter, and there is no essential core common to the entire text. Although this model of theology is, in my judgment, preferable to confessional historicism (postliberalism), I am less sanguine about its ability to take account of the multiplicity that has increasingly come to characterize identity in the modern age. Is this a sanitized historicism, a theological strategy that occludes the divergent currents that constitute the self? Further, does it paper over the extent to which communities and traditions are marked by dissonance and difference? Does it lend itself too easily to the presumption that individuals inhabit single communities, that traditions are monolithic?

The discipline of theology continues to reflect its origins as reflection on behalf of a particular religious community, what Anselm described as faith seeking understanding. Graduate training in theology remains wedded to a traditions model, with primary focus placed on gaining familiarity with the theological textual tradition. Religiously affiliated institutions typically hire theologians who will address audiences who share their religious heritage. What kind of theology would emerge if these institutional constraints were changed, and theologians attended more fully to the multiple social and cultural currents that constituted them? Escaping the grip of a single tradition need not necessarily lead toward the modernist focus on individual religious experience that is largely abstracted from a particular time and place. This is the type of theology that Lindbeck characterizes as "experiential-expressivism," and Delwin Brown has called "personal theology." The aim of personal theology, according to Brown, is the "development of a plausible and workable worldview for oneself."[24] Rather than focus on individual religious experience, or fashion a personal theological vision, I am suggesting that the theologian must be attentive to the multiple traditions and forces that are operative in shaping the lives of those to whom or about whom one is writing.

Generally speaking, theologians do not have much expertise in this domain.[25] Theologians are primarily trained to be philosophically sophisticated textualists, with the theological textual tradition as their primary datum. The analysis, assessment, and construction of arguments are central, as is command of the intellectual developments within a particular religious tradition. The contextualization of these texts receives little to no attention. Religious ideas as strategies with identifiable social effects do not really inform theological reflection. In short, one is trained to study the text, not the context, to construct a religious vision, not to investigate its reception or effects. Careful analysis of the economic, social, and political forces that shape contemporary society is not required. This prevents the theologian from addressing those currents that constitute identity, and hence insulates and isolates theology from the lived world. If the genre of theology is to be more reflective of the multiplicity that characterizes identity in contemporary, pluralistic cultures, then it must leave behind its rationalist abode that continues to reflect its authoritarian roots.

The failure to attend in a systematic fashion to the context renders much normative theological reflection irrelevant, if not counterproductive in its effects. Critical theory has raised a similar charge against philosophical and ethical thought, which rests on a separation of the *is* from the *ought,* and on a presumption that questions of the good life for the individual and society can be addressed abstractly without attention to what is the case. The result, as Seyla Benhabib expresses it, is a "normative naivete of evaluative theories prescribing an ideal ethics and an ideal politics" which can only be countered by the realignment of normative inquiry with the social sciences.[26] If "normative considerations, which are uninformed by a theory of present society, are futile," then theology clearly needs to incorporate a contextual focus if its contributions are going to be relevant and fitting.[27] With the rise of the social sciences and the academic study of religion, this focus can be far more systematic and disciplined than a theologian's intuitive grasp of what is going on in the culture.

Perhaps this point can be clarified by considering briefly the focus on community that dominates much theological reflection. Community is oftentimes advocated as an antidote to the individualism of modern life, as a template for the ideal ordering of social life, and proffered as an illuminating metaphor for understanding the divine. Its normative validity is all too often taken for granted, with little or no effort made to consider the way in which communities or discourse on communities actually function. Perhaps too there is a sense that utopian normative discourse is indisputably positive, perhaps ineffectual at worst.

But what might be missed by fixating too narrowly on the ideal, construed in isolation from the way things currently are? Consider the following sampling of relevant angles and questions. Some scholars have pointed to the way in which community correlates with the modernist construction of a coherent, unified subject. Communal pressures toward homogeneity are considerable and tend to undermine the freedom and creativity of the members. Moreover, because community is typically imagined as a relatively small group, in contrast to society, the ideal of community often functions more to strengthen the borders of particular groups than to facilitate the move toward a more universal community. The political economist Robert Reich, for example, has argued that the renewed focus on community in the past decade has been a dangerous and conservative ploy to limit the boundaries of solidarity and obligation.[28] Given economic and social realities in contemporary American society, the

embrace of community has functioned as a protective strategy to legitimate homogeneous units reflecting similarities in race, income, and education.

Or consider the work of Robert Fowler, who has explored the role and
function of religious communities in American liberal society.[29] He argues
that American religion in the twentieth century functions primarily to
reinforce American liberal society by serving as a needed haven from it.
Many people find in religious life the meaning, values, and community
lacking in the wider liberal society. But rather than challenge the liberal
order, religion primarily serves as a "temporary compensation" for it. By
functioning primarily as a haven, religion provides powerful reinforcement for the continuation of liberalism.

It is neither possible nor necessary in this context to consider the merits of these various contentions regarding the nature or function of community. Regardless of the validity of any one of them, however, they do
make clear that normative reflections on community fail to address more
contextually rooted analyses of the topic. The corrective to this failure lies
in addressing in systematic fashion the contours of the lived world within
which theological reflection is situated.

Theology would be more disposed to engage in this form of analysis
if it rested on a thoroughly historicist construal of personal and collective
identity. This means abandoning the presumption that personal identity
or communities or traditions are homogeneous or static. Individuals are
increasingly constituted by an array of practices, traditions, and collectives
that are continually negotiated in the ongoing project of selfhood. A
theology operating within this framework would avoid restricting itself to
a religious experience, the realm of religion, or the contours of an essentialized tradition, recognizing each of these as abstractions from the more
complex, messier tangle of lived experience. Although this model of theology would not be directly servicing a particular religious tradition, it
might well prove to be of greater service to the growing number of individuals who find themselves straddling and negotiating multiple streams
of interpretation and practice.

CHAPTER 3

Women's Experience between a Rock and a Hard Place

Feminist, Womanist, and *Mujerista* Theologies in North America

Serene Jones

THIS ESSAY IS DESIGNED to map out the different conceptual frameworks within which a new generation of North American feminist, womanist, and *mujerista* theologians are situating their constructive projects. Although there are, no doubt, a number of ways to draw this map, I have chosen to chart these theologians' positions by looking at the method-ological assumptions which have accumulated around their varied con-ceptions of women's experience. As an extremely open-ended category, *women's experience* serves as a useful starting place for mapping the theolo-gies in question because it functions as a theological flash point where one can see clearly both the similarities and the differences which mark their emergent perspectives.

In terms of their similarities, this new generation of texts represents the exciting culmination of the long struggle to place constructivist, nonessentialized understandings of *woman* at the center of theological reflection; and, as each of these texts illustrates, the fruits of this struggle are quite remarkable, opening these theological projects onto a richly tex-tured landscape where women's experiences are as multiple as their varied social locations, histories, and personal stories. At the same time, these theologians' shared affirmation of the nonessential nature of women is highly diversified with regard to the term *experience*—a notion which, in contrast to the term *woman*, remains methodologically essentialized by some while being radically historicized by others. On this score, there are thus significant philosophical differences between the texts, differences located in their disparate understandings of how one measures and defines this thing they call experience. Although much more should be said about the similarities between these texts, particularly their shared rejection of gender essentialisms, this essay focuses primarily on their differences, namely, their different theories of experience.

The map I have drawn to identify their varied theoretical perspectives divides roughly into two sides, the rock and the hard place. On the *rock* side, I place those theologians who continue to employ universalizing and/or ahistorical frames of reference to structure their accounts of human experience—the rock here referring to their penchant for analytic measurements which are solid, foundational, comprehensive in scope, and generalizable in character. In this context, I further identify three types of universalizing frames of reference: the *phenomenological* frame found in the works of Elizabeth Johnson and Catherine LaCugna, the *process/ psychoanalytic* frame developed in the writings of Rita Brock and Catherine Keller, and the *literary/textual* frame deployed in the analyses of Delores Williams and Sallie McFague. The advantages of these perspectives should be evident to those who engage their texts: the stability of their frameworks allows them to generate theological images which are resilient and visionary—no small accomplishment in a postmodern context. On the other hand, what they lose with this reliance on universalizing structures is, I will argue, a place for that which "does not fit," for the incommensurable experience, and thus for the marginal theological voice which defies the general and subsequently resists the closure of universal categorizations.

On the *hard place* side of the map, I locate the work of those theologians who self-consciously avoid universalizing gestures and opt instead for descriptions of experience which are historically localized and culturally specific. Here, I divide the map into two subgroups: those theologians who use the tools of *cultural anthropology* to localize experience, namely, Kathryn Tanner and Ada María Isasi-Díaz, and those who deploy *poststructuralist* gestures to uncover the play of language and power in the construction of identity, as seen in the work of Rebecca Chopp. This side is solid enough to be a hard place but its formulations are less stable than those of the rock. The challenges confronting those standing on such shifting ground are numerous: the status of normative claims, the limits and value of immanent critique, the viability of deconstructive rhetoric, and the still undecided fate of "truth" and its relation to doctrine.

As to which side of the map this essay favors, it will no doubt be obvious that my critiques of the rock are more forceful than my criticisms of the hard place. Let me say from the outset, however, that if this essay were focusing on the substance of the theological visions put forth by these texts, and not on their methodological appraisals of experience, my assessment would most likely be reversed, for it is clear that the six authors who fall on the rock side of the map take on substantive topics like embodiment and rework crucial doctrines like the Trinity with a theological boldness not yet found in the works of feminists located in the hard place. I therefore hope that my analysis and criticisms of these works will not be taken as a critique of their theologies as a whole, but rather as an attempt to map out the edges of a methodological chasm—between the rock and the hard place—which currently runs through our collective conversations, serving both as a divide that separates us and as a yawning gap which challenges us to daringly negotiate that still open space of "between."

The Rock

Phenomenological Accounts of Women's Experience

Let me begin with the universalizing (rock) side of the map by turning to two texts which announce a new generation of voices in Roman Catholic feminist thought: Elizabeth Johnson's *She Who Is: The Mystery of God in Feminist Theological Discourse,*[1] and Catherine Mowry LaCugna's *God for Us: The Trinity and Christian Life.*[2] Given the theological complexity and richness of both texts, it is difficult to limit my review of them to a discussion of their definitions of women's experience, for such a focus overlooks the enormity of their contribution to the fields of historical theology and contemporary Roman Catholic systematics. However, the advantage of focusing on their definitions of experience is that it highlights an aspect of their common heritage which is often overlooked in strictly doctrinal assessments of their work, namely, their shared commitment to the philosophical tradition of *continental phenomenology.*

What is significant about the fact that they both work out of this particular tradition? With regard to the question of experience, their commitment to engaging in phenomenological analysis points to their desire to describe women's experience by attaching it, at least partially, to a more general account of the basic structure of human experience. This attachment of women's experience to a broader phenomenology of the human is only partial, however, because both LaCugna and Johnson embrace a constructivist analysis of gender which rigorously avoids essentializing the term *women*. The same cannot be said for the term *experience,* which is described as having—in good phenomenological fashion—an "essential structure" replete with "universal features" and "constitutive dynamics."

When it comes to giving shape and contour to this essential structure, however, Johnson and LaCugna generate two very different descriptions: the former focuses on "the hoping subject" and the latter on "the radically relational self." In *She Who Is,*[3] Johnson presents an account of women's experience that is not only theologically insightful but poetically compelling, written in a language which invites the reader into an inclusive and hope-filled textual drama where God and the creature meet in an empowering embrace. Given that her feminist commitments are crafted into the very drama of this phenomenological account, her accomplishment in this regard is no small matter; she effectively writes a new script about personhood, history, and God, a script in which the insights of Paul Ricoeur, Karl Rahner, and Johann Baptist Metz are bound together and dramatically deepened by their encounter with feminism. This newly scripted theological anthropology also serves as the arena within which she introduces her readers to several major historical figures in Christian theology, bringing them as well into a reciprocally advantageous conversation with contemporary feminism. She further pulls into this drama of historical theology, continental philosophy, and feminist theory strands of the Sophia traditions in the Christian Scriptures. In the end, she leaves her reader with a complex and existentially compelling word about *She Who Is:* an "elusive female metaphor" which discloses "the mystery of Sophia-God as sheer, exuberant, relational aliveness in the midst of the history of suffering, inexhaustible source of new being in situations of death and destruction, ground of hope for the whole created universe. . . ."[4]

In Johnson's case, identifying the universalizing gestures which support the infrastructure of this project is not difficult; as I stated earlier, they simply come with her commitment to writing her new script of personhood in the language of phenomenology. Although these gestures are scattered throughout the text, they are most clearly evidenced at two points: first in her discussion of symbolic language and, second, in her description of essential human nature. With regard to the first (her analysis of the symbolic character of God-talk), she invokes Ricoeur's account of the mediating and paradigmatic function of image in experience and, in doing so, she also invokes his ontologically grounded hermeneutical understanding of how language as symbol acquires meaning. With respect to the second (her discussions of the human subject), she describes the frame of universal anthropology, wherein lie "essential features" and "anthropological constraints," which include not only the usual existential suspects but also a Rahnerian reference to an "orientation to hope and the pull of the future."

What is interesting about Johnson's invocation of these and other phenomenological "essentials" of human experience is that they stand side by side with her adamant refusal to essentialize woman and to eclipse thereby the multiple differences which structure the lives of women. In light of this refusal, one then wonders why the eclipses implicit in her structurally universal account of human experience and language are any less threatening to difference and particularity. In other words, why is her "universal subject" any less theologically suspect than the "universal woman" she so clearly rejects as essentialist? Given that feminist theorists have raised, in recent years, a number of critiques about the dangers inherent in this type of phenomenological universalizing—its resistance to racially historicizing identity, its idealist tendency toward expressive symbolism, and its potentially reductive drive to generate exhaustive accounts of experiential structures—Johnson's own use of feminist theory could be deepened by a response to such critiques. And with Johnson's facility for offering clear and accessible descriptions of theological problems, such a response would no doubt move us closer to understanding how one might deploy universalizing gestures or make generalizing statements without concomitantly invoking a conceptual apparatus which may be too restrictive and too totalizing to allow for the inclusiveness she so heartily applauds.

Within the category of phenomenological feminist theology, I also locate LaCugna's timely contribution to the unfolding renaissance of the doctrine of the Trinity in contemporary theology. Like Johnson, LaCugna falls into this category because she believes it is both possible and necessary to ground one's theological claims about the doctrine of God in a territory called "the universal structure of existence."[5] Unlike Johnson, however, she finds the territory traditionally occupied by the Western "subject" to be deeply problematic as well, both in terms of its investment in an individualized rhetoric of substance/being, and in its uncritical adherence to a notion of reflective consciousness. As a way of countering this view of the self, LaCugna positions her theological anthropology in another territory—one marked by a relational ontology in which "persons," not "subject," are conceived of in communal, nonsubstantive, dynamic, and agentic terms.[6] She develops this relational ontology by borrowing from and reworking several sources: the Trinitarian metaphysics of the Cappadocians, the agentic philosophy of John Macmurray, the neopatristic synthesis of Jean Zizioulas, the relational sensibilities of feminist thought, and the social-political analysis of liberation theology. When combined, these varied perspectives form a philosophical edifice which both sustains and is sustained by a doctrine of the Trinity wherein the event of communion—described as the perichoretic dance of divine persons—marks God's own being as agentic being-in-relation, being-in-communion, and being-for-us.

When it comes to defending the philosophical universals embedded in this creative account of "relational experience," LaCugna fends off prospective critics with a directness not found in Johnson. Her most decisive move in this regard is the assertion that her portrait of relational being reflects the dynamics of Trinitarian interrelatedness found in biblical and liturgical patterns of thought about salvation history. She thereby roots her analysis of being-in-relation in the language of historically particular communities of faith and not in the territory of an epistemically universal rendition of experience, a move which suggests that her philosophical commitments originate in communal narrative and are hence more pragmatic than philosophically foundational in character. As her description of being-in-relation unfolds, however, it often seems that it is a founding philosophical ontology and not a narrative scriptural drama which structures her analysis of both God-in-relation and persons-in-communion.

If this is the case, then LaCugna's text powerfully illustrates what is perhaps the most common universalizing tendency found in her generation of feminist theological writings: the tendency to critically dismantle the "modern subject" by positing a counterdiscourse in which relationality serves as the central organizing principle of one's theological anthropology—and in doing so, to posit *relationality* as the locus of a *new essence,* a new point around which the structural coherence of the subject (albeit a new subject-self-person) is secured. As a counterdiscourse to the old "essentialized subject," it is quite evident that this more relational framework works well as a means of conceptualizing women's experience in a more open-ended, historicized manner. There is, however, a double irony which attends this desire to open up the category *experience* by highlighting its essentially relational structure.

First, there is the ironic tension produced by the fact that, on the one hand, LaCugna remains committed to divesting the experiencing subject of its falsely inscribed borders and limits and to opening up theological anthropology to the coursing of history, difference, and community; and yet, on the other hand, she lifts these borders and removes these limits by positioning the experiencing self in an alternative structure called "relational ontology." As a universal structure, it thus continues to be a place where the chaotic tides of a thoroughgoing historicism are held at bay, where a new philosophical edifice called "relationality" holds back the potential of generating radically localized conceptions of experience and identity. It is also a place where the "unfitting"—the unmeasured, the marginal, and the silent—find a systematic home which ironically helps them "fit" into an inclusive understanding of community.

A second irony lies in that now old but still unsettling question: if women have long been cast as the bearers of being-in-relation, will ontologically valorizing what has been a "relational prison" really be liberating? With regard to this last question, LaCugna's discussion of "perichoresis"— the dance in which there is permeation without confusion—may suggest a way out of this prison and perhaps a way beyond the present ontologizing of relational talk. It may also suggest one way of negotiating the space between the rock and the hard place by marking the point at which relational ontologies (the rock) and poststructuralist discourses (the hard place) begin to overlap and mingle with creative but uneasy grace.

Process/Psychoanalytic Accounts of Women's Experience

This interest in exploring a feminist version of the "relational self," in both its ontological and historicist dimensions, also structures the reflections of feminist process theologians. As representative texts in this rapidly expanding field, Rita Brock's *Journeys by Heart*[7] and Catherine Keller's *From a Broken Web*[8] both offer influential accounts of this relation-seeking, "connective" self, accounts which, like Johnson's and LaCugna's, emphasize the interactive character of identity formation, the embodied quality of human experience, and the uniquely eschatological orientation of the self toward God. Insofar as they remain committed to describing such general features of human experience, they also share with Johnson and LaCugna universalizing structures which organize this relational self. As process thinkers, however, the conceptual resources which fund their depiction of the relational self are quite different from phenomenology. In the case of both Brock and Keller, these resources are of two basic sorts: *process metaphysics* and the conceptual world of *psychoanalytic discourse.*

First, let's look at the founding framework of their projects—process metaphysics. Although Brock does not develop her framework as fully as Keller, both construct theological visions undergirded by sturdy metaphysical structures of the pragmatic, Whiteheadian variety, structures which they argue are "true" because they fittingly pass the test of experience. Judged on such grounds, it is quite clear that both texts more than pass the test. Brock's richly pastoral accounts of the dangers which attend theological uses of abusive familial rhetoric have certainly moved and empowered many a reader. Similarly, Keller weaves an elegant cloth called the "serpentine self," brilliant in the fluidity of its shape and subtlety of its texture.

As the conversation between feminist theory and theology has developed in the years since the publication of both texts, however, several questions have been raised about the theoretical "fittingness" of metaphysical categories in general; and it is in conversations around these questions where new challenges for process feminist thought are emerging. These challenges meet the work of Brock and Keller at several levels. For example, along with the other authors reviewed in this essay, Brock and Keller both offer extensive critiques of essentialized notions of woman and argue against using static terms to describe the historical construction of gendered, racial, and class-configured identities. In light of these critiques, one cannot help but wonder why they both continue to uncritically deploy atemporal process categories like feeling, memory, and creativity without reference to the constructed character of this terminology. As long as this level of analysis remains absent, it seems that process feminists will continue to rely on a conceptual vocabulary which, ironically, in its abstracted, atemporal tonalities, cuts against the more historicizing aspects of their work.

These texts also construct process worldviews which, at times, appear to be restrictively totalizing in scope. This tendency is most evident in Keller's work, particularly in her use of repetitive patterning descriptions of "reality," where the patterning begins with historical-literary-psychoanalytic analysis of classical myths and is then mirrored in a broader anthropological account of the self; in turn, the latter is itself woven into a cosmological scheme which pulls all of reality (and beyond) into its purview. As she draws the circle wider and wider, these patterns mark the outlines of a conceptual system that is coherent, consistent, and whole.

This drive to systematize experience is nowhere more apparent than in Keller's relational ontology of "the oceanic, arachnean self" whose experience is framed by a structure of four different polarities. Given Keller's ongoing critique of Western dualisms as well as her appreciation for the repressive logic of philosophical binarisms, it is surprising to discover these dyads at work in her own constructive project. There are theoretical grounds for arguing that, in any form, this kind of binary patterning will be unable to admit the incommensurable differences of lived experience into its diadic patterns. Here, one again stumbles on a system wherein both history and difference are structurally eclipsed in the name of philosophically ordering the movement of "relationality" and "the self."

In pointing to these limits within process feminism's metaphysics—its atemporal habits of thought, its exhaustive drive to systematize, and its dyadic categories of analysis—I do not mean to overlook the fact that both Brock and Keller offer sustained critiques of earlier versions of process thought which did not pay sufficient attention to the sociopolitical and cultural dimensions of human experience and hence to the cultural construction of gender. As a corrective to this tendency, each theologian suggests that a psychoanalytic account of the play of gender coding in human experience might open their metaphysics more directly onto the terrain of history and culture. For Brock, the object-relations theories of Alice Miller and Nancy Chodorow supply the desired historicizing/psychoanalytic framework, whereas, for Keller, a feminist revision of Karl Jung serves a similar purpose. Here too, however, one finds that as feminist critiques of psychoanalytic categories have grown sharper in recent years, process feminists who have incorporated psychoanalysis into their theologies are being challenged to reconsider the cultural limits of some of their most foundational assumptions and ensuing insights.

For example, one might ask Brock if Chodorow's and Miller's analyses of "the family" might be too ahistorical to accommodate the historical differences that race, class, and ethnicity make in assessing the "norm" in familial patterning. Similarly, while it is evident that both Miller and Chodorow want to allow for changing models of parenting, the triadic family with distributed social roles still occupies an indisputably foundational position for them, one which makes it appear as a universal law or a natural given. This positing of a universal model is evidenced in Brock's move from Miller to a general anthropology in which broad claims about "true selves" and "false selves" are made.

Switching over to Keller's Jungian structures, one might ask if this general framework is conducive to historicizing feminism. Not only does the positing of archetypes lead to atemporal and dyadic habits of thought, it is difficult to imagine Jungian theory making sense apart from a structural commitment to a model of gender complementarity, albeit in Keller's case, the logic of complementarity has been not only inverted but cleverly skewed.

Literary/Textual Constructions of Women's Experience

The third type of situating framework used by womanist and feminist theologies is one I refer to as a *textual* or *literary* framework. In contrast to the two previous groups of books, the texts which exemplify this dynamic, Delores Williams's *Sisters in the Wilderness*[9] and Sallie McFague's *The Body of God*,[10] clearly do not employ methodological strategies that tie the notion of experience to either an underlying set of philosophical principles or a founding ontology. These theologies are thus remarkably free of references to the subject, the self, consciousness, and ontic relationality. Having detached experience from a static conceptual edifice, however, these theologies neither abandon it altogether nor leave it floating free and ambiguous. To the contrary, both Williams and McFague remain committed to articulating thick accounts of the multiple experiences which presently provide contexts for North American theology. Where do they turn to generate the material necessary for such thick accounts? To literature, to language, to the multiple fields of cultural production which—in all their variety—form the linguistic contexts or paradigmatic frames within which experience occurs.

As representative texts in this rapidly growing field of theological methodology, these books demonstrate how the term *experience* can be kept agile enough to travel across the differences of lived experience and yet historically thick enough—through literary analysis—to sustain boldly revisionist agendas. In the works of both Williams and McFague, literary materials—ranging in scope from scientific theories to modern novels—play a grounding role with regard to experience, insofar as they provide the historical substance which gives experience its unique character. For Williams, at issue is the historically eclipsed experience of African American women from slavery to the present; for McFague, it is the more culturally visible experience of North Americans responding to the ecological crisis. Given this description of their project, why then are they located on the rock side of the map? The agility of their conception of experience is constrained by universalizing gestures which attend their use of textual sources, gestures which relate to their understanding of how texts mean and how cultural experiences are discursively constructed and negotiated.

In *Sisters in the Wilderness*, Delores Williams offers her reader a deftly crafted and vividly painted account of the parallels between the biblical character of Hagar and modern "African-American women's social identity." As she moves between the biblical text and the modern context, she highlights a number of recurring themes which provide her with the basis for a compelling womanist critique of the servanthood/sacrifice images embedded in Anselmic strands of contemporary Christology. These resonating themes in African American women's experience—"wilderness experiences," coerced surrogacy, survival strategies, and "close personal relations with God"—are gleaned from several different textual sources which she combines to produce "an historically realistic model of non-middle-class black womanhood." It is a portrait which at once challenges the hegemony of cultural definitions of white, Victorian womanhood and gains critical leverage against persistent myths about black women's essential nature as mothers, workers, and believers.

Williams's contribution to contemporary theology, in this regard, cannot be overestimated, both with respect to the innovative method she offers and the doctrinal revisions she defends. In terms of method, Williams creatively demonstrates how diverse forms of African American women's literature (slave narratives, spirituals, novels, interviews, liturgies) can be used to reconstruct the lived experience of a community whose voice has seldom been figured into the dominant culture's assessment of "Christian truth" and "Christian faith experience." In terms of doctrinal revisions, the powerful vision of faith that she pulls out of these materials is certain to leave its mark on contemporary discussions of "the atonement" and "servanthood"—just as her treatment of surrogacy is sure to inform present-day theological discussions of the connections between reproductive rights and race. It must also be said that because Williams's book is written in such accessible prose and addresses a number of currently pressing social questions, it promises to be one of those rare theological texts which is read not only outside the academy but in communities where it speaks directly to the audience it describes. For a work in liberation womanist theology, no single accomplishment could be more important.

As I suggest earlier, however, her use of textual materials is also not without its limitations. These limitations are of two basic sorts: first, Williams's tendency to make the meaning of the texts appear overly static, and second, her correlative tendency to then define the experience of "black womanhood" in overly static—typologically rigid—terms. The first tendency is most apparent in the way she interprets the rich spectrum of literary materials which fund her descriptions of African American women's lived experience. Although Williams is sensitive to the context in which these various works were written, she often interprets these narratives as if they offer a transparent window onto a discursively stable reality, be it an antebellum tract describing "black motherhood" or a modern study describing African American women's "god-consciousness." When she does so, the meaning of these particular texts appears to be unambiguous. Thus, Williams's own narrative overlooks questions about the texts' original social functions and multiple audiences; it misses questions about historical and geographic migrations of linguistic usage; and it never asks questions about textual play, indeterminacy, and silence. As recent literary-critical study on the slave narratives in particular has illustrated, asking these sorts of textual questions can serve to deepen and advance the emancipatory agenda of works such as those by Williams.

Along similar lines, when Williams uses textual material in this manner, adopting a correspondence theory of language, she generates a picture of African American women's historical experience which is probably less open-ended than she intends. The social identity which she pulls out of these texts is construed in a fashion that leaves little room for experiences (past and present) which do not fit, only partially fit, fit all too well, or fit only by force. Likewise, she offers no analysis of the ways in which the texts she uses—as well as her own text—either contribute to or contest the ideological function of race itself as a diversely constructed category of social identity and not an essential, self-evident signifier. In Williams's case, addressing the status of racial formation by focusing on the specificity of culturally constructed identities would promote rather than hinder her commitment to challenging the reductionism embedded in the racism, sexism, and classism her text so compellingly critiques.

In *The Body of God,* Sallie McFague pursues a theological agenda which, at the level of defining experience, shares much with Williams's approach. Like Williams, McFague is interested in the myriad ways in which cultural images, stories, models, and paradigms shape Christian identity and practice. She shares Williams's historicist sensibilities about the dynamic construction of experience through linguistic gesture and social form. For this reason, McFague's text offers no rigid structural edifice to hold up a universal conception of the self. Instead, McFague offers thick descriptions of various stories which shape the way contemporary persons engage the world. Thus, McFague, again like Williams, removes experience from the realm of philosophical analysis and sets it squarely within the context of historically variant narratives. Having set it here, she crafts an extended theological meditation on one particular story—"the world as God's body"—a story offered in the hope that it might encourage a more ecologically responsible worldview.

This shift of conceptual emphasis from philosophy to story/culture/history does not completely free McFague's text from the weight of universalizing rocks, however. Again, in a manner not unlike Williams, McFague utilizes the notion of *story* or *model* in ways which suggest a literary essentialism—one which is not directly wedded to universalizing assumptions about human nature or consciousness, but instead results from textual-interpretive practices wherein an ossification of thick description occurs. For an illustration of this point, let us look at the methodological assumptions underlying McFague's telling of "the common creation story," the literary core of her project. Drawn from the insights of contemporary science, this story provides an organic model of nature which emphasizes two themes favored by feminists and postmodernists alike: relational interconnectedness and incommensurable otherness. In describing this organic model and its themes, McFague makes it clear that she is not presenting naively positivist statements of fact about nature; rather, she is describing the story that postmodern scientists tell about the world they study. She further suggests that it is a story which theologians need to consider not because it is objectively "true," but because it offers a discursive frame for reconceiving present-day doctrines of incarnation and creation in an ecologically responsible manner.

But having thus situated the narrative, McFague goes on to tell the story in a manner that suggests more stasis, harmony, and closure than one would expect—given her obvious bias toward postmodernist models. This stasis appears in her narrative recital at several levels. First, her text recites the postmodern "common creation story" as if it were a seamless, analytically coherent narrative. Given this account, one might be led to believe that this particular field of inquiry is a discursively stable and conceptually coherent whole. Her textual recitation leaves little room for a consideration of science's own internally generated epistemic ruptures, gaps, and anomalies.

Second, her textual rendering of this story seems to suggest that the story "means" in a rather straightforward narrative manner, one in which "true sense" can be traced back to a "scientific authorial intention" with a realist (though not positivist) referent. This assumption about narrative meaning is evidenced by the absence of any account of the different meanings the story might accrue when used in diverse cultural contexts. Similarly, McFague never considers the story as a site where cultural wars are inevitably fought and relations of power always renegotiated. Rather, the story appears as a universally intelligible and static site where global images "express" basic themes held by religions around the world.

Finally, in McFague's account of this story, one finds an example of a dynamic similar to LaCugna's and Keller's attempts to accommodate the possibility of marginality, silence, and chaos by structuring these terms into the very frame of their conceptual apparatus. Throughout the text, McFague clearly acknowledges the repressions which have accompanied the Enlightenment's scientific dealings with the chaotic, the novel, and the silent, and she remains committed to retelling the common creation story in a way which lessens the weight of these repressions. The narrative scope of her story is so comprehensive, however, that the only way to accomplish this task is to structure into the narrative a place for chaos, novelty, and silence. In doing so, she ironically brings order to the very thing that she celebrates as being beyond the boundaries of order and measure.

The Hard Place

Thus far I have described three different conceptual rocks (universalizing frameworks) to which the term *experience* has been tied in recent feminist theologies. In the case of the phenomenologists and the process feminists, I have argued that although they free the concept of gender from weighty essentialisms, they nonetheless keep their concept of experience attached to what has become the new rock of feminist theology—relational ontology. In the case of the theologians who engage in literary analysis, I have argued that although they clearly intend their analysis to assist in historicizing the concepts of gender and experience, they nonetheless seek to excavate static meanings out of the texts they use—an undertaking which runs counter to their otherwise deeply constructivist sensibilities.

These three essentializing frameworks, however, do not exhaust the conceptual possibilities presently available for theorizing experience in feminist theology. In the past five years, several texts have appeared in which "women's experience" remains a normative category of analysis but that emphasize the historical and cultural texture of identity and language. As I stated earlier, these texts can be roughly divided into two groups: those which use the tools of cultural anthropology to generate thick descriptions of communal experiences, and those which draw on the insights of poststructuralism to shape their analysis of identity, language, and power. Again, I refer to this side of the map as a hard place because the issues confronting those who stand here are numerous—establishing the status of normative claims, measuring the value of immanent critique, and assessing the political viability of localized descriptions and deconstructive rhetoric.

Cultural-Anthropological Accounts of Women's Experience

In the first group of texts, those which use the tools of cultural anthropology to analyze experience, I locate the recent work of Kathryn Tanner, *The Politics of God*,[11] and the work of Ada María Isasi-Díaz, *En la Lucha*.[12] Although these texts represent two distinct genres of theological discourse, they share a commitment to opening up the emancipatory potential of Christianity by noting the shifting cultural functions religious beliefs serve in different Christian communities. This shared interest also signals their general agreement on two related points: that experience is best described by reference to culturally specific forms of life, and that language is best understood by reference to the work it does—in other words, by reference to its sociolinguistic function.

In *The Politics of God,* Tanner develops a sociocultural understanding of doctrine by offering her reader a tightly argued, metatheoretical, and metahistorical analysis of the relation between belief and practice. Her analysis of this relation is based on the observation that in the history of doctrinal developments, the relationship between faith claims and social practice is ever changing. She argues this point by considering, as just one example, the diverse political sensibilities articulated by Christian communities who assert the absolute transcendence of God, and points out that when an oppressed group uses this belief to contest the absolute authority of an earthly ruler, its political use is subversive, whereas the same belief, when used by an elite to sanction its power, elicits social practices which support the status quo.

Tanner further argues that once one begins to appreciate the complexity of this relation between belief and practice, one's understanding of the meaning and use of traditional doctrines begins to shift. Tanner hopes that when this shift occurs, liberal Christians might begin to reassess their relation to oppressive doctrines within the tradition. To this end, she suggests that it may be possible to use seemingly conservative doctrines to bolster, in surprising ways, a progressive Christian ethic. As an example of such a use, she shows how the hierarchical logics of divine sovereignty and providence can be used, when effectively situated, not to foster a politics of exclusionary hierarchy, but rather to garner support for a constructive, feminist politics of difference.

However, just as Tanner's analysis of doctrine shows the agility of a theology which is not tied to essentializing rocks, her discussion also offers a glimpse of some of the hard places which attend theology of this type. In Tanner's case, two specific difficulties emerge. The first concerns the "meta" character of her postmodernist sensibilities. In reading Tanner's text, one cannot help but be impressed with her grasp of historic Christian doctrines and her subtle estimations of culture and language. But her facility for mapmaking keeps her strangely distanced from the beliefs and practices she charts. This postmodern version of a "view from nowhere" is evidenced by the fact that her map never dips into the messy lived experience of the cultural actors she describes—an odd absence given her insistence that cultural specificity be considered in assessing the function of doctrine. By holding the specificity of particular voices at bay, she prevents one from hearing the imaginative insights that such voices bring to theology, insights that often do not "fit" into the forms of traditional doctrines nor into her estimated calculus of belief and practice.

Second, Tanner's project provides an excellent model of how liberation theology might continue to profit from immanent critiques of the tradition using internally generated norms as the basis for a rigorous self-evaluation of belief and action. Alongside this view of tradition and critique, however, one might ask if there are other ways to understand cultural transformation. Is it possible to hold, as Tanner does, that the normative force of tradition/language can never be completely escaped, and yet simultaneously affirm the possibility of ruptures within the tradition, where fresh theological ground is broken—ground beyond the terrain of historical doctrines? Although Tanner herself would probably not reject this possibility, I use her text to make a point: namely, if the projects of feminist theologians who engage in internal critique cannot accommodate the new—the emergent voice—then they may well end up replacing the essentializing rocks of foundational philosophy with potentially rocklike descriptions of tradition and doctrine.

If Tanner provides an example of a theologian using a cultural-linguistic framework to chart grand maps, then Ada María Isasi-Díaz provides an example of a theologian using the same framework to opposite ends, using it to explore the particular, uneven, and conflicted terrain of a specific community's lived experience. In *En la Lucha,* Isasi-Díaz continues the task of engaging in a liberation theological analysis that avoids essentializing or universalizing experience by its focus on the unique ways in which cultural practices and religious languages have served to constitute the richly textured identities of North American Hispanic women. Her commitment to avoiding universal claims about Latinas is evident in the mosaic quality of her text, pieced together from the diverse voices of Hispanic women she interviews and from the different social theories which she uses to situate their lives. It is also a mosaic whose coherence rests in Isasi-Díaz's stated goal: to reflect back theologically to the community a voice that will empower its speakers to be subjects of their own lives and agents of their own history.

Perhaps the most remarkable methodological feat of Isasi-Díaz's book is the degree to which she keeps a notion of "women's experience" alive and working without anchoring it in any one analytic scheme or single textual meaning. This lively view of experience allows her to perform a difficult balancing act with regard to the relation between thick description and normative generalities. On the one hand, she adamantly refuses to eclipse substantive differences between Latinas. On the other hand, she acknowledges the pragmatic value of identifying shared "generative themes" which serve as the basis for a common, liberatory vision. Among such themes are first, the conception of *proyecto histórica,* a strategic eschatology of liberation; and second, the lived experience of *mestizaje,* the embracing and celebrating of diversity. Both of these themes provide Isasi-Díaz with a hermeneutical key for reinterpreting theological themes such as moral agency, truth, and difference in a manner which accords with *mujerista* experiences.

What remains to be seen, however, is how this lively conception of Hispanic women's social experience will fare when Isasi-Díaz, in her future work, turns her attention from theological method to theological construction. At this point, she has set the stage for such work, but what it will actually look like remains unclear. Will she be able to glean from her interviews with Hispanic women all the material she needs for rethinking such topics as creation, salvation, and Christology? If she can, will she be able to maintain such a deeply communal understanding of truth and value when dealing with topics which have traditionally required one to make not only universal but also objective claims about God and the world? And finally, if and when she steps onto the terrain of normative claims, will she provisionally gesture toward the rocks of essentialism (maybe even a relational ontology), particularly if they are communally generated essentialisms which serve the strategic ends of liberation? For answers to these questions, we will have to wait and see where her project will move in the future and where this ethnographic-cultural trajectory as a whole will lead as it develops in the context of *mujerista,* womanist, and feminist agendas.

Poststructuralist Accounts of Women's Experience

In addition to this sociocultural perspective, recent years have seen a flourishing of feminist and womanist texts which attempt to move beyond essentialized conceptions of experience by deploying the eclectic tools and insights of poststructuralist theory. I wish to highlight the term *eclectic* to emphasize that for the theologians I would locate here—Rebecca Chopp, Mary Fulkerson,[13] Susan Thistlethwaite,[14] and Emilie Townes[15]—poststructuralism provides, in broad strokes, the dramatic plot line of their analysis, but it does not serve the explanatory or empirically invested function that the cultural-linguistic tools give Tanner and Isasi-Díaz. For this reason, the theologians I locate here quite freely employ an eclectic array of conceptual tools whose final coherence rests not on an analytic scheme but on the ability of the tools to illuminate the central theological drama of their texts. For the purposes of this review, I will look at only one of these projects as a way of introducing what is still a nascent conversation.

In Chopp's text, *The Power to Speak,*[16] the theological vision stretches not only across a number of doctrinal loci, ranging from scriptural hermeneutic to sin and ecclesiology, but also into a number of modernity's favored themes: the subject, language, politics, history, and power. Chopp draws the basic insight which drives this vision from a gendered analysis of the structural drama of discourse. According to the French theorists from whom Chopp draws, the dramatic logic of Western conceptions of language is one in which linguistic definition and order are established by setting up margins and backgrounds which give "meaning" its contour and edges, but only by virtue of the position these margins occupy as "other" to the central term. Following the example of Hélène Cixous, Julia Kristeva, and to a lesser degree Luce Irigaray, Chopp attributes a distinctly gendered play to this dynamic, naming the ordered definition as masculine and the margin of otherness as feminine. She then makes the observation that in the discourse of "theology proper," as in all the dominant discourses of our culture, there is a repressed margin which, standing on the edge of language, marks the space of women's eclipsed theological voice. The task Chopp takes up in this text lies in articulating the emancipatory possibilities this voice from the margin holds for theology. According to Chopp, this emerging voice disrupts theological order and meaning and celebrates difference as it moves and dances on the borders of time and space. It is thus a voice which speaks freedom and authors new communities of emancipatory practice.

One of the most powerful aspects of Chopp's account of this voice is the lively presence in the text of her own voice—a voice which plays with genre in order to capture a cadence and a rhythm which contrast well with the disinterested, well-ordered voice of academic theology. In this regard, she shares Isasi-Díaz's view that feminist theologians need to honor, as best they can, the unique discursive practices of the historically marginal voices they seek to empower, for both believe that it is in the play of these voices that feminist theologians will find their freshest and most imaginative resources for a deep reconstruction of Christian doctrine. In contrast to the more static interpretations of McFague and Williams, both Chopp and Isasi-Díaz try to honor these voices by celebrating their instabilities as well as their thematic generalities.

Chopp's attempt to generate creative insights from the "other world" of marginal voices also stands as an interesting counterpoint to Tanner's strategic preference for critiquing the "tradition" *not* by speaking from its borders, but by recalculating the logic of its shifting centers. It is in the face of this strategic difference that the fragility and ambiguity of Chopp's project most clearly surface—just as Chopp's project betrays the limits of

Tanner's. From the perspective of immanent critique, there are at least two issues one must raise. First, although Chopp is not naive about the possibility of getting completely outside the constraints of the dominant discourse, there are points in her text where she seems to overestimate how far "out" this speaking voice of women is actually able to travel in its resistance. It is when she invokes a space not unlike Cixous's *écriture féminine* that this overestimated leap appears most clearly. In that space beyond— where bones dance and difference is celebrated—the rhetoric of the possible, the new, and the subversive becomes so strong that the burdensome weight of our constitutive histories, our institutional forms, and our tedious traditions and languages seems to fade and then disappear. While it is obvious that Chopp does not intend to underestimate the power of this weight, the aesthetic quality of the text may tend in this direction nonetheless and, in doing so, cut against the more pragmatic, historical dimensions of her analysis.

Related to this issue is a second one concerning the practical ends of this type of poststructuralist project. Is Chopp's "positionally marginal" voice capable of actually sustaining the strategic end to which it speaks, the goal of emancipatory transformation? Can this often ephemeral, fragmented, evocative—but slippery—rhetoric accomplish its tasks? Although there is obviously no one answer to this question, one must consider it carefully in light of two potential critiques of such endeavors. First, given the nature of her stated audience—postmodern, First World Christians— does she move too far beyond the strictures of tradition to speak to them intelligibly? Does her project work best for poststructuralist converts? The answer is not clear, for the book has already been used to great effect in contexts where the term *poststructuralism* has never been spoken. Second, is a rhetoric which celebrates the fragmentation of the subject strategically well suited for persons who are struggling to claim a sense of wholeness and stability, having been oppressively fractured by their time on the margin? Again, there is no obvious answer to this question, and because Chopp is most likely aware of both critiques, she does us a great service by presenting a text where these issues can be directly engaged.

Conclusion

Having come to the end of my survey of the methodological differences which divide the present-day terrain of feminist, womanist, and *mujerista* theologies, what can be said in conclusion about its two sides, the rock and the hard place? First, it is clear that each side has its own strengths. For those theologians who build their projects on universal, foundational rocks, their constructive work in the area of Christian doctrine is refreshingly solid, strong, accessible, and steadily visionary. These works thus bespeak the confidence of a movement come of age; in doing so, they offer hope in a form of enduring wisdoms and sturdy graces. For theologians who stand in the hard place, their work remains restless and, as yet, lacking in constructive solidity, marking a place of healthy instability. Looking behind truths, testing the strength of goods, and pulling back edges in search of ever-retreating margins, these texts offer hope in the form of rupturing voices and more particularized graces.

Residing within the respective strengths of endurance and restlessness, however, one also finds, secondly, positions that warrant serious critique. For those who stand on universalizing rocks, the challenge of women's experiences which do not "fit" into generalized categories of phenomenology, process metaphysics, psychoanalysis, or literary narrative will no doubt continue to make these foundationalists uneasy. Likewise, the pragmatic demand for sturdy visions and faith-filled truths will no doubt continue to keep those who stand in the hard places of cultural anthropology and poststructuralism wanting more substance than their methods seem able to deliver. In light of these tensions on both sides, it may well be that the still-uncharted chasm which stretches between the rock and hard place, a space which my map has only noted but not explored, will provide a space where our future conversations and struggles can unfold in as yet unexpected ways.

CHAPTER 4

SEEKING AND SUCKING
On Relation and Essence
in Feminist Theology

Catherine Keller

The Holy Spirit opened Her bosom,
And mixed the milk of the two breasts of the Father.
The Odes of Solomon, Ode 19

A FEMALE HOLY SPIRIT, a transsexual Father, and a rather intimate four-breasted milking procedure: not surprisingly, these gender relations did not congeal into the stuff of orthodoxy. But as attested in Irenaeus and Clement as well as the Syrian *Odes of Solomon,* early Christians indulged in some extraordinarily iconoclastic imagery. Especially in their eucharistic and trinitarian meditations, they could inscribe Christ the Word not just as the "Drink of Life" but, more specifically, as the breast milk of the Father.[1] "Seek and it shall be opened" means, according to Clement in his *Pedagogos,* "Seek Christ and the breasts of the Father will be opened unto you." Thus "seeking is sucking."[2]

In the present context I wish to reflect on certain nurturant practices of the young but sturdy subdiscipline of feminist theology. While the transgendering tropes of these pre-Constantinian fathers of the church deserve to be "opened" within their own historical setting, this paper only asks them to mirror the present bosom of gender theory at the end of the second millennium of the Christian epoch. Granted, these patriarchal moments of gender ambiguity not only appear intriguingly perverse within their own setting, but can only reflect the present moment through the glass of theory darkly. That darkness, a function of historical depth as

54

well as of the reciprocal distortions of present and past interpretations, may after all help to shade and clarify present issues of methodology.

As among the patristic tropes the father is both *tropheus* and *trophe*—both feeder and food, breast and milk—so as a feminist theologian I find myself both feeding and fed by my own community of discourse. The sense of a radical reformation through which a critical mass of Christianity has accomplished its own feminist rebirth has made the effects of feminist theology meaningful to a considerable public. But it is not as though we now need only suckle the "newly born" of Clement's trope to reach some fully integrated and reformed unity. On the contrary, the more feminist theology matures, the more open it grows to internal dissent and to multiple intellectual influences (the foremost of which at the moment is the poststructuralist range of theory we consider in this volume). Surely this complexification is for the good, if it is not narcissistic fusion with our own maternal or paternal origins that we crave. At the same time, a situation of relative strength for feminist theology allows us also to interrogate the politics, the economics, of our own role within the academy and religious communities, and in that light to question particular configurations of dissent and influence.

In brief, I wish to consider a feminist theological tendency to emulate too uncritically certain assumptions of postmodern feminist theory. At the same time I understand this transmillennial moment as precisely postmodern and requiring participation in those theories and movements that situate themselves at the end of modernity. I find myself in the awkward position of "sucking" from theories which still leave much to be desired, and therefore seeking an alternative path for feminist theology. My key examples for such theories will be Iris Marion Young, Julia Kristeva, and Elisabeth Schüssler Fiorenza. I will focus on their shared need to cut loose from certain feminist propositions concerning subjectivity: in particular those articulated variously as feminist relationalism, the ethics of mutuality, or the social ontology of the self. There is little disagreement regarding the need to unlock subjectivity, such that self functions as a fluid, internally diversifying, and temporally open-ended process rather than a product of some autonomous essence. However, the social ontology by which the fluidity was predicated has come under fire: its relationalism seems to entail a spurious, "feminine" essence.

I will question whether the emerging antirelationalism represents a maturation of feminist theology. That is, to what extent does it liberate us

from utopian fantasies of maternal suckle? And does it then return us to
"the breast of the father"? Would it be a defeat of feminist theology if it
did? More specifically, I suggest that the tendency to dispose of feminist
theories of relation in the name of antiessentialist "theory" may clog a vital
and fresh means of conceptual access to that "body" which we so much
desire and so much resist, a means which challenges traditional sex/gender
constructions and yet releases the energy of our carnal daughterhood.

I

In the ancient Christian context, a male author imbibes not just the
breast milk but the seminal Word, the Logos Spermatikos. But the
imagery of Christians directly feeding off of that pale male fluid may have
summoned impossibly gay associations. By contrast, the breast could more
legitimately be sucked or milked by either sex. Ancient science, according
to which both flesh and milk arise from blood, offered more palatable
tropes. According to Hippolytus, who offers the earliest attestations of the
baptismal Eucharist, water, milk, and wine were administered in three separate cups. The ritual milk was offered with honey in a facsimile at once of
the "land flowing with milk and honey" and of breast milk for the newly
reborn. By "the compound of honey and milk, with which He feeds his
own like children" it is said that the Creator "sweetens the bitterness of
their heart with the sweetness of the Word."[3] This early imagery, soon cov-
ered over by an increasingly monolithic masculinism, certainly presents
faith logocentrically: the cosmic logos Christology remained prominent
until the Son Christologies of Nicene orthodoxy came to predominate.[4]
But at that still-youthful moment in Christian history, at which baptism
largely involved adults undergoing a risky and transformative rite of
rebirth rather than literal infants being drafted unawares into a theocratic
institution, the symbolism of the initiation ritual provoked not a *phallo-
gocentric* so much as a *mammilogocentric* symbolism.

If there were a single, proper feminist interpretation for such imagery,
it would belong to that phase of second-wave thought in which we
rejected, as if in one voice, the possibility that "androgyny" encoded a liberating word for women. It was recognized as a patriarchal construction by
which femininity was, as Mary Daly put it, "scotch-taped"[5] together with
masculinity, for the enhancement of male "wholeness." Certainly these
images of an androgynous, or perhaps hermaphroditic, deity illustrate the

point. By appropriating to himself [*sic*] a defining female attribute, the male god assures the free flow of nurturant resources between generations of exclusively male authorities. Rebirth and suckle become spiritual substitutes for real mothers, understood as eschatologically expendable at any rate. But if God could absorb a certain symbolic maternity, women were offered at best the chance to become "like the male"—and that only in enclaves such as the one represented by Thomas Christianity. So the best breast adheres for the faithful to a Father.

But feminists more recently can argue for a less unilateral reading. While clearly in these proto-orthodox communities women were rarely coming to public voice anymore, that Nicene orthodoxy would later simply erase the vestiges of this hermaphroditic Father does not seem insignificant. A feminism less convicted than we once were of our own sex/gender "identity" need not seek an anachronistic feminism, nor even a subliminal protofeminism. But it may read in this fluid sexual imagery an inchoate yearning for freedom from the sociospiritual constrictions of mainline classical gender constructions. The imagery's gender subversion mirrors the still-dissident social situation of pre-Constantinian Christians, for whom power depended on communal nurture, powerful women within a weakened patriarchal circumstance, and a mobile fluidity of rhetorical forms, as perhaps it still does among feminist theologians, however close we may seem to stand to the center of power.

Here, at the other end of Christendom, we who have breasts have been coming to voice: we make public, publish, our *logoi*. At the intersection of academic and religious communities, precisely in the contradictions and convulsions characteristic of this space, we may have lucked into a peculiarly generative freedom. Whether or not we mother infants, we breasted theologians are able to suckle a new generation of pastors and professors, many, if not half of whom, are female. So what might Clement's trope open for us?

Perhaps this much: like the pre-Nicenians, feminist theory also finds itself at a point of gender fluidity. Subjectivity is "on trial"—*en procès*—in such a way as to question the alibis of an andromorphic ego. Its boundaries—or rather its Cartesian accounts of them—have sprung leaks. As Teresa de Lauretis put it in a near-classic definition:

> What is emerging in feminist writings is . . . the concept of a multiple, shifting, and often self-contradictory identity, a subject that is not divided in, but rather at odds with, language; an identity made up of

heterogeneous and heteronomous representations of gender, race, and class, and often indeed across languages and cultures; an identity that one decides to reclaim from a history of multiple assimilations, and that one insists on as a strategy.[6]

Specifically in terms of sex/gender, this means, as Judith Butler would have it, a replacement of those "naturalized" sex/gender essences so crucial both to masculine and heterosexual supremacy with shifting and parodic performances of sexual dissent. On the basis of her radical constructivism, that is, her understanding of our cultural preconstruction by discourse, she recognizes that there is no pure feminist or lesbian identity, no "outside" of the sex/gender system. Therefore the mobile mode of ironic mimicry, exemplified for her in transsexual performances, offers the best chance of resistance.[7]

Among early Christians, within their intensively cross-cultural, cross-racial, cross-class situation, women had temporarily erupted into positions of unusual prominence. While they certainly neither sought nor enjoyed a space outside of patriarchy as such, the cross-gendering of divine attributes and the infantilizing of the one newly born in Christ served to break down a certain impenetrable phallic-paternal ideal. Yet the dynamism of multiple and disputed rhetorics of salvation deferred any settled orthodoxy for a time—salvifically. Analogously, that ideal has broken down at the end of modernity. Yet feminists, in consciousness of the context of cultural diversity in which we move and think, also dispute our own orthodoxies, preventing any fixed unity of movement or theory.

At this level, therefore, the trope of the breasted father provokes reflection on theological anthropology. Indeed, as suggested before, the social ontology which supports practices of normative *mutuality* between subject and subject at the same time makes possible the *fluidity* characteristic of postmodern subjectivity. This is a somewhat paradoxical claim: I want to argue that rather than tossing out relationalist theories of subjectivity, postmodern theories may need them precisely in order to keep their own fluidity flowing.

For if "I" am partially constituted by you even as you partially constitute me, for better or for worse, that is, if I flow into, in-fluence you as you in-fluence me, then my subjectivity describes itself as radically open-ended in time as well as space. Otherwise fluidity would be discernible merely within my own internal multiplicity of moment-to-moment selves: now you see me, now you don't; what I was, I am not. That latter fluidity suggests, however, a state of pluralist autonomy doomed to entropy: I may be many, but if the many is merely a self-generated subjective mutability, it does not feed itself from others, nor feed them. Such multiplicity, usually the sort indicated by postmodern discourse of the carnivalesque, the fluid, the fragmentary, requires a less solipsistic setting even in order to sustain itself. In other words, the gender fluidity of an open-ended, unfixed subjectivity cannot be meaningfully construed merely as a matter of an independent set of personal performances.

If such subjective multiplicity is not to collapse in on itself, exposed as a mere set of colorful masks over a metaphysically quite substantial unity of essence, its multiplicity requires a social account. Such a requirement will not be satisfied, however, by simple appeal to "cultural construction"—which either explains too much or too little. Indeed the notion of cultural construction, fairly innocuous in itself, may well exhaust the explanatory power of any discourse which reduces meaning to discourse itself. For certainly the discursive consciousness which preconstructs all of our conceptions and thus all of our perceptions circulates within the terms of its given cultural-linguistic framework. But constructivism seems then to function as the poststructuralist compensation for the decentering fluidity of the subject. In other words, it is as though "culture" can now function as a kind of surrogate super-subject, imprinting us with our inherent diversities. But then we lose access to such limited realms of creative resistance as might enable us to question our respective cultures and their subjective formations in the first place.

Such constructivism, while it helpfully criticizes Enlightenment humanism, nonetheless remains by the terms of its own linguistic culturalism ineluctably confined to the anthropocentrism on which that humanism is based. I would think that no body-nurturant feminism would want to shirk androcentrism merely in favor of anthropocentrism, with its inherent alienation from our animal condition. That is, we will not want to reconstruct our intersubjective relations in merely interhuman terms, as though only speech can mediate an ethical posture, as though only human culture inherently matters, and as though human speech and culture could be understood severed from the vast, prelinguistic animal-emotive ecologies which contain them. The ecology of the suckling infant as well as that of the nurturant environment, which begins for us with our own bodies, suggest that an adequate social analysis cannot restrict its understanding of self-construction to human cultural relations. Or perhaps it must expand the notion of "culture" beyond its mind-numbing opposition to "nature," to include all the nonhuman cultures on which human ones depend. Such an expansion stretches the implicit social analysis into social ontology: or rather, demands the acknowledgment of the social ontology already complicit.

The key point here, however, remains a feminist one: gender fluidity, as we seek to articulate sexual difference without hardening it into new feminist dogmas, comes embedded in the social ecology of a relational ontology. Yet while ontology cannot function within an ecocentric account as a mere derivative of epistemology, it is certainly the case that any account of what we "are" will congeal into indigestible "natures" and cheesy "substances" unless it acknowledges its step-by-step interdependency with epistemology. The intellectual construction of what we seem to be, are, and might become produces schemas of objectification as soon as it neglects to reference the productivity of its own thought process. In other words, as soon as it abstracts its own language from the very social ontology here expressed, it begins to veil the responsibility and the relativity of its own standpoint to whatever "nature" it perceives. Being both precedes and follows knowing. But the being which follows the knowing is different from the preceding one.

The Father's breast intrudes into the matter of feminist theological epistemology. At an obvious and intractable level, that of the intellectual engagement of texts, feminists in academic theology study mostly male discursive formations, within still largely male-defined and even male-inhabited contexts. No matter how much feminist theory we read, we interpret it within a paternal discipline: sitting on the lap of the fathers, we seek and suck women's writings. While some (such as Emily Culpepper) might skillfully pursue a methodological strategy of reading only women, most feel compelled to engage for themselves the masculine sources cited by women authors, and may unapologetically acknowledge their attraction to them. Indeed as feminist theory increasingly tastes French, few of us satisfy ourselves with French feminists; we nurture ourselves from *les papas*—Derrida, Foucault, Lacan—whom *les mamas* both deconstruct and reconstruct. Additionally, the poststructuralism emergent within the U.S. reception of French theory itself serves as a primary source for the gender-bending pluralism characteristic of queer theory and what Susan Bordo diagnosed as "gender skepticism,"[8] which renders feminist source orthodoxy—any myth of a possible pure feminist origin—passé.

I derogate none of these possible reading strategies. I wish however to *interrogate* the epistemological tendency flowing from the father's breast of elite feminist theory. I would claim that this operative theory of knowing implies an asocial ontology. My concern is with its impact on feminist theological development. For if, as I suggested, the tale of the fluidity of subjectivity and thus of the fluidity of sex/gender is dependent on a social ontology of the self, we will want to be attentive to any tendencies among us to lop off the nodes of relation, the theoretical sites where a conscious affirmation of ontological dependency and ethical mutuality might be emerging.

II

Feminist relationalism counts at this point as a kind of tradition in its own right. It indicates the trajectory of the second wave's attempt to theorize sexual difference. It did this in resistance to what is generally now called "liberal" or "enlightenment" feminism, which had sought to liberate women from the traditional constructions of sexual difference as male supraordination. Through such analyses as Simone de Beauvoir's, *vive la différence* had lost its mystifying charm for this century. Only with fear and trembling did we risk again a discourse of difference, this time freed from any fixed "nature" of femininity, drawn mainly on psychological accounts of gender formation within the patriarchal Western nuclear family. Carol Gilligan's research into the emphasis on care and responsibility, in contrast to a more male-typified rights rhetoric, did not pretend to any grand theoretical framework for its own empirical explorations: it opened a possibility for inquiry into difference free of the hierarchical "complementarities" of *la différence*.[9] Nancy Chodorow offered a theory, derived from a carefully historicized, object-relational appropriation and critique of the Oedipal complex.[10] Jean Baker Miller simultaneously worked up the basis for the feminist psychology of the Stone Center, the affinities of which to feminist spirituality were immediately recognized.[11] While radical feminism devised its own spirituality of female difference, feminist theologians were quickly assimilating the relational model to other theoretical frameworks available to us at the time. This feminism still drew its major motivation from activist rather than academic sources. For instance, Rita Nakashima Brock's and my own early couplings of Whiteheadian theism with the above feminist psychoanalytic voices offered a clear political agenda for religious institutions and their theological ideologies,[12] an agenda influenced by but not identical with that of Mary Daly.

But the feminist tension between "no more difference" and "gender difference" soon gave way to the internal agonies of a women's movement which was not one—and had to recognize that white feminism could no longer set the agenda for a global sisterhood, relational or not. Connec- tions—however ineradicable in ontology—broke down in practice. At the same time the powerful new Eurocentrism of postmodernism/poststruc- turalism began to inspire a generation of academic feminists. Here, with the help of Derrida's pun on *différance,* "difference" became the motto— referencing, however, the entire range of human differences, sexual, mul- ticultural, idiosyncratic. Subsequent waves of critique seemed, as Bordo well remarked, to read a different Chodorow than she (or I) had read.[13] Missing altogether the revolutionary contextualization of the nuclear fam- ily in the trajectory of bourgeois Western modernity, academic feminists began to debunk anything smacking of Gilligan's and Chodorow's work as "essentialist." Thus, quite consistently, the very notion of "gender" became suspect, rightly questioned for its obfuscation of the differences between women, its tendency to absorb the biologistic construction of "sex." After all, essentialists philosophically are those who hold that some character is necessary to what something or someone is. And there is nothing more worthy of interrogation than any claim as to what femininity or mas- culinity necessarily entails. But unfortunately a welcome (if philosophi- cally hardly new) critique of essentialism seems to have fallen prey to its own essentialism. The "essential woman" it finds in feminist attempts to construct a model of the human subject emerging from its matrix of rela- tions may be a log in its own eye. That is, it necessarily obfuscates the dif- ference between feminist relationalism and those traditional subjectivities which undermine difference by the construction of unifying discourses.

Such homogenizing moves in the service of heterogeneity strike me as especially disheartening. Perhaps they count as an inevitable discursive mechanism, apparent in the other's moves rather than in one's own. Cer- tainly this slippery slope on which antiessentialism slides into antirela- tionalism can be found in carefully reasoned arguments. For instance, Iris Marion Young offers a brilliant challenge to communitarianism on the basis of its unifying ideal, saying that it is possibly healthy for affinity groups yet tempts totalitarianism when deployed as the ideal for national or international politics. Yet her needed critique of the sacred cow of the community ideal degenerates within one chapter into an undifferentiated polemic against all manner of feminist relationalism.[14] She seems to have in mind anyone—such as feminist philosopher Seyla Benhabib—who dares yet to draw on the Gilliganesque trajectory.[15] So while Young illumines the homogenizing dangers of the ideal of community (so dear to feminist theologians, for instance), she fails to note her own homogenization of all critiques of individualism. While I would certainly agree with her that the communitarian propensity is to set up a false polarity between individualism and its own unifying and occasionally reactionary ideal, I wish she did not ipso facto perform the same binary sleight of hand—with the other hand. Aside from appeals to her laudable theory of justice and difference, and an uncritical philosophical reception of Derrida's *différance,* she manages only to lump together and criticize appeals to the social nature of humans, while offering no account which could dislodge the much more dominant discourse of the autonomous individual. Perhaps this omission would be harmless, if it were not for the fact that liberal individualism in the guise of the *homo economicus* fuels the implicit anthropology of the entire neocolonial free market project.[16]

Of course, Young's political philosophy claims only national parameters for its ethics. But if we are claiming moral status (tropology) for any First World political ontologies, for any claims against and for certain constructions of the logos of our being, then must they not answer to *global* criteria of justice? For where else does our vaunted criterion of "difference" gain its vigor and its challenge—precisely if it does not merely refer to sex/gender—but from the transnational global circumstance of modernity and the multicultural complexity which it has thereby fostered? Pluralism, especially as it pertains to the suffering and contributions of minorities, can hardly be addressed apart from the global tracework of coercion and opportunity characterizing most paradigmatically the history of the United States.

While accepting Young's and other postmodern interrogations of the inherent homogenizing proclivities of relationalism and its communalizing impetus, especially as it makes unifying claims beyond its own "affinity groups," we must also question the viability of the "difference" which is preserved at the expense of relational width. The sensibility I am worrying about typically expresses itself as an enthusiasm for the "local" over against global metanarratives. Foucault's "insurrection of local knowledges" has indeed offered leverage against globalizing generalizations of both the metaphysical and the economic orders. However, it seems to have become a slogan serving not to unhinge global corporate empires of "free trade" but rather to breed indifference to their destructive hegemony.

III

The slippage of antiessentialism toward a postmodern individualism becomes overt in Alice Jardine's interview of Julia Kristeva. Opening with an allusion to her participation in a group grappling with the apocalyptic scope of ecological collapse and economic injustice, Jardine asks how to think about it. The answer is more or less "don't." "In my present state of mind," says Kristeva, "I think that all *global* problematics are archaic; that one should not formulate global problematics because that is part of a totalitarian and totalizing conception of history."[17] Apart from the disquieting sense that a great thinker has resorted to cliché, we must of course assume that she means to continue the salubrious critique of the universalizing and colonizing subject of scientific and state modernity. Freedom from the grip of overgeneralization purveys not only an antitotalitarian ethic but intellectual honesty. In its place, predictably, she invokes local knowledges. "Where are things actually happening? In specific regions in our intimate lives, or in different fragmentations of knowledge through very specific research" (84). So local knowledges, as the only nontotalitarian option, seem to boil down to psychoanalytic, anthropological, and linguistic investigations.

How does one attain to this particularity? "One must ask different specialists . . ." (84). In other words, leave it to the experts. Cultivate academic specialization. How does this deglobalizing, respecializing gesture apply to the construction of the self? She herself suggests the link. Noting that she considers it a good thing that the state has become a mere bureaucracy, she notes that "this technocratization . . . liberates us from the religion of the State" (85). By this she presumably applauds the death of state socialism, with its totalizing arbitration of moral values. Of the failure of its collectivism, she says

> so much the better. That way we will perhaps reach a point where these values, which are moral values, ethical values, will be resolved in smaller and smaller groups, and from there will move closer and closer to the individual. At that moment it may be the individual discourses which will acquire greater importance. (85)

So ethical values will at last be liberated from all communal constraints, not just from the state, presumably, but from relationship itself. In this inadvertent little postmodern teleology, Kristeva certainly exceeds Young's anticommunalism. Young only wanted to abort the inflations of the community ideal to larger civic structures—she did not question its local validity. But in Kristeva we seem to encounter the unfettered dream of the bourgeois academic: that after all these decades of intrusive social movement perspectives, we can get on with the performances of our individual verbal brilliance, unburdened by the clumsy weight of global concerns. Did Foucault's summoning of locality also contain this secret eschatology, this hope for the restoration of the full moral privilege of academic discourse, and thus its definitive emancipation from what, perhaps clunkily, differentiates itself as "praxis"? So we witness, in the end times of the enlightenment subject and "his" communist opposite and counterpart, not some dialectical composite of individuality and collectivity, but rather the vision of the victory of a shrunken residue of the first: no longer universally accountable, "the individual" is now the unaccountable one, the one whose virtue will be defined by the quality of his or her "discourses." By ignoring the global, indeed by appending to it the onus of totalitarianism and thus summoning the support of leftover Western anticommunist energies, a new, nominalist individualism comes to light.

Perhaps I am reading too much into the spontaneous overstatement of a brief dialogue. But because it contains a hope whose tugs and temptations I certainly feel as well, I consider my reading not damning of Kristeva (on whose written corpus I continue to draw) but illumining of a pervasive postmodern tendency. Certainly in the work of feminist theology, doubly accountable to practice (on the fronts both of church and women's movement), one tires of the dogmatic and contradictory stress of an oversimplifying discourse. Wouldn't it be refreshing just to specialize, to cut loose from all those global, save-the-world pomposities, those rather cardboard-sounding, ill-founded hopes by which we purportedly practice our accountability to our communities? Haven't those hopes been sucked about dry? Do they desiccate our own creative resiliencies? As to the great progressive schemes of social nurture and mutual responsibility, maybe the old deathbed curmudgeon recently portrayed by Jason Robards in Harold Pinter's *Moonlight* rightly wrote off his two wayward and unemployed sons for "living off the breast of the state." Certainly it is what the experts in economics tell us. Maybe a modest return to individualism would be more responsible and more interesting.

Unfortunately I cannot evade the global consequences of such a return. The more we detach our discourse from the frail global networks of accountability which the social movements have mobilized over a century, the more we suck at a certain breast. When Columbus on his desperate third journey first set eyes on South America, at the mouth of the Orinoco with the great peaks of his *otro mondo*—the other world—rising behind, he figured he had fulfilled the biblical prophecies of Isaiah and the Book of Revelation. Rather than awaiting the new creation, he had "discovered" the new heaven and earth. And though he fled in terror at the prospect of entering paradise unbidden, he recognized in it the shape of the world, roundish but like a pear, with the lost garden of Eden top and center, he said, like *una teta de mujer,* the earth a woman's breast, with paradise as the nipple. The nipple of paradise inspired his most brilliant cartography.[18] As we still suck at that nipple in the most voracious and material of senses—indeed as I gratify my oral addictiveness with yet another scholarly cup brewed from fine Colombian beans—how shall I claim that "all global problematics are archaic"? Does such an intellectual disappearing act make transnational corporate neoliberalism go away? Would I thereby disenfranchise the coffee plantations and their rabid ecosocial practices? Or does it rather allow me to consume the products of the southern hemisphere in peace, knowing that the ecological, economic, and political issues of neocolonial interdependency do not concern me?

To be sure, the site of "things actually happening" is always the microcosm—so then it behooves us to investigate the character of that individual or local actuality. Feminist theology so far has developed in disciplined attentiveness to these global "issues." We have been groping toward a narrative of the person as a labyrinthine interaction with these transpersonal issues, with sex/gender as our Ariadne's thread. To the extent that we have cultivated an ontology of relation, an ethic of mutuality, and a resultant ecofeminism of global interdependence, we have done so for the sake of situating the accountable individual at or rather *as* the node of intersecting "issues." Otherwise the truly "archaic" and still very powerful ontology of the autonomous, separate, and quasi-fixed individual will reign, adding the delights of mutability to that about which Fredric Jameson and David Harvey[19] have warned: that postmodernism will deconstruct any possible basis for a critique of global injustices, while in its stead offering a "fetishism of the local"[20] amidst the ongoing consumer feast on the body of the earth and its subject populations, human, animal, and vegetable. That critical theory includes a growing number of postcolonial critics itself is, as one of them, Gayatri Spivak, would be the first to note, no guarantee against its neocolonial convenience. Indeed she quiets any self-congratulatory academic celebration of "difference":

> Arguments from culturalism, multiculturalism, and ethnicity, however insular and heteromorphous they might seem from the great narratives of the techniques of global financial control, can work [to obscure such separations] in the interests of the production of a neocolonial discourse. Today the old ways, of imperial adjudication and open systemic intervention, cannot sustain unquestioned legitimacy. Neocolonialism is fabricating its allies by proposing a share of the center in a seemingly new way (not a rupture but a displacement): disciplinary support for the conviction of authentic marginality by the (aspiring) elite.[21]

When Spivak elsewhere proposes a "strategic essentialism," not to encourage the restoration of the old colonial identities but to contend with the decolonizing necessities of communal self-organization, she implicitly allows for a subjectivity founded neither on substance metaphysics nor on its mere disavowal.[22] In terms of gender, as de Lauretis has recently argued, antiessentialism among critical theorists has merely intensified the heterosexist identities of academic respectability (as the main examples of the "bad," that is, radical and therefore essentialist, feminism are invariably the lesbian separatists Mary Daly and Adrienne Rich). Antiessentialism as a criterion of theoretical correctness (T.C.) certainly achieved a preliminary loosening up of ontological presumptions and epistemological habits—to be sure, of the sort already achieved in the antiessentialism of, for instance, process metaphysics.[23] But such T.C. seems otherwise to have intensified rather than alleviated the self-destructive divisions within the potential coalitions of women among our own groups and with other social movements. And yet the only moral justification for the declaration of "difference" was, in Lorde's terms, to enable relationship across difference by acknowledging the differences by and through which we might connect. She early declared that

> it is not those differences between us that are separating us. It is rather our refusal to recognize those differences, and to examine the distortions which result from our misnaming them and their effects upon human behavior and expectation.[24]

IV

In terms of the first trope of this essay, we may be said to be sucking at the breast of poststructuralist theory; indeed, to be drinking father's milk through female authors. Yet as the trope itself confuses gender, so does the authorship of feminists who are no more or less dependent on malestream theory than any of us. The point is rather that the denial of relationality, with its heavily pre-Oedipal associations, smacks of what Kristeva (indispensably) called abjection—of a distaste for the maternal milk, a disgust with the fluid "issue" of issues, a histrionic desire to be free of all encompassing, "global" connections, of all that binds us to the (m)other in those bonds of mutual accountability that may prove suffocating.

I hear this tone especially in feminist antirelationalism, which is one but only a recent one among many species of antiessentialism.[25] Is tone too subjective and affective a notion for a theoretical critique? Musically speaking, of course, it is no more subjective than any other aspect of organized articulation, and for present purposes, it helps designate an affective cover for cognitive inadequacies. I hear this particularly defensive, dismissive tone more among feminist theorists than among our male counterparts, sounding like a denial of something that is not merely other, but self. Especially, or at least most relevantly, I read this attitude of abjection in a certain style of feminist theological reception of "theory." Given what I have described as a defining feature of feminist theology so far—its ability to reconstruct individuals as locally adherent intersections of global processes, by way of a reflective process at once material and spiritual—it would be a shame to surrender to the antiessentialist dogma just as women in philosophy are throwing it off. But perhaps it is inevitable that theologians lag behind the theoreticians they feed from.

I need to address more specifically the danger for feminist theology. I find the absorption of poststructuralist assumptions worrisome, not so much in feminist theology engaged in the explicit interchange with French and U.S. philosophical feminist theorists (as initiated in *Transfigurations*),[26] as in a certain trendy drift of thinking. That is, the more *casually* antiessentialist, antirelationalist, and antireferentialist reflexes that are beginning to show up in feminist religious discourse seem to denote a new discursive grid seeking to function like common sense—and therefore marking off a new sense of what is *au courant* and what is passé. These reflexes show themselves best in certain critiques of feminists by other feminists competing for the same theological turf.

One recent example will suffice, that of Elisabeth Schüssler Fiorenza's *Jesus: Miriam's Child, Sophia's Prophet.* As she pursues helpful hermeneutical investigations of the early Christian language of Jesus and its christological range, she marks herself off from various current feminist Christologies. Whether or not she would count herself a feminist theologian, she makes ambitious theological claims for this work. Therefore I consider her to have opened herself to theological critique, indeed, in such a way as to perhaps allow a certain helpful indirection in the assessment of our own tendencies. Her confrontation with feminist Christologies—which by definition occupy the turf of theology—is pursued, as we shall see, not as a complementary or even cross-disciplinary project but rather as strategy of supersession. In order to establish her own liberation-rhetorical epistemology, she targets what she dubs the "'canonical' position among feminist theologians," that of a "relational christology" as put forth by Carter Heyward and especially Rita Nakashima Brock. In Schüssler Fiorenza's reading, relational feminist theology succumbs to the "same discursive structures of the sex/gender system inscribed in 'heroic' christological discourses."[27] In other words, it reappropriates the very patriarchal constructions of reality it criticizes, by virtue of its relationality. This is the sort of circular deconstruction we all like to pull on our opponents. How well does it work in this instance?

Schüssler Fiorenza quotes Cathie Kelsey's critique of Brock with approval: "It is feminine to be concerned about relationality, so we have a feminist theology of relationship."[28] In other words, because women have been constructed as experts in relationship, any feminist rhetoric of relation represents a regression to femininity. Hence the critique of relationalism offers Schüssler Fiorenza the opportunity to deploy the rhetoric of antiessentialism: "[F]eminist theologians must no longer articulate wo/men's identity in essentialist universalistic terms" (*Jesus,* 188).

Inasmuch as it stimulates us to question continuously the temptation to acquiesce in traditional roles for which we have been often rewarded within the terms of the sex/gender system, her challenge to the possible essentialism of feminist relationalism is well taken. Certainly Brock and other relationalist feminists do make use of the interpersonal and developmental categories of psychoanalysis and feminist psychology (as do the poststructuralists whom Schüssler Fiorenza presupposes for their linguistic antiessentialism and critique of the sex/gender dogma, but whom she fails to engage in explicit exchange). Schüssler Fiorenza demands that feminist Christology "must not be conceptualized in personalistic, individualistic terms as connectedness between individuals. Rather it must be articulated in sociopolitical categories" (54). She proposes "that feminist theological reflection privilege soteriological over christological discourses and social-cultural over individual-anthropological theological frameworks" (89). By "soteriological" she seems to mean anything which serves "the struggles for liberation" (57).

The question is whether her binary opposition of individual versus sociopolitical, of feminine versus feminist, of anthropological-ontological versus liberation-rhetorical accurately captures any important relationalism. Or is it perhaps her very dualism which constructs for them their "essence"? I do not for the moment wish to belabor the improbity of this philosophically understudied tradition of essence-bashing, here uncritically adapted from poststructuralism. She seems to assume that her own appeal to "feminist movements around the world" represents an alternative to the supposedly essentialist and homogenizing move of which she accuses other white feminists, that is, of "reading or speaking *as a woman*" (188). (Hence her "wo/men" device, which might have worked in a more playful script.) Indeed the women of those movements do not want to be defined in terms of a universal white woman. Yet they would be appalled to learn that a white woman would deny them the prerogative of "speaking as a woman," let alone of strategically deploying the category of gender, so key in the nongovernmental organization and Beijing debates for the rights of women. Moreover, those other movements usually also refuse to be identified as "feminist." Her own soteriological criterion therefore poses a problem for Schüssler Fiorenza's attempt to evade an identity-political essentialist "woman's" stance while appealing to liberation rhetoric. While she like other U.S. feminists prefers "feminist" as a political-epistemological term to "women" with its potential biologism, the women of color to whom they appeal against other white feminists prefer "women's movement" to feminism. Indeed, when "struggles for liberation" become the ultimate criteria of justice, themselves therefore not subject to any ethical norms, it is hard to understand how one has evaded "identity politics," which names nothing other than the strategies of those movements.

A key point in Schüssler Fiorenza's argument lies in its caricature of relationalism as the canonical ideology of a new cult of the "white lady," "articulated with reference to elite white ladies" and held up as an ideal for all women (57). While I understand the temptation to join Thistlethwaite and other white feminists in attacking *other* white feminists for their racism (especially when those feminists are upholding a rival theory), Schüssler Fiorenza's main example of the white feminist essentialist-relationalist happens to be Rita Nakashima Brock. Unless race is a more shifting and disembodied category than even postmodern gender, Brock was still a Japanese and Hispanic American, with a powerful political identification with women of color, when I last heard. Is this misreading of Brock a matter of an empirical mistake? Hard to imagine, given the contents of all of Brock's recent writings. It seems rather the result of a systemic oversight—indeed of an epistemic "essentialism," if I may say so.

Most white women have (as Nakashima Brock, who is neither, often points out) continued to construct race as a matter of black and white. Does this exclusionary habit perhaps support certain binary oppositional thought patterns to which the "kyriarchy" still tempts us? The point of feminist relationalism, as I understand it in the authors whom Schüssler Fiorenza lambastes, has of course been precisely to criticize the binary oppositionalism of the dominant androcentric paradigm—including that of much modern liberation rhetoric. The heroic Christology which Brock has questioned tends to support messianic and warrior-centered emancipatory movements. Some of us cannot then consider mere "struggle for liberation" an adequate soteriological or even just ethical norm. We would surely want to be able to distinguish, for instance, between the appeals of the Shining Path and the FMLN, for example, or between different kinds of sex/gender arrangements within different U.S. social and religious movements.

Moreover, feminist theologies of relation, whatever their level of intellectual sophistication, had, more than other feminisms, already moved beyond single-issue feminism, single-cause theories of evil, and essentialist construals of femininity. Relationalism in theology was always based on a thoroughly historico-constructive view of selfhood, derived to some extent from the early and radical antisubstantialism of Whitehead, which long before deconstruction had deconstructed any notion of fixed subjects or their essences. Those of us (and I count myself among them) who explored these process-relational categories presupposed a critique of the dualism of individual/society and worked to channel and politicize personal and interpersonal intensities for the emancipatory struggle. We thought we were doing this precisely by refusing the sort of static opposition of the relational to the abstractly sociocultural which so much justice rhetoric demands. For already in the late seventies it became clear that such rhetoric, even in Schüssler Fiorenza's most recent appeal to "a permanent process of critical reflection and transformative solidarity," readily rings hollow. It lacks the recognition of interdependence and the hope for reciprocal and just relations between persons and peoples, between movements, between species, that lends "struggle" its motivating power beyond the sites of mere necessity to which white feminists are hardly privy—but also beyond the elite indignation of white spokeswo/men for liberation.

Schüssler Fiorenza has much to teach regarding the "rhetorical-symbolic" reading of early Christian texts. Indeed she has cast her lot with the popular presumption that language does not refer to the world: "If language is a sociocultural convention and not a reflection of reality, then one must theologically reject the ontological identification of grammatical gender and divine reality as well as grammatical gender and human reality" (162). That is quite a subordinate clause for a feminism engaged in theo-ethical discourse! She is not arguing (with Richard Rorty et al.) that language cannot "mirror nature" or that it cannot reflect its objects or represent their essences literally: rather, simply, that it does not reflect reality. This is the sort of casual, philosophically charged but philosophically unargued absorption of current cultural assumptions which worries me the most for feminist theology. Her point of course imbibes the larger poststructuralist theory of discourse, in which rhetorical analysis tends to take the place of historical or contextual, let alone ontological, reference. Indeed the centering of postmodern "theory" around language is the basis for both its helpful epistemological antiobjectivism and its troublesome anthropocentrism. In its American reception, this lingocentric bias believes it can do without any notion of the correspondence of language to reality. To critique delusions of objective reference is one thing; to blithely surrender to the trendy academic presumption that discourse reflects only itself is another. Without elaborating that argument in the present context, I duly note the perplexing phenomenon: that one who would found the legitimacy of her own discourse on "the struggles of social movements" is at the same time willing to throw out the capacity of discourse to reflect reality, that is, to address its world, as though that world of suffering and struggle *existed* apart from one's rhetoric about it.

What are we then to make of her own rhetorical strategy when it comes to reading contemporary texts? Again referencing Brock's proposal for a relationalist alternative to christological hero worship, Schüssler Fiorenza writes: "Feminist christological discourse must abandon and replace with an epistemology of liberation both the christology of Jesus the great individual and its corrective conceptualization as 'power-in-relation'" (57). In other words, her own rhetorical alternative, if one can find it, would supersede in one fell swoop both patriarchal Christology and the targeted feminist Christology. What sort of epistemology, what use of knowledge/power, does Schüssler Fiorenza's supersessionist rhetoric imply? *Abandon and replace*—a phrase consonant with the endless stream of "shoulds" and "musts," symptomatic of ethical imperatives unconstrained by the ambiguities of either a social ontology or a postmodern pluralism, let alone by any awareness of their own inconsistency. How consistent is the style with her discursive project? Perhaps such a commandment to feminist theologians to "abandon" their own methods and "replace" them with Schüssler Fiorenza's must be read at face value, as a performance of the antirelationalism of her content. Its epistemology then reads consistently as an oppositional either/or logic of subject/object, right/wrong, easily correlated with the dyads of public/private, liberation/relation, around which her logic pivots. Ongoing question and conversation are not elicited within such a model. Indeed even interdisciplinarity between feminist biblical hermeneutics and feminist theology, whose incipient Christologies she simply disses with nontheological criteria, is imperiously slighted. One is left only, as in traditional models of power as knowledge, with the choice of conversion to the correct side of the binary. Might one have thought such hierarchical dyads to be none other than a late modern form of the "kyriarchy"?

V

We have read rather closely two very different deployments of feminist postmodern epistemology. Both would reject any relational model of the individual, and therefore any social ontology. Indeed, both would reject ontological description out of hand, privileging instead a lingo-centric epistemology. But while Kristeva would liberally move away from "global" to "individual" preoccupations, Schüssler Fiorenza drives in the opposite direction, from the individual and the interpersonal to an abstract global liberationism. In other words, both reject the mediating realm of interdependent relations in favor of either a microcosmic or a macrocosmic social epistemology, one defined by the production of discourses.

If, however, one holds to a social ontology and its inherently mutualist epistemology, these opposite motions seem to mark differences along a single continuum of disrelation. For relation as I understand it only occasionally breaks into discourse, though it is precisely through discourse that we render its sentience *conscious.* Con/sciousness itself betrays its relational roots etymologically: "knowing together." There is no knowledge that is not an act of "knowing together," an interaction not of subject with object but of subjects reciprocally. Such reciprocity is neither good nor bad in itself but merely registers the impact of our actions as interaction. To the extent that such reciprocity is recognized, ethics is possible. To the extent that what Hegel called "mutual recognition" is achieved, ethics is satisfied.

A relational epistemology therefore understands itself to be engaged in descriptions of nondiscursive relations in a style and with a care which "theory" may render irrelevant. To put it clearly, mutual recognition demands more than talk. That nondiscursive zone of sentience, sensation, and sentiment presents itself at any given moment as the *pre*discursive zone of human self-consciousness. Any effectual social ontology must thus describe not just a prediscursive—indeed pre-Oedipal—matrix of human interactions but the vast ecological unconscious in which humans are embedded. It would follow that the anthropocentrism of the epistemological privilege of language precludes the social ontology of the subject. The entire haze of material and affective relations by which the moment is suckled into human form fades into oblivion within such lingocentric reduction. Or worse, it is captured within the realm of Kristeva's "abjection," a superb discursive tool for diagnosing matriphobia in less dualistic terms than feminism had initially enabled.

What does this abjection of relations mean for gender analysis? In Kristeva, feminism drops out as itself too global a discourse. Schüssler Fiorenza discursively breaks "woman" or "women" into the self-conscious "wo/men" while she nonetheless holds with white heat to the vastly more limited category of "feminism." Yet feminism should now supposedly float free from "reality." But then its entire claim to mobilize the best of the

Christian and Jewish prophetic and wisdom traditions for liberation and sex/gender justice lacks any reference—to or in "reality" at least. So the feminist theological concern for "power in relation," that is, for gender justice as implicated in multiple, crosscutting emancipatory movements, is broken at the joint by the incursion of "theory"—yet in the name of that very social justice agenda.

A more philosophically grounded theory (such as Kristeva's) might get away with its elegant political and global irresponsibility and its sublimation of cruder feminist movement agendas. But a Christian feminism is left looking rather foolish: clinging to social-ethical criteria which have lifted feminist discourse beyond white women's self-interest, it buys into the antisociality of postmodern individualism at the same time. That is, its antirelationalism may claim to be anti-individualism. But it must lodge that claim in the presupposition of that ontology of the separate self on which individualism depends. By so doing we lose our purchase on the rich and barely explored "relational" alternative to individualism—in the name of an unnamed collectivism still redolent of the messianically political metanarratives its French-derived theory is directed against.

By the same token, with that blithe gesture by poststructuralism which is dispersing itself among the humanities, Christian feminism sacrifices the capacity of its discourse even to discuss what Luce Irigary calls "sexual difference." It does this because it cannot distinguish between overuniversalized essences and relational conglomerates. That is, it cannot distinguish between an essentialist individualism, an essentialist globalism, and an ecosocial ontology. Inasmuch as it cannot make this distinction in terms of an ontology of the subject, neither can it do so in terms of sex/gender. Therefore attempts to think of sexual difference in its biosocial complexity will be a priori undermined.

Feminist theology, I would argue, does not benefit from boxing itself into the false binary opposition of either psychoanalytic individuals or liberation collectives. Such entities exist only in abstraction from the open flow of influences continually shifting the boundaries of persons and their social interactions. Those of us inventing relational feminisms had not, contrary to stereotype, been considering the dynamic interactivities of the self as a pretext for return to Victorian femininity or to the mother's breast. Rather, the social ontology of the subject allows us to acknowledge the potent influences of maternity on our own sexual self-formation, while acknowledging the maternal itself as the effect of multiply layered social formations. The point is that any intellectually credible relationalism is based on theories (yes, "theory" existed before the U.S. reception of French deconstruction) of any subject, human or otherwise, as intrinsically constituted by its relations. So of course relationalism has nothing to do with the charge leveled against it, that women are "essentially" more connective. Rather, all subjects are "essentially" but only partially formed by their connections (the social matrix is a defining part of who you are; it necessarily but partially determines who you are). Women, due to the particular sociohistorical pressure of our patriarchal connections, are simply more likely to bear the burdens of awareness of those connections. For in our capacity to give birth and due to early empathy with our mothers, we are simply more likely than men within the same system to become sensitive to the ebb and flow of relations.

Women, in other words, do not carry the burden of relations because of some relational essence, some necessarily more nurturant nature. Nor does external coercion explain our proclivity (i.e., a probability as opposed to a necessity) for greater connectivity. Rather, we have been socially and discursively molded to perform the intimately and consciously relational tasks which men of power could always abdicate. There is no intrinsic virtue to such performances. They may merely draw on the relational knowledge for questionable private ends, as through manipulation of family members; or for questionable public ends, such as greater white solidarity. Within the kyriarchy that zone of prediscursive connectivity remains the maternal abject (to combine Schüssler Fiorenza and Kristeva), and thus not surprisingly still repels many feminists, for whom the lure and the threat of a traditional feminine role remain far too close.

VI

Let the trope of the father's breast fleetingly encode for us here the still-confused, still-transformative desires of feminist theology. If the traditional questions of theology stem from the high patriarchies of Christian doctrine, they yield us little nutrition. Indeed they "express" the centuries of post-mammilogocentric theology, where gender lost its subversive openings into ambiguity. It is as we draw from other sources of theory that we seem to gain a sense of methodological renewal. For example, in the uses of poststructuralist theory, a certain conceptual Eucharist unfolds. Its gender skepticism contributes to the ongoing desubstantiation of sexual essences inaugurated by feminism. Yet I have suggested that at the same time it may also be congealing the liquid con/sciousness of a self-in-relation into substantial individuals or solidified liberation collectivities. So the milky fluidity internal to the postmodern "subject" may turn cheesy, that is, if it lacks the nutritive fluidity of a social ontology of the self, and instead presents ethically suspicious and philosophically deficient criteria.

I suspect that the epistemology which would support a sustainable emancipatory theology for women requires an ontology which exposes women to a peculiar version of what Harold Bloom called the "anxiety of influence." We are understandably allergic to a noticeably feminine "substance" of any sort; if feminist theories offer anything that seems to force the breast down our mouth it stimulates rebellion, an irresistance to suffocation. Thus Irigaray suggests we speak while feeding a baby, "so that the child does not feel that the milk is being stuffed down his or her throat, in a kind of rape."[29] Unfortunately the father's breast so promisingly proffered by the poststructuralist theorists, male or female, seems for all its speech to encourage among U.S. feminists mere matriphobic reaction. That effect is worth worrying about inasmuch as it invites a comfortable return to andro/anthropocentric rhythms of subjectivity: influence from the (m)other is minimized, autonomy maximized, and the pre-Oedipal/animal/prediscursive exhaustively superseded by the highly cultured discursive.

Yet as the Father's breast among early Christians perhaps briefly held open the unlikely possibility of female-bodied transcendence, so perhaps the ambivalence of feminist theory toward its own maternal matrix still holds open the dialectics of femininity: the possibility that a mother's embrace could encode thought and not only feeling, that a woman's breast could bring to mind the circumambient embrace of "reality," good and bad, global and local, political and private, social and ecological, pumping its in/fluency into our prediscursive beings and demanding the continuous reinterpretation of our own discourses.

Such mindfulness requires Sophia indeed. In Clement's christological poem at the conclusion of the *Pedagogos,* Christ as the milk now flows from the breasts of "the Bride"—apparently coterminous with the Father. Such a gender shift is possible by identifying divine wisdom as the source of the milk: "O Christ Jesus, heavenly milk of the sweet breasts of the graces of the Bride, pressed out of Thy wisdom."[30]

Within the currents of influential feminisms, we do not need to figure out whether the Father is really a Mother. Nor vice versa. Those sex/gender roles have forfeited any fixed metabiological meaning. Perhaps our maturation as a movement requires rather that in the spirit of "the powerful Child" we recognize ourselves in relation to each other in particular and to "reality" in general; that we at times may think like "Babes nourished with tender mouths, filled with the dewy spirit of the rational pap."[31] The "rational pap"—Sophia as food and as feeding—deconstructs the binarism of rationality and nurture which dictates not only gender stereotypes but transnational economics, where whatever is conducive to profit is rational, whereas whatever makes basic human welfare a priority appears to breed irresponsibility, socialism, and dependency.

Nor do we need to "get in touch with the child within"—if that means a regressive return to a surreptitious archetype. Nonetheless there is something to be said for overcoming at once the glorification and the fear of the childlike. How else would we deconstruct the traditional discourses of maternity and paternity which we have imbibed as infants? Feminism's coming-of-age means outgrowing late-adolescent revolts against mom as well as dad. It also thus facilitates in its margins the unprecedented theological evolution that becomes possible when we cease to replay endlessly our version of the modern Oedipal revolt against "God." To outgrow the androcentric discourse of separation and independence, we need to understand that connectivity cannot be equated with femininity or dependency. Relationalist insight needs maturation through constructive criticism, not abandonment. By inscribing channels for the world's inflowing juices and our own outflowing contributions, it begins to trace an ambiguously gendered possibility for intimate and global relations. Such social ontology does not determine, suffocate, fuse, or ensnare—precisely because it can tell the difference between sociality and homogenization.

Perhaps such differentiation, more than a matter of philo/sophia, depends on the guidance of "She who milked Him,/ Because His breasts were full,/ And it was undesirable that His milk should be ineffectually released."[32] At the present moment in our own history, in which mothers appear as fathers and fathers as mothers, in which genders divide, multiply, cross, and mutate, it is undesirable that our fluid and nourishing feminist gift to theology and to theory be ineffectually released.

CHAPTER 5

THE SELF BETWEEN
FEMINIST THEORY AND THEOLOGY

Thandeka

THE HUMAN BODY is the magisterium of human knowledge as both teacher and student, subject and object of life. Our bodies expand beyond their physical boundaries as the touch of another becomes a sweep of feeling, a flux of sentiment, a current of ideas, the matter of engagement first felt. What this feeling means will be determined by a system of cognitions, a nexus of feelings, volitions, and muscular tensions related to a social history of attitudes, expectations, disappointments, and derailed affect-laden feelings.[1] An account of this nexus is a story of the way in which the interpersonal becomes intrapsychic, the cultural becomes personal biography, the psychic becomes social history. This account is both psychological and theological because the *cognitively* dark, affect-laden core of human relationship is also the hallowed ground of human engagement.[2] In this domain of our lives, the human body meets the expanse of life as a mutual embrace.

I call this domain of our lives the embodied self. My article is an investigation of this domain. This inquiry will identify the way in which the embodied self establishes the relationship between what we envision (theory) and what we believe (theology). To this end, my account is a story of the way in which the embodied self is found. I have undertaken this project because of the present state of feminist theological discourse.

Currently, feminist theologians often construct their theories of the self using ideas embedded in a "mechanistic metaphysics"[3] with a concomitant psychoanalytic-mechanical model of the self inspired by nineteenth-century physics. Not surprisingly, such constructions confound the theological claims feminists wish to affirm. In a word, the discrediting of feminist theological agendas has been, at times, an inside job. This is not a new insight. In 1987, Sheila Greeve Davaney called our attention to the conundrums wrought by feminist theologians' use of theories from the received tradition of modern thought.[4]

The agenda of the Iliff conference was a collective call for a critical assessment *and* reconsideration of our use of such theory. I presented my work in this context as a method for the construction of a theory of the embodied self. Noting that feminist theologians have formulated embodied theologies as sexual theology,[5] ecological theology,[6] process theology,[7] and womanist theology,[8] I argued that we do not have a systematic, intersubjective theory of the embodied self which affirms the human body as the magisterium of human knowledge.[9] "Body knowing" has meant "carnal knowing," which usually denotes sin rather than grace, fallen flesh rather than spirit, the scorned body as impediment to one's spiritual journey.[10]

To correct this systematic degradation of the body in much of modern thought, I chose to investigate the "ambiguity of embodiment." This ambiguity is the felt connection between the body as both site and sign of human knowledge.[11] My investigation entails a standpoint epistemology because it is both a critique of the modern notion of objectivity that separates subjective, embodied experience from objective, abstract claims and an affirmation of the efficacy of socially situated knowledge.[12]

The embodied self is defined in this article as *the felt congruence of mind and body with the surrounding environment as one moment of lived experience. The "feeling" of this congruency is cognitively empty but affectively full as an immediate, nonreflective, lived moment of life.* My definition of the embodied self unites intersubjectivist psychoanalytic notions of both embodied (mind-body cohesion) and embedded (the sustaining caretaker milieu) experiences of the self.[13] As an intersubjective description of the self, this definition identifies the way in which the gap between the interpersonal and intrapsychic realms of human experience is closed, as a moment of lived experience. My definition also affirms the first principle of a quantum systems theory of the self.[14] The rule of any such system is mutual complementarity: the observer and observed form an indivisible whole.[15]

The first section of this article is a brief introduction to the trinitarian heresy entailed in my theory of the embodied self. Without this context, the systematic oversight of the embodied self found in Western thought cannot be adequately explained.

I

The Gospel of John expresses Christianity's most basic understanding of embodiment.[16] According to John 1:14, the Word (logos) became flesh in one man: Jesus Christ. Christian theology's subsequent attempt to explain *how* this union occurred split the church into Eastern and Western orthodox traditions and divided Western theology into acceptable and heretical standpoints about God's internal relationship to the Son and the Holy Spirit. As a speculative *theory* about the way in which God became man, the culmination of this doctrine within Western Christian thought is found in the Hegelian system. Hegel made the Trinity the basis of his dialectic. The Holy Spirit's awareness that the Father and the Son are the same became the movement of spirit which propels the Hegelian dialectic. The essence of this spirit, according to Hegel, is self-consciousness.[17]

According to Hegel, "The Trinity is the speculative part of Christianity, the means through which philosophy can discover the Idea of reason in the Christian religion too."[18] From this standpoint, Hegel could claim that the content of his *Science of Logic* "is the exposition of God as he is in his eternal essence before the creation of nature and a finite mind."[19] Hegel claimed that his logic was the delineation of the internal trinitarian structure of God. Simply stated, Hegel's logic and God's logic became one.[20] For Hegel, the relationship between theology and theory (qua philosophy) was self-evident: it was the Holy Spirit. His dialectic, as such, was a trinitarian doctrine. This is not surprising because Hegel was both a philosopher and a Lutheran theologian.

Hegel's project was ambitious, but an ambiguous success.[21] His inability to demonstrate the necessary link between *Geist* (mind/spirit) and flesh (nature) also reaffirmed the split between mind and body he had attempted to bridge. Hegel's own post-Kantian attempt to bridge this gap in German idealism—which began with Fichte's discovery of the gap between the empirical and transcendental selves in Kant's theory of the self[22]—did not achieve its goal. Hegel's apparent failure brought this project to an end.

Kierkegaard's celebration of this breach as the gap between reason and faith into which one must leap, and the subsequent postmodern affirmation of this rent in Western theory, set the stage for a "radical" Christology in which the gap between mind and body—as the absence of cognizable identity—is construed theologically as man's new cross.[23] The repeated modern and postmodern returns to Hegel's system are part of a tradition in Western theory that keeps philosophy within the field of trinitarian concerns even after such a position is no longer speculatively tenable.[24] Without the middle term (spirit) affirmed as the link between mind and body, trinitarian doctrine is expressed as blind faith in the absurd (Kierkegaard) and the preponderance of difference wrought as the rupture of the integrity of identity and the propriety of person (Mark C. Taylor's a/theology).[25]

Friedrich Schleiermacher, who today is recognized as the father of modern Protestant theology, was Hegel's colleague at the University of Berlin.[26] Schleiermacher rejected Hegel's use of speculative reason (that is, his dialectic of spirit) to resolve the gap bequeathed to philosophy by Kant's flawed theory of self-consciousness.[27] Schleiermacher's solution began with feeling (*Gefühl*),[28] the embodied human experience of immediate self-consciousness. In Schleiermacher's dialectic, feeling became the content of the gap the Kantian "I think" could not grasp. By means of his own dialectic, Schleiermacher constructed a new theory of human experience. His theory explained human self-consciousness as a body-affirming feeling of congruence.

Karl Barth's most basic objection to Schleiermacher's theology is the central *theological* role given to this *human* experience of coherence. Schleiermacher, Barth argued, had compromised "a proper theology of the Holy Spirit" by propounding a "theology of [human] awareness." Human consciousness rather than the Holy Spirit was now the theme of Christian theology.[29] Simply stated, Schleiermacher had stripped theology of its "third" element, its principle of mediation: the Holy Spirit.[30] This absence of the mediating third stripped Schleiermacher's standpoint of a way to keep the distinction between "man" and God absolute.[31]

Barth called this non-trinitarian place in Schleiermacher's work its mystical element.[32] For Barth, this mystical element broached heresy. Schleiermacher's human link "cannot be," Barth argued, because the absence of the Holy Spirit prevents "man" from hearing the Word of God.[33] The heretical standpoint[34] *implicit* in Schleiermacher's theology challenged the relationships among *Geist,* flesh (the human body as part of the physical, organic world of nature), and the godhead proffered by the received traditions of Western Christian trinitarian theology and theory.

Contemporary discussions that remain focused on the absence of a necessary connection between mind and body continue a trinitarian agenda. This absence (of spirit) is affirmed as difference. This affirmation of difference is a continuation of a failed trinitarian speculative project. In other words, with the "link" (of spirit) lost, there is a determined effort *not* to find another way to affirm the bond between empirical and transcendental consciousness. Both the affirmation and the replacement of a trinitarian metaphysic are proscribed.[35] From this perspective, the contemporary problem of a lost foundation for absolute claims of truth is a postmortem legacy of the loss of this Christian, trinitarian spirit. By fixating on this loss, the postmodern agenda becomes a requiem for and thus a tribute to trinitarian speculative thinking.[36]

The theoretical conundrum of feminist Christian theologians who wish to affirm a link between mind and body can now be more adequately understood. Using the received tradition of a failed, trinitarian-informed, speculative philosophy in the Christian West, feminist Christian theologians find it difficult, if not impossible, to establish an internally coherent, theoretically respectable position which affirms *unity* as well as *difference* as core to human experience. The relationship between feminist theology and theory, from this vantage point, is paradoxical. Feminist theology cannot affirm the integrity of women's experience using ideas embedded in or fixated on failure, loss, and death.[37]

II

The contemporary feminist turn to Freud (and subsequently Lacan) for assistance in extricating theory from the conundrums wrought by the use of Western Christian trinitarian thought in feminist theology has further confounded the problem.[38] Ironically, Freud's work has been used by feminists to affirm the gyno-centered self discounted by a phallocentric theory of human development.[39] The work of Paula M. Cooey is useful in understanding the way in which the use of Freud (as well as Kant) has exacerbated feminist theological claims.

Cooey, in her book *Religious Imagination and the Body: A Feminist Analysis,* reaffirms Davaney's delineation of our use of the conceptual tools of modern Western thought. Cooey rightly notes that we as feminists "live with the legacy of Kant, even when taking a direct stand against him." Our theories affirm Kant's delineation of human experience and knowledge as always conditioned and structured by human modalities. This affirmation is "the default assumption" for many of us.[40] Coupled with the feminist use of Freud, whom Cooey characterizes as "one of the master architects of the deconstruction of the human subject" (68), feminist theory is in disarray. Cooey contends that the use of the conceptual tools of this received tradition by feminists has resulted in a complexity of epistemological debates within feminist theories over contending essentialist and cultural determinist positions, the former beset by tendencies either toward biologism or supernaturalism and the latter by idealist oversights of human physicality.

One source of the complexity of these debates, Cooey argues, is "the ambiguity of the body." These ambiguities in our theories are the result of the fact that our bodies are both a cultural artifact and the embodied sentience of our lived experience as subjects (111). We lack adequate theories that take this ambiguity into account. Notions of a noncomprised state of "woman" are dissolved in this mix of site and sign. Cooey calls for a theory of experience to bring balance to the current stock of feminist theories about women's experience. Cooey, however, does not construct such a theory. Rather, her task is to caution restraint by delineating the constraints imposed on our discourse by the ambiguity of our bodies as both site and sign. As we shall see, my theory of the embodied self is a theory of experience designed to fill in this gap in contemporary feminist thought.

For Cooey, the link between this polarity is mapping, an analysis conducted at a "micro-logical level of human existence that refers to the interaction between body as site and body as sign in the making of the body's significance for human experience and identity" (119). To elaborate this point, Cooey cites a passage from Jonathan Z. Smith's description of religion as practice and exercise in mapping. Writes Smith: "Religion is the quest, within the bounds of the human, historical condition, for the power to manipulate and negotiate ones [sic] 'situation': so as to have 'space' in which to meaningfully dwell."[41] Cooey affirms this call to map out the terrain of feeling as the link between site and sign, body and mind.

In the work that follows, I give an account of the way in which this "space" in which one can meaningfully dwell is established. This space is both the impetus for as well as the desired end of mapping. I shall give special emphasis to the work of D. W. Winnicott, Heinz Kohut, and Friedrich

Schleiermacher in my account of this "space." I do so because each of these theorists sought to find this space by retrieving the self overlooked by Kant (Schleiermacher) and Freud (Winnicott and Kohut). Although each undertook his search using a different set of methodological tools, I will argue that all three found and affirmed the same place: the field of human experiencing that is the center of human meaning and agency. Winnicott called this place the intermediate area of human experiencing; Kohut called it the nuclear self; Schleiermacher called it the natal hour of everything living in religion.

III

Psychoanalytic theoretician, analyst, and pediatrician D. W. Winnicott, until his death in 1971, was England's equivalent to America's Dr. Benjamin Spock. Winnicott endeavored to find an aspect of human nature classic Freudian psychoanalytic theory had overlooked: the link between subjective and objective human experience. Winnicott did this by dividing human experience into three realms: inner, outer, and between. He called the "between" area the intermediate place of human experiencing and peered into it to correct an inadequacy found in the standard psychological delineations of human nature. This place, according to Winnicott, is neither the inner subjective world of human experience nor the outer objective world of our experience. It is the place between the two that cannot be ignored.[42] This place, according to Winnicott, is the "space" in which we meaningfully dwell.

Not surprisingly for Winnicott the pediatrician, this place is first established as the field between the infant's lips and the mother's breast, the place aptly characterized by analysts Marion Milner and Clifford Scott as the body boundary discovery of "the me" and "the you," the place where the illusion of union and the fact of contact meet.[43] Winnicott did not intend to reify either the mother or the infant as the locus of this field. Rather, he wished to establish the expanse *between* them as a relational matrix of identity that is the center of the human self. As we shall see in the next section of this article, Kohut was much more self-consciously aware of the risk of reifying the mother and eventually chose gender-neutral language to describe the role of the infant's caretakers.

Winnicott characterized this place of engagement as the place of magic, mystery, and creation, the place of illusion where the infant discovers its power to create what it needs to satisfy itself. He constructed his theory around the notion of the "good enough mother" who initially makes an active, almost 100 percent adaptation to the infant's needs by affording the infant the illusion that her breast is part of the infant.[44] This adaptation by the mother makes it seem as if the mother's breast is totally controlled by the baby in a magical way (*Playing and Reality,* 11). The infant becomes the omnipotent magician, the creator *ex nihilo.* The infant experiences the external world as if it corresponds absolutely to the infant's own capacity to create (12). From the standpoint of the infant, it is hungry and cries and "voilà!" a breast is there to feed it. This experience is obviously illusionary, because the breast is not controlled by the infant. The baby is not omnipotent. The mother's task is to wean the infant from this experience of her breast as something created and controlled by the infant—but not right away.

According to Winnicott, these earliest experiences of the baby aligned with its mother create and develop into a subjective phenomenon within the baby called the mother's breast (11). From the infant's psychological standpoint, it has taken from a breast that is part of itself. From the psychological perspective of the mother, she has given milk to an infant that is part of her self. Thus, from these two standpoints, Winnicott argues, there is not really an interchange between them, because one is taking itself and the other is giving itself. The psychological overlap of these two experiences is the primal referent for what Winnicott calls the intermediate area between inner and outer reality: the between (12). Here we find the human experience of the unity of the act of creation and the thing created; here the creator and the created are one. The infant initiates the process that creates the breast and experiences its creation—the breast—as that which is itself. Psychologically, this is the space of confidence, the space out of which self-esteem emerges.

For Winnicott, this field of relatedness is "the basis of initiation of experience" (14); it is the place from which we become aware (27). This field is a cooperative space, the space where contact is experienced as union. Not surprisingly, Winnicott identifies this field of human experience as the place of congruity between our inner and outer realities: the place where apperception and perception meet. Here, the mind learns how to keep inner and outer reality simultaneously separate and interrelated. This simultaneity of keeping the internal and external worlds of experience together and apart is the linchpin of intersubjective psychoanalytic theory.

Psychoanalytic theorist Jessica Benjamin expands Winnicott's notion of the intermediate area of experience in order to embolden and add cogency to the way in which *both* identity *and* difference are maintained in the *same* moment of experience. In her essay "Recognition and Destruction: An Outline of Intersubjectivity," Benjamin does this by postulating not a sequential relationship but a lived "tension between asserting one's reality and accepting the other's [reality]."[45] This tension is the content of the "paradox of recognition" in which both denial and affirmation of self and other are entailed. These mutually contradictory feelings are experienced as the tension between them. This simultaneity of mutuality and complementarity, Benjamin contends, is the hallmark of the intersubjective perspective. Benjamin, by means of this emendation, affirms Winnicott's basic insight that "complementarity of the intrapsychic and intersubjective modalities is important" (52).

Benjamin justifies this emendation to Winnicott's work in noting the perspective which most psychoanalytic theories of infant development overlook: that of the mother. Benjamin's fine analysis of the infantocentric and androcentric standpoint embedded in much of current psychoanalytic theory carefully delineates the way in which the androcentric perspective renders male dominance the mediating third between child and omnipotent mother through the intervention and internalization of the Oedipal father. When the symbolic father is substituted for the space between mother and child, Benjamin argues, the mother's existence as an object of desire remains terrifying; the Oedipal repudiation of femininity, with its disparagement of women, then becomes a further obstacle to the creation of intersubjective space (55, 57).

An intersubjective perspective, by contrast, "shows that within the maternal dyad mutuality exists alongside complementarity" (55). Benjamin affirms the claim by psychoanalytic theorist Thomas H. Ogden that "the space between self and other can exist and facilitate the distinction, let us say, between the real mother and the symbolic mother; this triangle is created without a literal third person."[46] Benjamin concludes that "the existence of this space is ultimately what makes intrapsychic capacities creative rather than destructive; perhaps it is another way of referring to the tension between using and relating."[47]

What exactly is this space of relationship, this tension wire linking ourselves to others? We know what it is not: some thing. Neither Benjamin nor Winnicott has affirmed some "bit" of essentialist stuff such as the Holy Spirit, the soul, a spark of the divine, or a small particle of matter as the content of this field of experiencing. Rather, both theorists have described a process, a field of *human* experiencing, a range of relationships which assure the infant that its needs can be adequately addressed and satisfied. As we shall see, various types of air, water, and land metaphors can be used to characterize this space. Winnicott uses air metaphors. For him, this space is best conceived of as an environment, the self's oxygen, its breath of life. Without it, the psychic health of the baby is asphyxiated; its emotional life becomes contorted.[48]

This environment is our actual experience of relating to others. As a nourishing environment, this locus of activity with another is the infant's first experience of the congruence of inner and outer reality as one unit of experience. Here, inner and outer experience are one. This "between" is the referent for the embodied experience of wholeness. It is the living experience of unity, continuity, and coherence. This is an *embodied* experience because it is more than an idea. It is *felt* identity, *the link* that combines body, mind, and others into one unit of lived experience. It is, to use an air metaphor, our breath of life.

I call this congruency of self and other, mind and body, the embodied self. The embodied self is a lived moment of human experience as the continuity of our inner and outer life. This congruency is our most basic experience of the integrity of our life: the experience of the self at one with its surroundings.

The nineteenth-century German philosopher Wilhelm Dilthey argued that this self is beyond the grasp of the researcher.[49] Dilthey referred to this "psychological life unit," which he called self-consciousness, as "the stream of life itself."[50] For Dilthey, water metaphors best characterized this realm of human experience. Of this living moment of human experience, Dilthey wrote:

> The stream of life itself never stands still for observation, but courses ceaselessly toward the ocean. We can never grasp nor express it as it is, but we fix its partial contents. We break up what is flowing into firm discrete parts. From a reality whose complicated character we inadequately designate as complexity, many-sidedness, multiplicity, we select individual aspects as partial contents.[51]

This stream of life is the embodied self, the experiencing self. Continuing Dilthey's use of water metaphors, we can say that each of us is a wave of life, a crest of this stream of life. At any moment of our lives, each of us is a splash of eternity.

For Jungian theorists Ann and Barry Ulanov, their metaphor of choice is the anima and animus which "touch all aspects of our identities in the most intimate ways. They charge our body reactions with sexual feeling. . . . Their embrace is large enough to encompass truth, justice, and beauty, and find meaning in them as in ourselves seeking experience of them."[52]

Winnicott studied the contours of the human experience of this life-full engagement. The shapes that emerge from this intermediate area of experiencing, Winnicott argued, are the infant's first "objects." Winnicott used the terms "transitional phenomenon" and "transitional object" to refer to the sequence of events which represent and give specificity to this otherwise "neutral" field of relationships. The "objects," Winnicott argued, sustain the infant and allow it to expand its activity of relating inner and outer reality while maintaining an intermediate area of relief: a resting place. These objects are site-specific to the time and place of the infant's life. The infant, for example, will not have a teddy bear in a society in which such objects do not exist. But the infant will have something that serves the same function. This is Winnicott's point.

As the child matures, other cultural objects configure the intermediate area of experiencing Winnicott called "the between." Using mapping metaphors, these configurations are the bold relief, the topographic contours of this field. One such cultural object, Winnicott suggests, is art. Another is religion. The religious object as a transitional object—the Holy Spirit, for instance—is culturally determined. Such an object of religious devotion, is not, however, the field itself. It is an aspect of the field mapped or configured as contour lines. All trinitarian debates, from this standpoint, can be explained as discussions about the importance of this particular transitional phenomenon. Such discussions are examples of the way in which the field of human experiencing has been mapped, how it has been conceived of and simultaneously experienced as life itself. In other words, the mapping determines what an experience *consciously* means and thus the way in which it will be conceived.

We can now identify the inchoate form of the trinitarian heresy embedded in a theology which entails such a theory of human experience.

Within the locus of this intermediate area of experiencing, the Holy Spirit functions like any other transitional phenomenon: it is the means by which the human being *consciously* expresses its actual coherence and continuity as the congruence of inner and outer reality, one unit of experience.[53] Doll, teddy bear, Holy Spirit—each phenomenon is an expression of the way in which the self affirms itself in a determinate moment of consciousness. The experiencing self, however, is a wider and richer terrain than the contour lines and other determinate mapping expressions which "fix it" as a graspable subject and object of thought. One such mapped experience or "transitional object" of devotion is the Holy Spirit. For Winnicott, what is important about *all* such objects is the way in which they function for a person and whether they are respected by others. The center of the theory, as we can see, remains focused on human experience.

Our attention must now turn to an analysis of how the simultaneity of incommensurable events occurs as the same moment of human experience. This focus takes us into the realm of feeling. As we continue our discussion, we must keep in mind a crucial distinction made by Winnicott. The *field* of experiencing and the *objects* he refers to as *transitional* are not the same. We must also remember that Benjamin emboldened this distinction by reaffirming the independent center of activity of the (m)other. In sum, the cognized object is not the same as the embodied self. It is also not the same as the other the self encountered in a moment of lived experience. It is not the primal *reality* of the self's living encounter with another as a cooperatively lived moment of life.

IV

Heinz Kohut, as the founder of psychoanalytic self psychology, has been counted with R. D. Laing and Jacques Lacan as one of the three major psychoanalytic theoreticians who have widened contemporary concepts of the self.[54] Kohut's most basic claim is that empathy must be experienced and affirmed if the patient is to be cured. First empathic understanding, then explanation. Kohut called the field of empathic understanding "the nuclear self" and identified it as the self Freud had not taken adequately into account.

Traditional psychoanalytic theory, Kohut argued, has focused on the object as the target of the infant's needs. Kohut wished to emphasize the needs of the infant and the experience of the caretaker as a part of the infant's self. Kohut thus referred to this unit of the infant and its caretaker as the self-selfobject unit[55] and characterized it as the energic continuum, the empathic milieu. This empathic milieu is first felt by the infant as an affect, an immediate body-based awareness of the self as a feeling, a rush of sensations, an emotion, a sentiment, a vitality signal that life itself is present.

We must pause here and examine more precisely the content of the empathic milieu. As we shall see, this milieu has a cognitively "dark core." The "dark core" of the empathic milieu, as developmental psychologist Daniel Stern has pointed out, is interaffectivity. According to Stern, interaffectivity begins as a body-based awareness of another. It is an exchange of affective states. Empathy cannot parse the early stage of this exchange because empathy involves the mediation of cognitive processes.[56] Empathy thus is an abstractive process. It is the abstraction of empathetic knowledge from the human experience which precedes it: emotional resonance, the resonance of a feeling state. This is the (cognitively) dark core of intersubjective experience.

Stern identifies the earliest stage of the infant's "domain of core-relatedness" as "the physical self." Sometime between the second and sixth months of life, infants sense that they and their mothers are quite separate physically, are different agents and have distinct affective experiences and separate histories.[57] Between the seventh and ninth months of life, the infant discovers there are other "minds out there." The domain of intersubjective relatedness, Stern concludes, begins here.[58]

Jessica Benjamin provides us with an important emendation. Again, she focuses on the mother's perspective. This perspective, Benjamin argues, alters Stern's theory as to *when* the infant's intersubjective experience begins. Benjamin contends that from the mother's standpoint, whose infant returns her smile, affective sharing is already the beginning of reciprocal recognition. Benjamin thus reconceptualizes Stern's claim that affective attunement develops around eight or nine months, and argues that at this age intersubjectivity "proper" begins. Benjamin, wishing to emphasize the developmental transformations which take place *within* intersubjective experiences, writes, "I would rather conceptualize a development of intersubjectivity in which there are key moments of transformation."[59]

We must now understand the way in which such "key moments of transformation" occur. Our discussion begins with Kohut's analysis of the

way in which the infant's *body-based* feeling of unity is subsequently idealized as empathic bonding. We begin with Kohut's theory because of the
emphasis on the role of empathy in psychoanalytic cures. In this article,
particular attention remains focused on an analysis of feeling and the various ways in which this realm of human experience has been theorized.
Kohut's self-psychology theory about the importance of the role of empathy in cure brought about a sea change in psychoanalytic theory.[60]

To vivify an important transition point in the child's development
and the way in which empathic bonding functions in this moment, Kohut
offers the example of a baby girl

> who is picked up by her mother and thereby feels herself part of the
> omnipotent strength and calmness of the idealized selfobject. Later in
> childhood, however, when she walks away from her mother for the first
> time, the little girl will try to maintain the bond to her mother by turn-
> ing around and looking back at the mother's face. If she is an emotion-
> ally healthy child who has been surrounded by a milieu of emotionally
> healthy selfobjects, she will do so not primarily because she is afraid and
> needs to be reassured that she can return, but rather to obtain the con-
> firming reverberation of her mother's proud smile at her great new
> achievement.[61]

Kohut now makes an extremely important claim. The psychic content of this new step forward for the child is not adequately described by
saying that the self has separated itself from its selfobject. This new move,
Kohut contends, is not the breakup of a relationship between objects.
Rather, it "*embodies* the shift in an essentially persisting self-selfobject relationship from one level to another" (emphasis added).[62]

Kohut uses the term *embodies* to refer to this shift for three reasons.
First, he wishes to identify the deepest source of our personal integrity: the
way in which we experience body contact with another as the ground of
self-identity, cohesion, and coherence. Second, he uses the term to delin-
eate the way in which the experience of body contact shifts from the first
stage of the infant's physical contact and psychic merger with another, to
later stages of affect attunement in human development. Third, the term
embodies identifies the way in which the self's experience of fusion with
another links body, mind, and world into one unit of experience. Here,
self, object, *and* other form a coherent whole through empathic bonding
grounded in our organic reality as beings who first know (that is, carnal
knowing) through feeling. The term *embodies* focuses attention on the primary locus of feeling: the body. Kohut uses the term *embodies* to remind

us of our nature as part of an organic world that first knows right relationship through feeling the supportive, empathic presence of another. This embodied bond is transmuted, but it remains grounded in our experience as beings whose identities are built up through feeling.

As we have seen, the feeling of empathy is not the first experience of core-relatedness. This experience begins with the (cognitively) dark core of relatedness, interaffectivity. "Attunement," as Stern notes, "is a distinct form of affective transaction in its own right."[63] This link to another can be present without being cognized.

Interaffectivity, as such, is the "dark core" of the intersubjective experience of the other as an "intrinsically significant human presence."[64] It is the mutual regulation of affective experience within the developmental system of human interaction.[65] But how can we *feel* something that is not conceivable? How do we feel a relationship we have not first thought? To answer these questions, we must again go deeper into the structure of feeling. This exploration leads us to Friedrich Schleiermacher's original insight about the nature and structure of feeling at its most primordial stage.

V

Friedrich Schleiermacher, like both Kohut and Winnicott, was interested in the noncognizable field of human experience. As a philosopher and theologian, Schleiermacher found this field of human experience in the place *between* thoughts as the mind shifts from one determinate moment of conscious experience to the next. Schleiermacher called this moment, because it is noncognizable, the "nullpoint" of thinking. Concerning this moment of human experience he said: "[We] always experience [it] yet never experience [it]"[66] because it is the Whole of life—too vast to be encompassed as a discreet cognizable thought. Schleiermacher called this noncognitive experience of wholeness *feeling* (*Gefühl*).[67]

Schleiermacher developed his theory of this infinite moment of human experience "between thoughts" as a way to counterbalance Kant's rational, "one-sided" theology. Kant, Schleiermacher argued, had reduced religion to the concerns of speculative reason and turned God into a human idea. Such misadventures, Schleiermacher noted, would result in atheism. Kant's work was incomplete because he had failed to identify the "common seed," the point of transition by means of which the logical, ethical, and physical aspects of human experience could be understood as interrelated facts of human nature. To find such a transition, Schleiermacher concluded, a new paradigm for human nature must be developed.[68] In a word, Schleiermacher went looking for the embodied self and found it.

Schleiermacher reported his findings in his *Dialektik,* six series of lectures given in Berlin between 1811 and 1831.[69] In this work, Schleiermacher identified the state of nonsensate feeling as the place of convergence in which mental and physical events meet. These discrete events meet because they are touched by the infinite expanse of life itself. Life, in this moment, is without limit because thinking has not reduced its expanse to something cognizable. In this primordial moment, nothing in life is excluded. Nothing is left out. No one is a stranger. This infinite expanse of life thus includes the opposing shoals of our existence. Our experience of an unencumbered moment of life is the experience of life's infinite sweep. In this moment, the self and the universe, mind and body, inner and outer reality, are swept up together as the same rush of life.

This experience, Schleiermacher argued, can be described from two perspectives: mind and body—the intellectual and organic foci of human experience. From the standpoint of the intellect, this place is empty. Nothing can be known about this place because the mind is at its transition point: the place between thoughts. From the standpoint of our organic reality, however, everything is present because in this moment we are an indistinguishable part of life. Here, neither I nor you but *we* exist as one unit of experience.[70]

The feeling of this expanse is the source of our love of life. In this moment the infinite expanse of life is the current of our lives. The life of the infinite world courses through "our innermost nerves."[71] Life in this moment is a bridal embrace. This flow of life absorbs all, including ourselves, into eternity. This flow of life is the embodied self, the magisterium of being that exceeds the limits of reason.

This is the mystical element Schleiermacher discovered at the center of human consciousness.[72] It is also the core of Schleiermacher's incipient trinitarian heresy. By replacing human consciousness of the Holy Spirit with human consciousness of limitless life, Schleiermacher affirmed the integrity of the experience of human cohesion without making a theological claim about God's nature and revelation as the source of human cohesion. Concerned by the *absence* of a firm distinction between Christian revelation and human feeling, Barth asks bitterly in his book *The Theology of Schleiermacher:* "Rightly understood, is not *everything* revelation, and again rightly understood, *nothing*?"[73]

A theology of the embodied self reaffirms Schleiermacher's basic insight that *everything* in life as mutual and complementary embrace is indeed an occasion for revelation. From within this noncognizable moment of revelation, such a standpoint cannot claim that revelation is God showing God's self to the religious community. Rather, a theology of the embodied self claims that the *experience* is *thought of* by a *believing* community as God revealing God's self to the faithful. A theology of the embodied self can thus affirm with Ann and Barry Ulanov in their book *Religion and the Unconscious* that

> Revelation as a means of knowledge is the ultimate source of religious community. One must share the good news of the gospel—that God has shown himself, that from the other side of being the divine has reached forth in word and flesh to shape the invisible, inaudible, formless, bottomless expanse of our human being. Scandalous knowledge—that infinity addresses itself to finitude and finds lasting significance in human persons! How can anyone really contain such a thought? If grasped, this "news"—always newer than other news—must be flashed forth to the world. (18)

A theology of the embodied self affirms this claim as the way in which a *believing community understands itself when awash in the eternal waters of creation.* An intersubjective theological position, however, makes a distinction between the actual experience of the believing community and its claim of revealed knowledge. Human knowledge is always mediated by a determinate moment of human consciousness. This is Schleiermacher's point. The experience of a lived moment of creation is not mediated. The feeling is thus infinite. Thinking, in this moment, has reached its null-point.

From this standpoint, the term *God* cannot be used as the absolute reference for human truth claims. This is Schleiermacher's heresy. As Terrence N. Tice notes in his interviews with Barth, "Barth wanted absolute truth claims instead, whereas Schleiermacher felt he could not offer them. Barth believed that Schleiermacher therefore offered 'no external giveness of God,' that his was not a theology that relied on the 'truth of Christian revelation.'"[74]

Barth, of course, was right in this characterization of Schleiermacher's standpoint. The term *God,* from the standpoint of this experience of life itself, is a conscious cognition which describes the experience of being embraced by the eternal. The term expresses this moment as the first *cognized* referent for life. It is the first *idea* that arises from the immediate experience of the infinite expanse of life found between the restrictions of thought. This idea, however, like all ideas, has a culturally determined human history. It is a narrative about how experience can or should or must be thought. Barth characterized Schleiermacher's "inbetween place" as the absence of "Trinitarian thinking."[75] Without trinitarian thinking, Barth argued, humans as unpardoned sinners could not know God. Barth concluded that Schleiermacher's standpoint challenged "the decisive premise of all Christian theology"[76] that we begin as unpardoned sinners. This is not a claim an intersubjective theology of the embodied self can affirm.

An intersubjective theology of the embodied self affirms life in its fullness as the primordial experience and ever present moment of release from the constraints of human bondage. It affirms this experience as the felt embrace of life itself. This embrace is the experience of the infinite as a moment of one's life. Intersubjective theology calls our experience of this infinite moment of our life *grace*. Grace is the liberation of the self from the confines of conceptual schemes, socially constructed identities, public policies, and private strategies that have reduced the expanse of the self to the submissive/combative strategies of a tributary. These human-imposed restrictions of the self are sin. Human beings are not unpardoned sinners. Rather, they have committed unpardonable sins that result in a shutdown of our inner spaces.[77] There always remains, however, a tributary of life, some aspect of an "undestroyed capacity for love."[78] This pool of life is the embodied self.

We can now understand the way in which the embodied self is the link between theory and theology. The link is our experience of the discovery of ourselves as a moment of creation in which we exceed the confines of oppressive expectations, repressive social definitions, and egregious political practices. This font of experience is the healing waters of eternity, a moment of eternity awash in us. This moment, to use another metaphor, is our breath of life. In this moment we are the expanse which embraces more than we can say.

Such experiences demystify all socially constructed claims that reduce us to transitional objects and reduce life to transitional phenomena. When this experiential ground is present as the referent for our analysis of the self, we know that our lives cannot be reduced to the sum of our socially constructed identities. We know that we are too vast to be ultimately encumbered by the terms of our oppression.

A theory of the embodied self constructs conceptual schemes that account for this ongoing experience. It explains how incommensurable thoughts and feelings are reconciled in the same unit, the same moment of life. Where the theory breaks down into contradictory claims, the theorist laughs. She remembers Walt Whitman's words from his song to himself: "You say I contradict myself? Very well then, I contradict myself. I am vast. I contain multitudes." *And, she organizes. She has found the source which can sustain her as she says, "Never again!" to those who would oppress her and deny her the right to her full humanity.*

A theology of the embodied self offers rituals and beliefs that affirm life as always a moment of something more. It calls on this "something more" using sacred words as a litany to life itself. Always at the center of this theology is the recognition and affirmation of the inherent dignity and worth of every person. Each of us is a living moment of creation.

VI

In this last section, I shall briefly mention three immediate benefits to feminist theorists and theologians who affirm the embodied self as a central reference for their work.

1. The issue of essentialism will finally be laid to rest. The self affirmed by a theory of the embodied self is an intersubjective self. It is a process self.[79] This self is not some*thing,* but the experience of cooperative, mutually enhancing encounters with others as the core of self-cohesion, congruence, and coherence. Accordingly, debates as to whether we should refer to ourselves as "woman" or "women" will be seen for what they are: discussions about transitional objects. We must give such objects respect but we must not confuse them with their ground, the intermediate area of experiencing which is an experience of life-full encounter. This field of experiencing need no longer be mistaken for the particular cultural shapes (gender, race, class, and so forth) of our cognized identities. Our central task will be to promote and facilitate encounters which are mutual, cooperative, and complementary.

2. The Jewish/Christian debate in feminist discourse will reach a new accord. The removal of implicit trinitarian dogma from the theories used by Christian feminist theologians will allow them to recognize the common *ethical* agenda they share with their Jewish sisters. The ethical agenda of the embodied self affirms (with Martin Buber) that all real living is meeting. Ethics will assume a more central place in our collective theolog-

ical and theoretical concerns. The standpoint of a theory of the embodied self will help Christian feminist theologians overcome a cardinal sin in some of their work, as identified by Susannah Heschel in her article "Anti-Judaism in Christian Feminist Theology": Christian supremacy as the "sole and ultimate religious truth."[80] Intersubjective theology, as a theology of the embodied self, affirms the experience of inclusion as the hallowed ground of our humanity as moral agents.

3. The rift in womanist/feminist discourse will be healed. From the standpoint of a theory of the embodied self, the field of relationship is affirmed as the terrain of our humanity. A theory of the embodied self provides women with a set of conceptual tools needed to understand right relationship as an interactive and inclusive embrace of irreconcilable differences. Our relational bonds as embodied beings sanction Katie Geneva Cannon's claim in her book, *Katie's Canon: Womanism and the Soul of the Black Community,* that "every reflective and well-intentioned African American scholar who is consciously concerned with 'the liberation of a whole people' must work to eradicate the criterion of legitimacy that implicitly presumes an *absolute* incompatibility between Womanist critical scholarship and White feminist liberationist sources."[81] The claim of absolute incompatibility denies the expanse of human engagement which always expands beyond the limits of our categorical identities. Incompatibilities are always relative. Our humanity never is. How else can we explain to ourselves and others our surprise when we find ourselves affirming the value of persons whose ideas and practices we despise? The attitude of the Reverend Dr. Martin Luther King Jr. toward segregation is useful to recall in this context. Dr. King did not hate segregationists, he hated their policies and practices.[82]

In sum, both a theory and a theology of the embodied self affirm the place in our lives where definitions that restrict our bodies and restrain our minds lose their grip. The majesty of this place is our life, infinitely filled with the splashing waters of creation. In each of these moments, subject and object, observer and observed are one. In this sweep of feeling and thought, we are swept beyond first explorations, as Audre Lorde has said, and discover ourselves "in a landscape the rest of our lives attempts to understand."[83] Intersubjective theology is a systematic exploration, explanation, and delineation of the religious meaning and significance of this experience. In this life-full experience of encounter, the grace note of our life resounds. Our movement toward liberation has begun.

CHAPTER 6

CONTESTING THE GENDERED SUBJECT
A Feminist Account of the *Imago Dei*

Mary McClintock Fulkerson

THERE IS NO BETTER PLACE to look for the intersection of feminist theological and secular thinking than at the problem of the gendered subject, one of the most important and contested issues in current feminist thinking. Referring to the ways a subject comes to be defined as *woman,* the gendered subject first arose as a challenge to the false universal *mankind.* Early criticisms from women of color, lesbian women, and class-based feminisms noted the false universal in feminist appeals to woman. The recent jargon of feminist theory calls these problems of essentialism and the politics of identity. Feminist theologians need to care about the gendered subject because secular feminist accounts of the subject are unavoidable and embedded in our thinking. Put simply, the dilemma is how a feminism defined by the desire to alleviate women's oppression can avoid being hopelessly hegemonic with its focus on a limited subject.

My point of departure for this topic is theological feminism and its liberating frame for the gendered subject, the *imago Dei* of women. When we assess feminist theories of the subject, some of the problems related to hegemonic difference appear in the classic feminist theological treatment of women as *imago Dei.* However, a poststructuralist intervention offers a different kind of "difference" worth consideration, which can helpfully chasten a reconfigured story of the *imago Dei.* Finally, my assumption that feminist theory and theology are social-change practices leads me out of the potential paralysis of poststructuralist destabilizations to argue for the distinctive contribution provided by new Christian feminist narrations of

99

the creation of a loving, just God. I begin with a quick review of major feminist accounts of the gendered subject.

The Subject Changes

Contesting the notion of the subject is definitional to feminist explorations. This is best illustrated in the elegantly simple statement of Simone de Beauvoir—"One is not born a woman"—an insight which originated all modern feminist accounts of gender, says Donna Haraway.[1] Major types of feminism have explored the "constructed" character of the designation woman to varying degrees over these past decades. To see the emancipatory implications and problems of this development, we begin with nineteenth-century liberal feminism.

The now-familiar subject of liberal feminism emerged out of the "woman movement" in the United States. Defining women as potential citizens and rational creatures, this group thought education and legislative action would solve women's problems. This rationalistic notion of woman as person assumed masculinity and femininity to be secondary attributes of human being, a position that implied the existence of a common humanity. This generic concept has been judged suspect by later feminisms, and it is fair to say that many view this as an androcentric rather than a generic notion of human nature.[2]

A feminist alternative to the ostensibly genderless liberal subject emerged in the late 1960s when use of *gender* as a term for language forms was overtaken by its use to refer to constructions of maleness and femaleness.[3] Although its early expression in "gender identity" studies (focused on normal gender "roles") had a conservative effect, the possibilities for social criticism opened up with this change in definition. This work assumed that a biological difference grounded accounts of masculinity and femininity (a view that characterized feminist theorizing into the early 1970s).[4] However, even with its limits, an impulse toward more radical possibilities of criticism is evident in this move to constructionism in the treatment of gender.

Feminist thinkers developed these possibilities in the 1960s and 1970s, when the concept of gender could increasingly "contest the naturalization of sexual difference in multiple arenas of struggle," as Donna Haraway put it.[5] Marxist and socialist feminisms expanded feminist constructionism on the basis of Marxist, historicizing concepts of human nature. Human being as maker is *being made* in history in these systems.[6] Although such feminisms get stuck in the problem of expanding production to include "women's work," and continue to assume a biologically sexed subject, at their best they define human nature as *in process.* They thereby imply that historical change could (potentially) challenge even that binary subject, particularly if reproduction could be detached from women's bodies.

The expansion of the category *gender* takes a slightly different turn in lesbian and radical feminism.[7] These feminisms correct the Marxist failure to interrogate constructions of sexuality properly. From some radical feminisms we also get a revalorization of the female body. With that recovery radical feminism offers a notion of the subject that is sometimes judged to be essentialist. Such a view assumes that the authentic human is a woman, defined as a naturally gendered/sexed body. Despite this continuing naturalization, these feminisms expose the centrality of sexuality and heterosexuality, in particular, in the oppression of women.

I offer this hasty and unnuanced sketch of feminist accounts of the gendered subject to highlight the ways they employ the idea that a subject is *made a woman,* as de Beauvoir put it. Gender is a moving concept. It extends de Beauvoir's modest pronouncement by pressing the question, How are subjects constructed into something called woman? What it means to be a woman has increasingly been understood by feminists as a function of social definition rather than a natural essence or subjectivity. As such these accounts are exercises in social constructionism, asking how ideas about reality are products of their contexts and how they reflect the biases, limits, and possibilities of their contexts. They assume, then, the finite or partial nature of constructions such as gender. Although each feminism considered has a different frame for defining women's oppression and liberation, to some degree each assumes the emancipatory thrust of constructionism: that to recognize the *made* character of the female/male is to create an opening for things to be different.

This expanding application of the sociology of knowledge to the concept of the gendered subject does not, however, exempt these feminist interrogations from hegemonies, that is, from commitments to particular identities that deny the validity of the Other. According to a liberal feminist notion of the subject, one is a woman but aspires to be a neutral citizen; the stable, unacknowledged hegemonic subject is still white male. Marxist/socialist feminisms define the production of the subject through social and historical conditions, but remain generic on gender. Despite the expansion of feminist concern into the production of sexuality, for significant forms of radical feminism authenticity is ostensibly classless and colorless. The continual use of "woman" as a nonclassed or nonracial category to which class/race can be added is, according to Elizabeth Spelman, clear evidence of the serious ethnocentrism of feminism.[8]

Yet a commitment to women or to any group brings assumptions that cannot be avoided. Social constructionism, which is emancipatory for feminists, implies that it is impossible to produce liberatory discourse without particularity, which is necessarily a choosing of this and not that—a kind of exclusion. By virtue of being historical and contextual, the particular is partial and finite. There is, then, a risk entailed in any feminist commitment to particular accounts of women, at least the risk of partiality.

However, to further characterize and identify the nature of this risk we need to know feminists' visions of their emancipatory subjects. Only that knowledge would tell us what counts as the relevant form of hegemony. At least two possibilities seem likely for the reach of that vision. If the vision of feminism's emancipatory subject includes all women, then we would expect that its account explaining the basic oppression of women should be adequate for all women. Or at least we would expect that it had a frame for expanding the horizon of concern beyond its particular focus and analysis. However, the primary frames for feminism are specific accounts of the oppression of women. A liberatory discourse must analyze the constitutive parts of oppression and how to address it. It is clear from the continual criticisms that none has yet accounted for the oppression of all women. Only secondarily do these feminisms show how the category woman could expand beyond its limitations to recognize the subject who is different, particularly that woman not subject to the particular form of oppression under discussion. Implicit frames for humanism employed in feminist thinking and the potential to add categories (race, class, and so forth) via the logic of social constructionism strike me as the basic frames for expansion.

Although this assessment needs further argument, I find these treatments less than satisfactory for answering how feminism can expand its focus beyond a particular subject. While explaining the specific conditions that make woman an element in an oppressive set of social arrangements is the lifeblood of feminism, feminists should also enable the focus on the particular to resist rather than create new hegemonies. It is not clear to me how feminist commitments to the particular satisfactorily address the production of those capacities.

This is not the end of feminist theory's interrogation of the subject, however. An alternative to these approaches to the subject woman is poststructuralism, in which antihumanism effectively destabilizes the notion of subjects altogether. Feminist poststructuralist interventions will confirm my suspicion that constructionism is inadequate for a nonhegemonic account of the gendered subject and that a feminist theological project should be simply a project of inclusion. With it, feminist thinking about difference becomes more complex.

The Subject Disappears

First, I offer some background to poststructuralism. With the term *poststructuralism* I refer to a set of discussions about signification within but not identical with postmodernism. With roots in the linguistics of Ferdinand de Saussure and structuralism, *post*structuralism developed from thinking about language as an organizing structure or process of differentiation rather than a set of labels that reflect or mirror reality. Out of his realization that the synchronic (present structural) relations of words are more important for understanding language than their diachronic (historical, temporal) relations, Saussure determined that language makes meaning through differential and arbitrary relations of sounds and concepts which are ordered by systems.[9]

Poststructuralist corrections of Saussure's structuralism include the view that these relations do not occur simply in structures that function as closed or self-contained producers of meaning. Rather they intersect with and unravel into endless processes of differentiation—a mark of deconstructionist poststructuralism. Departures from his work also include attention to practices of meaning production rather than formal systems of relations—a mark of liberationist appropriations of poststructuralism.[10] However, what continues to characterize poststructuralism of all sorts is the gap between signifier and signified.

So far I have made poststructuralism sound like simply another, more far-reaching version of constructionism in the nonnecessity of signification. In fact my argument is that poststructuralism exposes the inadequacy of the latter. To suggest the difference I will explore an insight of Saussure's that endures in these interventions and constitutes the move away from or beyond social constructionism. The force of this move is to open up the possibility of epistemological nonfoundationalism and an alternative account of difference. Saussure explored the mechanics of the claim that differential relations constitute meaning. It is the differential relation between sounds that produces meaning at the level of the sign, the relation between the signifier (sound image) and signified (concept). At the semantic level another differential operates, but a differential all the same: that between the meanings of the signs. *High* makes meaning by virtue of its difference from *low, woman* in differential relation to *man.*

In this view the *foundation* of meaning is neither the external referent of a sign nor the context. Insofar as there is a foundation to meaning, it is the unheard, the unsaid reality *between* sounds, between signs, and between whole patterns that buttress the said and the heard. Otherwise put, it is the differential relation that makes concrete meanings possible. One can distinguish and understand the signs *pat* and *bat* because of the difference between the /p/ and the /b/. That difference is not heard, for it is not sayable. As Jane Tompkins puts it, "Rather than the differences themselves, you hear *the words that the differences make available.*"[11]

Similarly, one understands *woman* from the differential relation between it and its opposite, *man.* The distinction is the "unsaid." Thus knowing what the word is *not,* neither *man* nor those things that define maleness, is the closest we come to knowing what *woman* is. This semantic difference can be said, in the sense of unearthed, in contrast with the phonetic difference. Yet in both examples the unsaid is the basis for the possibility of meaning; it is the *outside* that accompanies the understanding of these or any signs.[12] Difference operates not simply in phonetics, but throughout an entire structure or language game to produce intelligibility. By offering the possibility for relations of contrast and similarity, Tompkins says, difference is "that which makes any such opposition come into being."[13] The instability of language becomes a metaphor for the instabilities of all discursive systems and practices in poststructuralism. Again, Tompkins puts it well by saying that language "becomes a metaphor for understanding or intelligibility itself."[14]

In a sense this inescapable connection among meaning, difference, and exclusion appears banal: meaning simply depends on exclusions and "nots," somewhat like the notion of the particular implied by the constructionist view. However, the understanding of partiality and exclusion, and the implications for defining difference, are not the same. Let me explain.

The Other that is created by the exclusion of *woman* in the identification of *man* as human is not simply a word not chosen or a different perspective that can be added; it is a foundation of sorts on which the systems that define *man* as ideal human rest. That foundation is a source of destabilization, not of the "truth" in the sense of bare reality behind the signifying systems. We might say that the *excluded* or the outside in poststructuralism becomes a metaphor for the Other, as the constructions of reality that threaten the unity of the reigning arrangement.[15] The kind of foundation offered by such an outside is not that of particular knowledges acknowledged as finite or partial—for such are always pieces of a potential explanation that may become certain. Unlike the theories of feminism as social constructionism, there is no fixed knowledge base in poststructuralism, however transient, from which to explain or to dissect the causes of a phenomenon. There will be no explanation that is not subject to destabilization. For what we might take as particular discourse is part of a configuration, a system, that always dissembles, that always hides an Other.[16]

The contrast between the treatment of a particular discourse as finite or partial and as a system of exclusion is helpfully illustrated with the work of feminist Judith Butler. Butler investigates the power/knowledge arrangements and cultural specificity that constitute binary gender difference. Her criticism of the identity *woman* is exemplary feminist poststructuralist investigation yielding new terrain for liberation, specifically, the previously occluded "outside" that supports the binary man/woman. Her argument challenges the view we found persisting in feminist theories that, regardless of how expansive gender became as a critical category, never questioned the givenness of male and female sexed bodies.[17]

Butler poses a poststructuralist inquiry: what is being excluded, unsaid, in the assumption of bodies divided into male and female? The outside that she uncovers has two elements. First, the conviction that there really are men and women rests on the hidden notion that being a man/woman is a deep truth about one's body and psyche, that it is, in fact, "the supreme secret (the 'mystery of sex') and the general substratum of our existence"—a complex of notions that are now recognized as modern Western ideas.[18] It does not rest on the access to the prediscursive bodied reality of real men and women that our language provides, but on the notions that sex *causes* desire and that desire is binary and naturally directed toward the opposite "sex." These are the hidden conditions of a discursive system of binary heterosexual definitions of human subjects.

This destabilization also exposes the outside or the excluded as "perverted" or "abnormal" subjects. Bodies with desires at odds with the oppositional arrangement fall outside the system of heterosexual binarism. The multiply sexed subject of Foucault's writing, Herculine Barbin, is used by Butler to display the outside of the heterosexual binary and the cracks and slippages in the heterosexual regime that s/he represents. These slippages give the regime away, just as authorities attempt unsuccessfully to unify features of Barbin's body and to match that unity with a gender and a deeply inscribed source of sexual identity. However, her/his body refuses to be unified satisfactorily under the binary options—male or female. Barbin is the outside to this regime, and s/he puts pressure on the inside, even as s/he is counted by that regime as the "abnormal," the pervert (or the lesbian/homosexual).

Butler's work rearranges "common sense" about binary, gendered subjects. The power of heterosexuality is not the power of the natural—the real apart from its being signified. It is the power of the dominant systems of discourse—the power of hegemony. From her analysis Butler argues that soliciting women to join the politics of identity through feminist theory or practice functions as an appeal to the real that is, in fact, an appeal to a discursive power regime. It is a regime of heterosexism that reinforces and reproduces the connections between binary, sexed identity, the collapse of sexual desire into gender, and the normative linking of desire with the opposite (binary) sex. To reiterate "woman" is to support and maintain heterosexual, binary arrangements.

The point here is that Butler's work is not a relativization or contextualization of oppressive views of men and women. Her poststructuralist intervention assumes an inextricable connection between specificity of meaning and exclusion in a way that constructionism does not. To make Butler's case in the terms of constructionism, the assumption that a view is a perspective and that what is excluded might be added, is to suggest that the categorical system man/woman of the heterosexual regime can accommodate the bodies and desires that fall outside. However, the Other, in these terms of difference, would be defined *in the categories of the dominant regime,* and virtually obliterated.[19]

What we can learn from this account of poststructuralism is that an identity is a function of a position within a system of differences. Subject identity does not depend on substance or natural essence, just as it does not depend on the sameness of the body. Rather it depends on the outside on which it rests. That outside supports the specificity of meaning, man/ woman, and provides pressure to move out of the established definitions, thereby offering the possibility of a reconfiguration of differential relations. In contrast to constructionist criticism, the poststructuralist intervention requires us to look at the relation of identities to dominant constructions of reality and to ask what they occlude. This is why it contradicts what is implicit to constructionism, namely, that we might combine relative perspectives. Not only will they be mutually exclusive, but the addition of another Other woman to the feminist account of the subject will likely be a process of *saming*—of *incorporating* the Other under the terms of the current discursive regime. My earlier question about the risk entailed by the commitment to finitude has a preliminary answer. What is risked by a feminism operating with tools of constructionism is a notion of identity, which, however much it confesses its partiality, deploys operations of equivalence and, therefore, hegemony.

Feminist Theology and the Imago Dei

In the hands of feminist theologians the Christian belief that all are created *imago Dei* becomes the application of the "feminist critical principle" to issues of the gendered subject. Articulated by Rosemary Radford Ruether, the feminist principle states that the "promotion of the full humanity of women" is normative for theology.[20] One of the most cited ideas associated with feminist theology, this formulation of the woman-centeredness of theological feminism is rendered distinct by the grammar of Christian theology. Central to theological thinking about the human is this *imago* doctrine, which operated classically to identify the features of human being which are most like, or in the image of, God. Thus it refers to the idea of an original authentic human nature which is fallen or damaged in "man" and authentically displayed in the person of Jesus Christ. The *imago Dei* indicates the attributes of human being that make it capable of a relationship to God. Most important, it conveys the theologically appropriate affirmation of the goodness of finitude—of creatures. There is, then, an incipient universal referent to the *imago;* by definition, to be creaturely is to be worthy of regard. The important question is how the notion of *authentic* is defined, and that depends in no small part on the way the Jesus figure is used to define ideal human attributes.

The feminist charge is that tradition's compliment to humanity with the *imago Dei* has never been fully paid to women. Instead, Jesus' maleness has long been used to characterize authentic human being and to limit the implicit universal reach of *imago Dei*. The beauty of its formal grammatical function, however, is that the *imago* can warrant the correction of centuries of misnaming the ideal human as male. Employing this doctrine to expose the "false generic" of mankind, Ruether (and others) have a theological warrant for liberation of women. As a naming of subjects of God's saving care, the *imago Dei* entails no essential definition of the subject, characterized only by finitude and God-dependence. This is how feminists can use it to create a woman-affirming anthropology that never existed. The doctrine's basic work is to say that being female is "like God," too, even as it is God-dependent, and in so doing produce new insights about creation.[21] As such, feminist theologians employ a traditional frame to focus on a particular subject, woman, and enhance the potential reach of that frame by inserting woman in the category of finitely good human subjects, exposing the problematic character of the male-identified constructions of *imago Dei.*

Feminist theological use of the *imago Dei* appears to work well. It would seem that the previously ignored "outsiders" to Western Christian hegemonies might easily be added via the *imago Dei:* the subjects whose race, sexuality, or class has been deemed less than human can be affirmed as good in their creatureliness, just as woman are. However, feminist theologies are at risk along with feminist theories. Ruether, to continue my example, criticizes many of the contributions and inadequacies of the very feminist theories considered here. She enhances social constructionist critique of gender, which is crucial to her work, to uncover gender asymmetries. Refusal of idolatry strengthens the theological strategies and authorizes the addition of women to the class, "ideal humanity." Missing only a poststructuralist take on difference, she calls for consideration of racism and class. Her summary portrayal of the subject walks a careful line between recognizing psychic and biological tendencies of male/female and calling for a transformation of both.[22]

However, with a poststructuralist intervention, occlusions appear. In Ruether's terms males cannot be absolutized as authentic human beings, so the argument proceeds that we, *too,* are of value; we, *too,* are created *imago Dei.* However, the converse is also true. She says, "Women cannot affirm themselves as *imago Dei* and subjects of full human potential in a way that diminishes male humanity."[23] The feminist appeal to *imago Dei* becomes, then, affirmation that the world is divided into two kinds of people, and what we want is respect for both kinds.[24] But this implies that gender criticism is a kind of "me, too" theory. Taking Butler's view, what is going on here is the deployment of the heterosexual binary. The continual affirming of man means that, minimally, what lurks behind the sign "woman" in Ruether's formulation are certain constructions of heterosexual, male-desiring subjects who know their deep identities to be sexually female. For that is all that can be accommodated by the system of discourse that Ruether leaves in place. We remember that poststructuralism assumes that occlusions support this binary, and we might fairly assume they are racial, too.

Producing Antihegemonic Positivity

With a destabilizing of the feminist theological option, we seem to be at an impasse. But the real question is how such destabilizing can be understood to converge with positive commitment to concrete *women.* Here my view is that feminisms are social practices for change; thus we are not guided by some frame of permanent deconstruction. The function of a liberatory poststructuralist intervention is to identify the outside or the Other that is being occluded. What it does not do is frame the inevitable commitment to a particular with a "why" and a "what for." For that some of the early investigations of the instabilities of signifying are again helpful.

We see how meaning can be claimed even in the face of the pressure to destabilize by looking at what happens in actual communication. Two processes are important. What Saussure called the associative or similarity-based linguistic operation, which refers to the paradigmatic axis of language; this is analogous to the process of identity/difference. For a speaker it is the capacity to make identity or similarity/contrast judgments. This means that one can *substitute,* which is a process requiring the relating of elements of meaning according to their degrees of similarity. The paradigmatic operation allows one to have categories, that is, to use and understand the sign "man" in a particular communication and to recognize the same sign in a different context. It is, in short, to know what "the same" is.

The speaker/hearer who cannot make similarity or identity associations is unable to carry out operations that require some distance from
context, such as beginning a conversation, or dealing with metalinguistic
discourse. S/he is unable to make connections between the same word
when it is used in different contexts and, thus, can only be reactive.[25]

The capacity to make identity judgments (or substitutions), however,
is not enough for communication. To communicate, one needs the syntagmatic axis of language as well as the paradigmatic axis. The syntagmatic
refers to the capacity for discerning relations of *contiguity,* that is, the con-
stituents of a context, in Roman Jakobson's terms.[26] This is the capacity to
combine the "next to's," whether successive or spatial/simultaneous, that
is, to know how words are to be properly ordered in a particular language,
to know what words should come next in a sentence, and to know what
response comes next in a particular communication. One exercises the
capacity for contiguity relations by knowing how to respond when greeted
by "May I help you?" on entering a shop.

Without this capacity (contiguity aphasia), a person cannot make
connections. S/he can only speak in terms of categories or identities. Since
context is a multilevel phenomenon, from the context of words in a sentence to that of gender in a specific social code, contiguity judgments obviously differ according to the complexity of a situation. What is shared in
the deficit is the inability to respond to context.

These capacities are suggestive for thinking about feminist theology
as a social-change practice. Poststructuralist interventions, again, are for
the identification of the refused outside; they are not to disable us.[27] To
depend on these alone would be to create an analogous deficit in the
ability to communicate. We need not be paralyzed by poststructuralism.
Clearly both communicative capacities are necessary to and implicit in
feminist theological and secular practice. Both have facilities for selection
and combination. Knowing what counts as a proper substitution for the
word *God* in a particular community, for example, must come with knowing how to use *God* in a sentence or with how an account of *God* is contextually useful in a situation of poverty.

Let me illustrate further. Knowing what could count as *imago Dei* is
an exercise of the capacity for distinguishing similarity or identity/differ-
ence. What *is imago Dei* rests on differential relations that produce what is
not as the necessary outside of the definition. (It is obvious that knowing
a situation or a system of rules is necessary to the capacity to make specific

intelligible identity judgments.) The feminist principle is based on an ability to read situations, to interpret contiguity relations as well. On the basis of that ability, the feminist judgment is that the claim of traditional theological rules, that any subject is a proper candidate for the *imago,* has been false. The system of differences of traditional theology has rested, we might say, on an outside—the domain of women (but also on pagans, and Jews). In Ruether's and others' work with the *imago Dei,* feminists have displayed their analogous facility to make "good sentences" by exercising capacities for paradigmatic and syntagmatic relations.

It may be that capacities for identity/contrast and contiguity judgments move us away from the suspicion that the enterprise is dissolved by destabilizing identities. (They also lessen the threat of the crime of essentialism; saying "woman" in a particular context may be the exercise of contiguity judgments.) However, the question of antihegemonic response to context requires consideration of what *connects* these episodic situations.

Now we take up the earlier question of the *why* or *for what* of a social-change practice, after a summary of the clues thus far. It has been the capacity to see the excluded, the outside, in what counted as ideal human being that has led feminism to become a powerful liberation movement. There is, in short, some operative notion of how to use *woman* in a "better" sentence going on in the practices of feminists. Their "better sentences" break through these exclusions, a facility I see in the theological vision of feminist theologians such as Ruether, Daly, and a host of foremothers. Minimally this is to say that facility with context or contiguity is necessary to the employment of poststructuralist interventions. But it is to say more. Neither a poststructuralist flair for destabilizing, contextual skills nor their combination can account for or extend feminists' gift for recognizing the excluded.

Feminists must be able to trace connections between episodes in the life of the church and society in order to work for change. The missing piece in a frame of communicative practice is *narrative.* With this category for connection we can answer the question of how feminist theology refuses hegemony.

Narrating Imago Dei *in a Story of the Outsider*

Again Saussure's founding destabilizing move is helpful. By bracketing the temporal, historical trajectories of signification, the focus on language as a system of differences sunders the relation of signification to fixed referents. Analysis of the synchronic brings into view a freeze-frame or a still life. To get the temporal and successive back into the picture requires the discursive form of connection. According to Fredric Jameson, this is the rhetorical form of story. Story brings the two dimensions of meaning together in a display of history.[28]

By "history" I mean something rather simple. We do history in order to look at two situations together. Relating the situation of white middle-class women in the nineteenth century to that of twentieth-century women is a historical project. However, we can only make the connections discursively, or rhetorically. Narrative is the rhetorical mode that relates the two situations synchronically: it is the rhetorical mode that makes meaning by finding the similarities/differences of various situations. It is in some sense where we answer "why it matters." Explanation is the rhetorical mode for history in its diachronic or successive sense; it relates episodes causally. While these are surely more complexly related, we might say that narrative offers us the rhetorical mode for transformative connections.[29]

That feminist theology tells us about the different conditions of being woman is the discourse of doing history; it can be done as an explanatory science. *How* it relates those conditions is a story about the world and God's relation to it. It is displayed through a particular rhetorical mode, and it is necessary to an assessment of how feminisms invoke a trajectory beyond the particular system of differences. Feminist theology looks at different conditions of being woman and interrogates certain similarities/contrasts to display how women should count in the class of ideal humanity in those situations where they do not. The logic that has allowed them to "pick up" woman as the outside is not one of explanation, but a story that has an imperative to change, a commitment to value denigrated forms of creation.

Similarly, stories are working in secular feminist thinking, whether acknowledged or not, because episodes of defining woman are connected and ordered toward the evoking of change; they are not simply explained. It is these narratives that shape our notion of hegemony and suggest the expansiveness of the emancipatory subject. My earlier criticism of secular feminisms resulted from my judgment that they offer ambiguous narratives to this end. My point here is not to dwell on that case, but to suggest that narratives are endemic to social-change practice and that poststructuralist intervention has exposed the risk of overreliance on explanatory discourse. Without a story that universalizes the emancipatory subject for new discernments, feminisms are best at offering explanation. As important as these explanations are, they may "same" the outsider, even with expanding trajectories of humanism.

My point relates to Butler's work, as well, but raises another issue. Despite poststructuralism's aversion to grand narrative, her account invokes a logic of liberation, however modest. It must make the connections to which "history" aspires. The "story" that implicitly connects Butler's episodes is an impulse to better human social arrangements, or one she may count on readers to contribute. However, when one unearths the excluded, as she has done, one has not successfully applied poststructuralism and found the basis of oppression. One is able to see this outside, the heterosexual regime, because *one is already governed by another system of differences,* another outside, which, by definition, *cannot be seen.*[30] What narrative of liberation remains after the defeat of this first oppressive regime, heterosexism, given that one has, in fact, simply moved to another, possibly more pernicious one?

The implications of this investigation of the gendered subject are several. I will close with suggestions about what needs to be different about feminist theological use of the *imago Dei,* and what feminist theologies contribute. To review, I have suggested that the hegemonies recognized in feminist appeals to woman are best taken up through poststructuralist questions. These help expose the potential hegemony in social constructionist or explanatory grids, for the latter account for difference by accommodating the Other to their categories. Yet I have argued that destabilization is insufficient for communicative and social-change capacities. I conclude that stories are the way that we make connections between situations and invoke change. The final question, then, is what counts as a good story, and that will differ between secular and religious feminist communities.

I am not arguing for a false universalizing narrative, or that secular feminist theories should commit to humanity rather than to women. Any commitment to women is an exercise of one's sense of episodic contiguity. One resists particular hegemonies by saying what needs to be said in a particular setting and marks the refusal of hegemony in one's discourse when occlusions are exposed. My point is that commitment to woman may not be the adequate *connecting* story, even though the discoveries that emerge through this commitment should change the traditions of the stories. Insofar as secular feminists need to tell stories that compel a sense for the outside, I am suggesting that they need to examine the limits of humanism as a story for doing that. Minimally, this is what poststructuralism requires. Donna Haraway comments, "Gender is a category to explore what counts as a woman, what has previously been taken for granted, and to problematize what counts as a human."[31]

What I propose for feminist theological use of the *imago Dei* is development of its strength—stories, rather than explanations. Feminist theologians must develop stories of a God of justice in light of poststructuralist destabilizations. A narrative of this God-creation relation cannot use *imago Dei* to add women to the class of human creatures. Poststructuralism reminds us that there must be a purely negative function for the claim that woman is created *imago* and a story that tries to match it. The work of Ruether's principle should be that "men are not" *imago Dei* because the need to affirm *women* is constructed out of a pernicious system of significations which constitute *men*. This is not to say that woman is the real image of God; it is not even to say that both are. It is only to say that in this particular set of discursive arrangements, in this context of male dominance, what the reigning discursive system means by *man* is not the *imago Dei*. It is to make a contextual, contiguity-based judgment about the effects of the reigning hegemonic (white male) identities that control the current accompanying contrast/exclusion. If this is not recognized, then the exclusions operative in any definition of *woman* and its supporting discursive setting will continue to go unrecognized.

A good feminist theological story will be an incomplete story of a God-loved creation, a creation for which the only requisite features of imaging God are finitude and dependence. That story must allow the commitment to the particular situation to develop new sensibilities for the outside, defined as violations of the goodness of the finite, God-dependent creation. It must sponsor the capacity for total self-criticism, for commitment to the goodness of the partial, and for the possibility that all is redeemable. For the outside, as a place where the occlusions of a situation appear, is not a stable foundation. A theological story might name it as the lure of an eschatological future, but, by definition, it will require disruption of the present system. Therefore it will not look like God's eschatological future to many.

Such stories will not, of course, escape hegemonies. Those who tell them must mark the occlusions when they appear, but know that they are already determined by others. Thus, Ellen Armour suggests that we speak of "whitefeminism" to mark that system of discourse that is only able to see Other women as having race.[32] Because of the new knowledges from "whitefeminist," womanist, and other liberation critiques of the tradition, this is a story, a set of stories, that Christians must construct anew.

These stories have hegemonic ones to replace, of course, given that the formal constructive function of the *imago Dei* is shaped by the relation of authentic humanity to Jesus. The implicit universal referent in the story of the God-loved and dependent *imago Dei* can become a form of hegemony in a number of ways. However, it does not always. Even an outsider to Christianity hears the possibilities in a newly told Jesus story. Haraway tells a story of the suffering servant as trickster figure, as the "original mime" who "redeems" the hegemonies of humanism: Jesus the "original mime" is "the actor of a history that mocks especially the recurrent tales that insist that 'man makes himself' in the deathly onanistic nightdream of coherent wholeness and correct vision."[33]

If there is insight in telling Christian stories, it might be that they can invite us to move ceaselessly toward the discovery of new "outsides," new strangers and the conditions that support them. It is not a story for all feminists, but it raises questions for their stories as well as for Christian communities. We do not abandon particular commitments, or particular stories; we simply expect that they will always contribute to dissembling. The best we can do is tell stories that enable us to confess that and to hear from rather than explain the Other.

CHAPTER 7

THE BODY POLITIC VS. LESBIAN BODIES
Publics, Counterpublics, and the Uses of Norms

Janet R. Jakobsen

I HAVE TAKEN THE OPPORTUNITY provided by this conference and anthology to reconsider contemporary feminist theories in relation to my own implication in both the structure of the discipline of ethics and the contemporary public sphere. Thus, I focus not on feminist theology, but on the associated discipline of ethics by addressing an issue that has proven consistently problematic for me as someone disciplined in ethics: that is, norms. I'm very suspicious of norms, as are many feminist and lesbian theorists.[1] Needless to say, however, this suspiciousness has created some cognitive dissonance with regard to my work within the discipline of ethics.

I undertake an exploration of norms through a second and interrelated issue: the implication of my own, specifically lesbian, body in a series of public-sphere discourses. How do the norms that constitute the "public" also constitute and contain lesbian bodies in public? I wanted to explore these issues, in part, to comprehend better (if such comprehension is possible) my own position as an out, publicly lesbian employee of the state of Arizona. In order to join the faculty at the University of Arizona I had to sign a loyalty oath to uphold and defend the laws of the state, one of twenty-six states in the United States that criminalize sodomy. At first, I wanted to get out of the oath on the grounds of religious freedom, but my colleagues convinced me that the claim that I was religiously lesbian would not serve as the necessary grounds for protection from this particular brand of loyalty. Thus, with no little sense of irony I signed the oath.

This irony intensified for me, however, on arriving at the University of Arizona and finding my body, and specifically its public lesbian status, tokenized in a number of ways in the service of the university and, thus,

of the state. In a story that is all too familiar given this type of tokeniza-
tion, my body took on a form of overrepresentation, of hyper- or surplus
visibility. Within weeks of arriving on campus, I was faculty adviser to
three student organizations that seemed to have nowhere else to turn. I was
called when virtually any issue related to lesbian, gay, and bisexual politics
came up; I was poster girl in the city newspaper for domestic partnership
and asked to join the Diversity Action Council to represent my "diversity";
when lesbians or gay men visited campus or interviewed for jobs I was
called by people I had never met to make sure I would have time to talk to
them; and, of course, there were those hesitant voices on the phone—the
sure indicator of a "lesbian" call. "I'm doing a research project on lesbians,
can I interview you?" "My students are interested in aging and gay people,
do you know of any resources?" "My students want to know what the parents of gay people think, can you tell me?" Finally, by the second semester
I was swept up into a movement for queer studies on campus. I began to
wonder about the political effects of these forms of visibility and about the
ways in which lesbian and gay politics has focused on visibility, particularly through an emphasis on the importance of "coming out." Was my
being "out" really a political challenge to the state of Arizona and its
sodomy laws? My suspicion that visibility was not automatically subversive
was only furthered by the fact that at the time of my annual review I wrote
all of this work down under the category of "service." Whose interests were
truly being "served" if the University of Arizona needed the visibility of my
body in all of these different ways?

By raising this question I don't intend to suggest that visibility is not
an important social and political good or that I was anything other than a
joyful coinstigator of the Committee for Lesbian, Gay, and Bisexual Studies, or that public visibility is not a necessity for political survival. The constant reiteration of silencing techniques directed at controlling if not
eliminating queer bodies, techniques which indicate that queer in-visibil-
ity also serves the state, became all too apparent the following year when
moves toward queer studies around the state came to the attention of the
powers that be. The governor attacked a course being offered on transsex-
ualism at Northern Arizona University, requesting that the course be can-
celed despite the fact that it was taught through the unpaid labor of a
transsexual graduate student. While the class was defended on the basis of
academic freedom, the controversy became so heated that a police officer
was present the first day of class to prevent potential "violence" (by whom
was never directly stated). Similarly, the state legislature's budget commit-

tee looked into a lesbian studies course, demanding to know how tax dollars could be spent on such an undertaking. My interest, then, became how to examine *visibility* as the interface between lesbian bodies and the construction of the public.

Framing the project in this way led to one further irony, however. In the public discourses over sexualities where it seemed logical to undertake such an investigation, discourses such as the recent debate over "gays" in the military, lesbian bodies remained all but invisible. Despite the fact that, in the Marine Corps, for example, African American lesbians are statistically more likely to be discharged from the military on the basis of sexuality, the debate focused on white, male officers.[2] This invisibility, I will argue, is not just a form of gender and race discrimination, although it is that. It is also reflective of the mechanism by which public visibility is so frequently turned into invisibility and conversely public invisibility—being "unmarked" by gender, race, or class—becomes public visibility.[3] Through this mechanism white men are supposedly nowhere in particular, and yet are virtually all we see—in the media, in government, in business, in the academy—while people of color are invoked as the ever-present threat to (white) society despite invisibility in and even physical removal from (white) society through entrenched forms of institutional segregation (including the welfare and prison systems). Similarly, through this mechanism, the supposedly new policy of "don't ask, don't tell" becomes a method of allowing participation in the public service of the military only in exchange for a commitment to the invisibility of the closet, an invisibility which doesn't so much hide gays and lesbians—who continue to be discharged—as it hides, and makes lesbians and gays particularly vulnerable to, the operation of power.

These questions of visibility are deeply tied to questions of norms because of the ways in which norms materialize bodies. Judith Butler describes, for example, the operation of the category of "sex" as a norm which is also "part of a regulatory practice that produces the bodies it governs, that is, whose regulatory force is made clear as a kind of productive power, the power to produce—demarcate, circulate, differentiate—the bodies it controls."[4] Thus, the production of bodies takes place through highly regulated practices which are "the forcible reiteration" of ideal constructs or norms. In this way, norms materialize those bodies that can be seen in public, delineating which bodies meet the standards for recognized activity in the public sphere. Norms also materialize the social body which is the public itself, the body politic, further reinforcing hierarchies of visibility as some public bodies come to represent the body politic while others, even when visible in public, are located outside of (and frequently as threats to) this particular body. So, when the *Today* show opens in 1987 with the question, "Is AIDS spreading into the general public?"[5] the speaker publicly invokes particular bodies, those with HIV infection, in order to locate them outside another body, that of "the general public," which is at risk of infection if these two types of bodies—the particular and the general—are not kept apart.

Here we can begin to see some of the ways in which the contradictions of visibility are produced. The political implications of public visibility are dependent not simply on an opposition between visibility and invisibility, but also on the relationship between various public bodies and the body politic, a relationship that materializes through normative invocations and enactments. This relationship is further complicated because of the multiple interlocking normative matrices which variously structure the public visibility of particular bodies along the lines of "gender," "race," "class," and "sex." The interrelations of these normative matrices mean that the body politic is not just produced through an opposition between the visible and invisible, but also through oppositions among various public bodies.

In order to investigate the mechanisms through which the uses of norms produce both public bodies and the body politic, I will pursue an analysis of the videotape "Gay Rights, Special Rights," produced in 1993 by the Traditional Values Coalition. This is a videotape in which lesbian bodies are barely visible and which juxtaposes the public bodies of white gay men and straight African American men to produce a body politic that ultimately excludes both, and is represented through the visibility of one person in particular, Edwin Meese, attorney general during the Reagan administration. Meese has embodied the public at discursive moments which have proven crucial for those social movements forming my communities of accountability, feminist and lesbian and queer and antiracist:[6] first through his (anti–)civil rights record, then through the Attorney General's Commission on Pornography (Meese Commission) in 1986, and then again in "Gay Rights, Special Rights."[7] I'm interested in the rightwing strategies that led this particular public body, Ed Meese, also to be the body politic, but I'm also interested in the ways in which counterpublic social movements through "our" uses of norms have contributed to the body politic being represented in this particular way. Now admittedly, this videotape represents a right-wing appropriation of counterpublic discourses, one which "we" cannot control. Nonetheless, I think "we" have not been careful enough in fully heeding the dangers implicated in the uses of norms. Thus, I turn first to the question of norms and the problems that they have presented to feminist and lesbian and queer theories and ethics, and then I analyze the videotape to see the uses of norms in the production of the public and various counterpublics.

The Uses of Norms

Norms have been a particular site of feminist concern because they are frequently read as constituting prescriptive codes of action. For example, Marilyn Frye suggests in reviewing *Lesbian Ethics* that lesbians might do better without an "ethics," because ethics plays into disciplinary ideologies about right action.[8] Problems arise, as Drucilla Cornell points out, when ethics becomes the practice of judgment within a system of "moral integration" which purportedly "can give us the last word on the Right in the strong Kantian sense."[9] For Cornell, in contrast to "morality," which is a system of rules or standards by which to justify disapproval of others, the "ethical" indicates "the aspiration to a non-violent relationship to the Other and to otherness in the widest possible sense."[10] Given these suspicions that acceding to moral discipline through the use of norms only entraps lesbians and feminists in a system of control which they wish to critique, do norms have any role to play in feminist and lesbian ethics?

In the introduction to her important book, *Critique, Norm, and Utopia,* feminist and critical theorist Seyla Benhabib attempts to chart a new course for uses of norms. Benhabib argues that critical theory distinguishes itself from both "neo-Kantian foundationalism" and "contemporary contextualism and post-modernism" in "its insistence that criteria of validity, ascertained via non-foundationalist arguments, can be formulated."[11] In casting her argument in this way, Benhabib names the hopes and fears of many feminist theorists caught in between dominant modern and postmodern projects, neither of which fully articulates feminist positions or values. The fear: if we fully pursue a feminist critique of modern, Western rationalism, will we, in the process, lose the criteria which establish the very values necessary to make this critique meaningful and/or meaningfully feminist? The hope: that we can fully pursue this critique and simultaneously articulate a (utopian) vision of community, thus enabling social movement toward a future which we normatively know to be a better future, specifically one liberated from or at least resistant to domination. Without normative criteria we could find that we have no legitimate basis for critique or that the future that we pursue is in fact no better, no less dominating, than the one we have criticized. To put the matter succinctly, without criteria can we have a feminist politics?

For Benhabib, norms provide a means of mediating the relationships between critique and community (utopia), as well as a means of mediating across differences and conflict. Through rational, but nonfoundational, criteria we can convince those who disagree that our vision of the world is not just an expression of our interests, but is in fact better for us all.[12] Thus, the public is constructed as the space in which various persons and communities can participate in the project of forming and giving criteria which will guide us (as a whole) toward the future. This space is also "critically" important to various counterpublics, those social movements which run counter to the dominations and distortions of the contemporary public sphere: "[C]ritical social theory turns to those structures of autonomy and rationality which, in however distorted and imperfect fashion, continue in the lifeworld of our societies, while allying itself with the struggles of those for whom the hope of a better future provides the courage to live in the present."[13]

Here, Benhabib makes a move which is both full of hope and ultimately problematic. Through her appeal to normative criteria, Benhabib is able to hold together a space of both public and counterpublic possibility. In Benhabib's terms, she is able to hold together two poles of community formation, the universality or *generalized* terms of a lifeworld (public sphere) open to all and the specific, *concrete* claims of those social movements (counterpublics) which continually challenge the dominations of false universalism in the name of the public.[14] Despite the promise of Benhabib's project, however, I fear that her invocation of norms is not as free from or resistant to the dominations of the contemporary public as I, at least, would hope.

The problem arises, perhaps not surprisingly, at the point of the production of the "we" who is the public. Benhabib is clear that in order to uphold the possibility of norms which are accountable to both public and counterpublic, we need both the generalized focus of a "polity of rights and entitlements" and the specific focus of "communities of needs and solidarity."[15] These sites of association and community are structured by norms, thus naming the relationship between norms and community formation as one of materialization. Norms materialize, and are materialized by, communities:

> The perspective of the generalized other urges us to respect the equality, dignity and rationality of all humans qua humans, while the perspective of the concrete other enjoins us to respect differences, individual life-histories and concrete needs. Such communities, in my view, are not pregiven; they are formed out of the action of the oppressed, the exploited, and the humiliated, and must be committed to universalist, egalitarian, and consensual ideals. Traditional ethnic, racial, and religious communities are neither necessarily nor primarily such communities of needs and solidarity. They become so only insofar as they uphold the ideal of action in a universalist, egalitarian, consensual framework.[16]

A given community only becomes a community through normative enactment. The body politic and the public "we" which it embodies are produced through norms.

Benhabib attempts to hold together a general public and counterpublic movements by emphasizing the need for the perspective of both the general and the concrete other. Problems arise at certain points in her texts, however, when the tension between the general and the specific is resolved in favor of the general. This resolution arises specifically at the point of judgment or adjudication. In her 1992 book, *Situating the Self,* Benhabib states that general norms can trump the specifics of, for example, the care perspective: "Considerations of a universalist morality do set the constraints within which concerns of care should be allowed to operate and they 'trump' over them if necessary . . . ; and considerations of care should be 'validated or affirmed from an impartialist perspective.'"[17] Benhabib nowhere argues that care might similarly trump universalism. Thus, we find not mutual critique, but universal norms which form a framework for particular norms, delineating the constraints "within which" particulars must operate.

Benhabib argues that Western rationality can form the framework for moral interaction in a "global community" because persons and communities materialized through other normative traditions can question any aspect of this rationality.[18] In order to do so, however, they must ultimately enter into the "universalist, egalitarian, and consensual" framework of Western rationality. Once again, there is no indication that Western rationality must similarly enter into, be subsumed within, other normative frameworks as part of interaction or negotiation. Rather, "we" must "judge" others. In *Critique, Norm, and Utopia,* Benhabib addresses the question of judgment, specifically whether we can judge other cultures on the basis of the norms of Western rationality:

Suppose, however, that one were to raise the following objection: whatever one's evaluation of this process, it may be said, the argument concerning the binding nature of reflexivity begs the question. Certainly self-questioning, the justification of one's standpoint through reasoned argumentation, analysis of implicit and explicit presuppositions, and the like have been ideals in Western culture since its inception, but in what sense can they be universalized and applied in judging other cultures?[19]

She concludes that this question has only one possible answer.

In conclusion, then, it must be said that one can only give one answer to the critic who accuses us of begging the question in positing the bindingness of reflexivity: yes indeed, there is a circularity in our argumentation, but this is not a vicious circularity. It would be a vicious circle only if presuppositionless understanding, an understanding that could divest itself of its own contextuality, were also possible. Since, however, this cannot be the case, it follows that reflexivity is binding for us. To want to divest ourselves of it may be like wanting to jump over our own shadows.[20]

Benhabib here concludes that "we" who recognize ourselves within a normative tradition of Western rationality must use these norms to judge "other" cultures, because we cannot divest ourselves of the cultural context or the normative tradition that has made us who we are. In other words, in Benhabib's texts she connects the work that norms do in constituting communities and providing criteria for action with the need to judge. It is this move which I want to question, not the need for both the concrete and the general, but the specific relationship established between them at the point of adjudication. I want to question the slippage(s) in the uses of norms that supposedly have a universal validity, and yet, which materialize a "we" who judges "others." A simultaneous inclusion and exclusion occurs in the construction of adjudication. A "we" is constructed which excludes certain "others" and, yet, those "others" are included within the normative purview of the "we." "We" can judge "them" as if they were subject to our norms; in fact, we have no choice but to do so. The problem here is twofold: the slippage involved in judging other cultures as if they too should recognize themselves in a Western context, and the assumption that cross-cultural interaction necessarily involves judgment of others.

This relationship between the general and the concrete is embodied in the relationship between the body politic and bodies in public which I mentioned in my introduction. Because the body politic is constituted so that it is not bound by the specifics of particular bodies but will instead offer an overarching inclusion, it too forms an overarching framework for particular bodies rather than articulating a mutual tension between the two terms. It too enacts a simultaneous and mutually constitutive inclusion and exclusion, one which is particularly dangerous because the body politic embodies a "general public" that legitimates the disciplinary power of the state. The threat carried by these forms of inclusion and exclusion means that some counterpublics (persons, movements, communities) are induced to identify with the public on behalf of what Minnie Bruce Pratt has so usefully termed "threatening protection."[21] In other words, if one doesn't identify with the public, then one will face social sanction and quite probably violence. The simultaneous exclusion occurs as part of this same interaction, in that it is rarely the public itself that is the agent of the violence it protects against; rather it is some "other" (and, of course, the stress is on other here) counterpublic that threatens to do so. Thus, we have actually a three-party interaction—two counterpublics which are placed in opposition, in fact in violent stances toward one another, and an unnamed public which adjudicates between them on behalf of the good of all.[22] This third, unspecified position is, of course, the position of privilege, privilege which operates precisely because this position and the violence on which it depends are never specifically identified, never openly embodied.[23]

A simple illustration of threatening protection at work is provided by a reader's response to a paper of mine which questioned Benhabib's appeals to universal norms and adjudication in contrast to Susan Thistlethwaite's concept of "truth in action."[24] "But, what about gay-bashers?" the reader asked. "Aren't they just performing their own truth-in-action?" Here the reader has invoked this three-party interaction. If I don't accept the adjudicatory protection of universal norms, then my lesbian body is placed outside of the normative "we" and threatened with violence, not directly by the reader, but by an-other group of outsiders, the putative gay-bashers. I was rather struck (shall we say) by this question, and it evoked a number of responses in me: "Well, yes, they are performing their truth-in-action." "Are you telling me I'm supposed to be afraid?" "If I agree with you am I supposed to feel protected?" "How exactly is my accession to universal norms (the disciplinary response implied by the question) supposed to protect me?" I have never quite understood this implication. When approached on the street do I say, "Excuse me, but I'm a believer in universal human rights—yourselves included—thus, obviously you should not at this time do harm against my person because of my sexual identity"?

Of course, the protection is not supposed to come from the power of my own belief system, but from my agreement to participate in the protections of the liberal state (which replaces the reader as the privileged third party); specifically, in this case I accept the protections of a police force empowered (supposedly) to control the actions of gay-bashers.

I think this line of reasoning might be more effective with those persons and groups who feel that the police actually act to protect them, but as recent events, particularly the Rodney King beating, have so visibly demonstrated, police "force" is not exactly the site of protection for all those persons who are supposedly members of the "general" public, and certainly, queers cannot depend on any such benevolent use of "force" by the state. In fact, the dilemma of the loyalty oath to the state of Arizona is a dilemma precisely because, even if I accede to the state's protection and sign the oath, the protective force to which I accede—the adjudicatory power of the state—can be brought to bear against my lesbian body. The threat of gay-bashing does, however, highlight the three-party interaction which makes threatening protection an effective inducement to accede to the actions of the liberal state. Liberalism produces a body politic by giving specific public bodies someone they wish to adjudicate against, for example, gays and the Christian Right. By focusing on the opposition between these public bodies, a body politic is created which effectively excludes specific bodies while appearing to be indispensable to or the protector of those very bodies that it excludes. The normative concerns of my lesbian body may be excluded from the universal norms promoted by the reader, the laws of the liberal state, and the citizenship of the body politic which legitimates the state, and yet, I am still expected to view each of these sites as my protector whether from the physical violence of gay-bashers or the political violence of the Christian Right.[25]

Through this magic act, the public is established as a body politic which is at once a phantom and occupied by certain bodies.[26] The phantasmic nature of the body politic is its supposed ability to embrace all bodies and no particular bodies at one and the same time. Certain persons can articulate this phantom body precisely because their bodies are not marked as specific. Rather these bodies are taken to transcend the particularities of embodiment and, thus, to articulate publicness and generalizability. Those bodies which threaten to undermine the phantasmic nature of the body politic, which are, for example, too visibly embodied cannot, however, articulate the public.

Within Benhabib's understanding of norms, the creation of this phantasm, the "general" public, is necessary because without a normative framework to materialize generalizability there will be no general criteria to mediate across differences. Without such criteria there can be no normatively constituted "we." For Benhabib these norms and the "we" they materialize are historically (not naturally or foundationally) constituted, yet this particular form of constituting a "we" continues to be (historically) dangerous to some, if not most, public bodies. While the perspective of the concrete "other" may challenge given embodiments of the public, particularly through counterpublic social movements, as long as the general supersedes the concrete at the point of adjudication, rather than remaining in tension with it, the dangers of a body politic that disciplines public bodies remains. The videotape "Gay Rights, Special Rights" effectively shows the potential containment of counterpublic movements by disciplining all those bodies which deviate from the white, male embodiment of the "general," all in the name of protecting "civil rights." While this result is perhaps not surprising in a right-wing video, I think it is worth exploring further, in part because Benhabib so clearly articulates the uses of norms in relation to the production of the public, and in part because there is no easy solution to the dilemma which Benhabib's appeal to adjudication presents.

"Gay Rights, Special Rights"

"Gay Rights, Special Rights" is a 1993 production of the Traditional Values Coalition, headed by right-wing Christian Lou Sheldon. The video is in many ways a sequel to "The Gay Agenda," which was used successfully by the Coalition for Family Values in the Colorado campaign for Amendment Two and in the controversy over gays in the military. "Gay Rights, Special Rights" was initially used, once again successfully, in the battle to repeal the Cincinnati ordinance that prohibited discrimination against lesbians and gays. The video promotes the racist, anti-Semitic, and homophobic aspects of the Christian Right agenda, while posturing as an alliance between conservative whites and people of color. The videotape argues on behalf of protecting civil rights, but also promotes the (re-)Christianizing of "America," in part by narrowing the legacy of the civil rights struggles of the 1950s and 1960s to recognize only its Christian aspects. The conjoining of racist and homophobic agendas explains why Ed Meese, principal deconstructor of affirmative action under Ronald

Reagan, and Trent Lott, a notably anti–civil rights senator from Missis-
sippi, appear in a video which supposedly creates a cross-racial alliance.

The entire premise of the video is that "homosexuals" want the same
rights as racial/ethnic "minorities" were granted in the civil rights legislation of 1964 and 1965. The video argues, however, that to grant "homosexuals" these rights would be to grant "special rights." This logic
effectively implies that the rights granted in the Voting Rights Act and
Civil Rights Act were also "special rights." The video reasserts white, heterosexist Christian supremacy by positioning rights that are not "special"
as those rights which articulate a disembodied public, while almost obses-
sively focusing on the visible embodiment of racial/ethnic "minorities."
Perhaps most tellingly, people of color are only visible in the first quarter
of the videotape. Having used a multicultural alliance to establish the
legitimacy of white, male authority in the persons of Ed Meese and Trent
Lott, we see only two token people of color as representatives of authority
after the first nine minutes of this forty-minute videotape. Thus, the video
constructs an opposition between racial/ethnic "minorities" and "homosexuals" in order to establish Ed Meese as the representative of the disembodied (general) public. This opposition is normatively materialized
through the establishment of a legitimate minority, which simultaneously
delegitimizes other, specifically "homosexual," minorities. Once they are
normatively constructed in this manner both counterpublics are effectively contained so that there can be no crossover between them or
between "minorities" and the "general public."

The video opens with a reference to the 1963 March on Washington
as the disembodied voice of Dr. Martin Luther King Jr. is heard giving part
of the "I Have a Dream" speech. This is followed by a visual of the 1963
march and then a visual of Larry Kramer from the 1993 March for
Lesbian, Gay, and Bi (march organizers purposefully omitted the *sexual*)
Equal Rights and Liberation. The crucial aspects of the right-wing strategy of this video are here highlighted. First, the 1963 Civil Rights March,
leading to civil rights legislation, is set up to contrast with the 1993 march
and the possibility of a Lesbian and Gay Civil Rights Bill being passed by
Congress. Second, King's voice is disembodied, telling us that the appropriate dream of civil rights is the conservative one in which embodied
characteristics, in this case race, should disappear. The dream, thus disembodied, establishes the framework for the double containment of "minorities" which the video accomplishes. Once we see Dr. King and the
assembled crowd at the march, we see what a legitimate minority looks

like, and it doesn't look like Larry Kramer. In fact, Kramer's body dissolves into King's, while we are told that "out of pure logic . . . it was wrong to discriminate against black people simply on the basis of skin color." Thus, race is reduced to skin color and racial domination to discrimination. This use of Larry Kramer's body also enacts the anti-Semitism of the videotape as the Jewish Kramer dissolves into the Christian King, implying that "true" minorities can be recognized by the general public through a shared Christianity (and reenacting Christian supersessionism).[27]

Here, movements for racial justice of the 1950s and 1960s and those which followed are placed within classical liberal ideology at its most conservative. The goal of social change is not fundamentally to change the structure of the U.S. public sphere, but simply to integrate "minorities" into the already existing body politic so that embodied characteristics like race won't matter anymore, an interpretation which does violence to the heritage of civil rights struggles in its breadth and challenge to the dominant general public. Because racial/ethnic minorities are always contained in the video as the visible opposition to "lesbians, gays, bisexuals, and transgenders" (the vocabulary which the videotape uses), they can never truly enter the body politic. Instead, white men, such as Ed Meese, become the unmarked representatives of the public while racial/ethnic minorities are at best a legitimate counterpublic, and lesbians, gays, and bisexuals their illegitimate counterpart. Thus, ultimately the video constructs not only gay rights, but any civil rights, as special rights. The video thereby reenshrines the invisible rights of white men as the only truly universal and, therefore, public rights. The invisibility or unmarked status of these rights is so crucial to the argument that at one point Ed Meese claims that "as a white male" he has no rights.

An analysis of the narrative structure of the video will demonstrate how shifting forms of (in)visibility contribute to the construction of Ed Meese as the body politic. The video is structured into four parts: the first establishes people of color as members of legitimate racial/ethnic "minorities" and delegitimates claims to civil rights by lesbians, gays, bisexuals, and transgenders (in other words, queers) because they do not appropriately embody "minority status." Here we see a multicultural array of people of color (presumably straight) contrasted with a virtually all-white array of queers, mostly white gay men, many of whose bodies are out of control—disrobed, acting sexual, screaming, or simply marching and dancing.[28] This first section establishes the clarity of the opposition between the two counterpublics, implying that there is no confusing diversity within or between these two groups, that there can be no such thing as a legitimate, "homosexual" person of color. Lesbian and gay people of color appear only half a dozen times in the entire video (Ed Meese alone appears four), and the placement of each reinforces the idea that these persons have been deluded by the larger (read: white) "gay community," thus establishing that they, rather than the categories themselves, are confused.[29]

This first section also establishes the unmarked status of white, straight men, thereby initially establishing Ed Meese's claim to have no rights, at least no "special rights," and to be the voice of the general public. Thus, the video tells us, the general public has a racially unmarked body, while legitimate counterpublics have visibly marked bodies, a point which is established by an obsessive focus on race as skin color and only skin color. Other counterpublics, which are marked only by their behavior, are both illegitimate and particularly insidious because you can't tell who they are unless you catch them in the act (one of the services the video provides to the unsuspecting general public). The distinction between visible marking and behavior is further secured by a conflation between ethnicity and race, as representatives of the "Hispanic community" and The Chinese Family Alliance argue that ethnicity, unlike homosexuality, does not constitute a "behavior-based group." By implication in this configuration ethnicity, like race, is conflated with visible marking. Significantly, the question of women's rights in relation to gender discrimination and their inclusion in civil rights legislation is never engaged by the video, because to do so would complicate the opposition between racial/ethnic minorities and homosexuals. Thus, in this first part of the video racial/ethnic groups may be "deserving" in their claims to (special) rights, but they are never fully public.

The containment of racial/ethnic groups is furthered in the following sections of the film as the public role of straight, white men takes center stage. There are thirty-five appearances by white male authorities, two by the token white female, and in the final three-quarters of the film two token appearances by people of color. The second part of the video is still rhetorically directed at delegitimizing lesbian and gay claims to civil rights as a minority, but it visibly concentrates on the bodies of (supposedly straight) white men who represent the public, in contrast to the still out-of-control bodies of mostly white gay men. Here the apparent obsession which powerful, supposedly straight, white men have with gay white men is played out once again. Just as in the debate over gays in the military, in which Sam Nunn and colleagues focused on white male officers in the shower when white male officers are the least likely to be discharged,[30] so also the video turns its attention to white men when queer people of color and white lesbians are less protected by economic privilege and, thus, more likely to suffer from discrimination on the basis of sexual identity and to need access to civil rights claims.

The third part of the video heightens the stakes of argument, claiming that gays aspire not just to legitimate status as a counterpublic, but to take over the public. The demands of the 1993 march are listed, but the focus is also on the possibility that white male homosexuals, sometimes visually indistinguishable from straight white men, might take over. Here we begin to see the threat to society as a whole if minorities, in this case gay men, are not controlled. This potential threat is connected to the threat already posed by racial/ethnic minorities in the fourth and final section. In this section the authoritative representatives of the general public point out that gay rights would simply extend the problems faced by white men as a result of racial/ethnic claims to civil rights. Ed Meese argues that small-business owners might actually have to go against their (Christian) values and hire "such people." The "economics expert," Grover Norquist, speaks of just "one more reason" to sue the beleaguered business owner on the basis of discrimination, and Trent Lott claims that moral values would be "*further* degraded" by any more antidiscrimination restrictions. Thus, the video concludes that the real threat of civil rights is to the natural rights of white men. In fact, one authority argues that the real problem with antidiscrimination education in the public schools is that young boys, who naturally prefer boys to girls, might mistake this natural inclination for the unnatural attractions of homosexuality. At the end of the video the construction of the unmarked general public is thus established not only on the basis of the visual opposition between race and homosexuality, but also on the need to contain both minorities for the sake of society "as a whole."

Thus, the video promotes the racist, homophobic, and anti-Semitic aspects of the Christian Right agenda by reasserting Christian whiteness, specifically straight white maleness, as the only form of embodiment which is unmarked and, therefore, representative of the body politic. Moreover, the Christian Right is particularly adept at the magic act which constructs the body politic, by managing to be in two places at once, both public and counterpublic, like a phantom which rises behind and, thus, manages to overshadow each. Whenever opposition to the Right is raised by a particular counterpublic, an opposition which appeals to the dominant culture to stand against intolerance, the Right positions itself as a counterpublic which is oppressed by intolerance. In this way the liberal public is paralyzed because it cannot distinguish among counterpublics that it is committed to "tolerate."

"Gay Rights, Special Rights" articulates the other side of this strategy. The Christian Right positions itself as the public by materializing oppositions among other bodies—in this instance, people of color and lesbians, gays, bisexuals, and transgenders—and claiming to be the voice of those few values which the liberal public has left. Here the "Christian" part of the Christian Right is brought into play as those white middle-class liberal Christians, who fear that tolerance has evacuated all possible values, are reassured by the possibility that the public is normatively structured after all. These public norms can be materialized by disciplining and containing minority bodies. The video needs racial/ethnic bodies (at least at the beginning) to establish the white public, just as the United States has always used the labor of racially/ethnically marked bodies to establish white culture and society, but it reassures the "public" that these and other bodies can be contained. The effectiveness of this strategy is that it repeatedly induces white, Protestant, middle-class America to accede to this program without having to acknowledge itself as the voice of intolerance. Rather, middle America is simply asked to insure that no one gets special rights.

Publics and Counterpublics

Although the construction of the public in "Gay Rights, Special Rights" is obviously a right-wing appropriation, it is important to analyze because its assumptions, particularly its assumptions about publicity and visibility, are not found only in right-wing discourses. Unfortunately, as strategized by the national lobby groups which were its primary sponsors, the 1993 March on Washington for Lesbian, Gay, and Bi Equal Rights and Liberation accepted the two primary assumptions that I have criticized in the agenda of the Christian Right: that the public is the disembodied space inhabited only by those bodies which can aspire to the phantom status of unmarked (in)visibility, and that legitimate counterpublics are inhabited by visibly embodied "minorities."

In a somewhat paradoxical strategy, the march organizers focused on establishing the invisibility of "lesbian, gay, and bi" bodies by developing a media strategy of mainstreaming which promoted white, middle-class family lesbians and gays as the true, but invisible, face of lesbian and gay sexual identity, while downplaying those visible queers which the media had focused on in the past. Diversity in this strategy is used to highlight the visibility of "mainstream" white people. Queer people of color are nearly as problematic for this construction of lesbian and gay politics as they are for the Christian Right. Rather than showing queer people of color as deluded by the white "gay community," this politics shows people of color to be contained by the dominant white, gay community.[31] For example, in the video "Prelude to Victory," by the Human Rights Campaign Fund, Tori Osborne, then director of the National Gay and Lesbian Task Force, proclaims, "Look at our great diversity," and the videotape cuts to a white man. In the series that follows tokenized people of color are represented, but always contained between representations of white people. In "Marching for Freedom," produced by the National Gay and Lesbian Task Force, civil disobedience—a form of civil rights activity which through its embodied disobedience challenges the nature of the body politic—is contained within the category of "individual expression" and is presented through digitized effects of video production which obscure both the bodies and their actions.

Having thus aspired to inhabit the body politic by forefronting unmarked lesbian and gay bodies, the march relied heavily on analogies between lesbian and gay oppression and racial oppression, particularly on analogies with the 1963 Civil Rights March, in order to establish counterpublic claims for minority-group oppression and the need for a lesbian and gay civil rights bill. Thus, for example, in the portion of Larry Kramer's speech shown in "Gay Rights, Special Rights," Kramer is paraphrasing King to say that one day men and women will not be judged by their "sexual desire," but by the content of their character. In using this analogy in this way, Kramer accedes to the conservative reading of civil rights, appealing to those norms which make the body politic a social space inhabited only by those who can, phantomlike, disembody themselves by proclaiming that sexual desire shouldn't matter.[32] Simultaneously, Kramer depends on the visibility of bodies marked by racial difference to promote the claim that sexual identity, like race, should be a "protected category." There is a lot going on here, and just as with civil rights, there is more to Larry Kramer than this conservative point. It would be dangerous to define Kramer or queer movements, including ACT UP, which he helped found, by this moment alone, which "Gay Rights, Special Rights" clearly wants to do.[33]

The problems with the march strategy are multiple and interrelated. The analogy with race not only erases the historical differences between racism and homophobia, as well as antiracist and antiheterosexist struggle, but accepts the assumption that race is in the United States a protected category (a site of special rights)—as if to be racially marked in the United States is somehow to be protected. Perhaps even more problematic, once conservative assumptions about the public are accepted, particularly the assumption that the body politic is constituted by overcoming the particular embodiments of race and sexual identity, then racially marked bodies can at best claim the contained space of a counterpublic minority, while white lesbian and gay bodies can aspire to the public only by denying visible queerness and acceding to the unmarked categories of the white, middle-class family. Thus, for example, I was once told by a white gay man that "we" shouldn't use the word *queer* in public organizing because "we" needed to show that "we're just like your father, just like your brother." While these are not the two people in the world I find myself to be most like, I also took this remonstrance to be saying that making my white lesbian body a visible site of queerness threatened to exclude me—and, through guilt by association in a potentially shared queerness, him—from the public which he hoped to join.

"We" the People

Thus, I return to the production of "we" and the question of norms. As I wrote this essay I was repeatedly pushed toward the position—appealing in its clarity—that "we" must give up on the "we." Certainly, this is the tack which several scholars have taken with regard to queerness, that to be queer is a resistance, not just to heteronormativity, but to normativity itself.[34] The hope here is to resist the entire process by which norms constitute a "we," and, thus, to resist the type of inclusions and exclusions which I describe in this paper. This reading of queer is in many ways useful. It provides a fulcrum from which to question the mainstreaming of "lesbian, gay, and bi" identity into a public just like my father's and brother's. Yet, as partially indicated by the social location from which the movement to reclaim queerness emerged—young, urban, white, gay men—appeals to the queer in us all have the potential to reuniversalize a disembodied "we," once more inhabited by those whose bodies are the least marked by the normative constitution of the public.[35]

I would like to raise a related question: whether "we" could constitute a queer body politic and what it would look like. I think that such a project can only be effectively undertaken if the relationship between the body politic and public bodies is also challenged. As long as the body politic is a phantom body that coherently includes and supersedes all public bodies, the norms which materialize it will continue to represent certain bodies through the visibility of other bodies who are contained and disciplined by these same norms. Thus, even if this body politic is named *queer,* if it does not rework the relationship between the general and the particular, the same magic act of visibility and invisibility is likely to be replayed.

Returning to Benhabib, she argues that feminist or lesbian or queer or antiracist or any other politics requires normative criteria which may be developed in dialogue among particular bodies, but which can also be used to adjudicate among the specific norms which regulate these bodies, whether individual or communal.[36] A slippage takes place in Benhabib's texts in which the "we" who is formed in the specific context of Western rationalism and from this context judges "others," slips into the "we" who is the universal ideal of Western norms so that, although for Benhabib general norms come out of the negotiations among/between different particulars, these negotiations can only take place within the framework of modern, universalist rationalism.[37] When Benhabib states that "interactive universalism is the practice of situated criticism for a global community,"[38] the word *universalism* performs this framing function for an otherwise situated or contextual interaction. When she says, "[Communities of needs and solidarity] become so only insofar as they uphold the ideal of action in a universalist, egalitarian, consensual framework,"[39] the norms which she lists are not simply a part of, or representative of a party to, these negotiations; they are its frame, and the simultaneous inclusion and exclusion which constitutes the general is repeated in relation to "other" norms.[40] "Other" norms become differences *within* this frame—a pluralism of particular (communities) who share the general norms of universalism, egalitarianism, and consensuality and, thus, who do not fundamentally challenge the frame—while any excess, any exteriority which exceeds this framework, is an "other" to be judged.[41]

Benhabib adopts this position because without a framework of general norms we would be criteria-less at the point of moral diversity and conflict—the point at which she turns to adjudication. Are, however, the two central terms of this formulation—the need for a moral framework and the move to adjudication—the only, or even the best, possible understanding of and response to moral diversity and conflict? I would suggest that they are not. Similarly, I would ask, is the phantom public from which "we" judge a useful imagination of community? Can we imagine another type of community? What if the norms which materialize particular bodies were not necessarily superseded in the development of the public? What if we were to maintain the tension between the concrete and the general, even at the point of diversity and conflict? What would a public look like if it were made up of public bodies which did not constitute a single overarching body politic or which constituted a body politic differently? Would, then, the norms which materialize these particular bodies be general as well as particular public norms? Then, perhaps the problem with giving up on the framework that Benhabib finds necessary is not so much that we will be criteria-less, but rather that we will have more criteria than we know what to do with.

Here I think is a potential point of intervention. We should not give up on these multiple norms or their publicity by consigning them to a position in which they can be trumped by the general. If we were to abandon the project of developing a singular set of overarching norms with which to adjudicate among particular bodies, could we then build a different type of body politic based on the diverse and complex norms which materialize particular bodies, both individual and communal? I am not suggesting that we give up on the idea of the public, or of general norms; rather, I am suggesting that we locate the "we"—the community or public which brings together diverse and complex particulars—in a different place than in an overarching framework. I have suggested elsewhere that the spaces in between (in and between) differences are alternative sites to locate public activity, sites which allow both for the recognition of specific (differences) and for community building which challenges and reworks the boundaries of the specific.[42] The spaces in between shift the location and practice of normative interaction in that there is no single set of norms within which different normative discourses interact, but rather the spaces in between these discourses are spaces where articulations, connections which do not constitute an overarching frame, can be built.[43] Moreover, these spaces open possibilities for a variety of approaches to moral conflict, including mediations which are not adjudications.[44] Interaction in the spaces in between does not, however, consist only of conflict resolution; rather, conflicts at various sites must themselves be seen as part of the process of democratization among diverse and complex publics. Conflicts are not simply disturbances to be resolved, because conflicts are productive of democracy.[45]

I find this possibility an intriguing one. If the body politic is made up of, but does not supersede, diverse and complex particular bodies, then the site of imagination and of community/ies greater than any particular body would be at the points of connection and conflict between public bodies, rather than in a space based on the dissolution of visible embodiment (think of Larry Kramer's body dissolving into Martin Luther King's). The relational labor of value formation would take place in between, rather than above, particular persons and communities. The public would not be conceptualized as an overarching singular body—one public which corresponds with one nation-state—but would rather be conceptualized more as a network of interrelations among "multiple, sometimes overlapping or contending public spheres."[46] The normative question for feminist and lesbian and queer and antiracist theories is how should these publics be interrelated?[47] The ethical question that public bodies face is not so much how do "we" judge (others) as what values can "we" make among our (diverse and complex) selves?

The fundamental shift I am suggesting is from an understanding of feminist or lesbian or queer uses of norms as ultimately building a normative *framework,* to one of building a *network* among diverse and complex sets of norms, bodies, and publics. In this reading, then, the necessary relational work highlighted by resistance to the constructions of "Gay Rights, Special Rights" would be in and between queer movements and movements for racial justice, work which would need to make visible those lives and bodies at the intersections and interstices of these constructions of social movement. Through a focus on intersections and interstices such spaces allow for the articulation (in both senses of the word) of the type of diversities which subvert the oppositions on which the general public constructs itself.

Thus, I end not with an answer, but with a relational question. What are the possible uses of the diverse and complex norms which materialize our bodies? Can we focus on these uses and, thus, shift our public imagination from the phantom of a singular body politic to the possible relationships among diverse and complex, but nonetheless public, bodies? Here I am asking for a project of political imagination, one which through political struggle might lead to an alternative constitution of the "public."[48] Can we reimagine queer and public in an embodied way, in a way which recognizes queer bodies in public, not just a queer body politic? I can only conclude by stating that I hope so. My lesbian body (subject to the regulation of the state of Arizona despite the fact that as lesbian I am always already excluded from the norms that legitimate that regulation) depends on it.

CHAPTER 8

BAD WOMEN
The Limits of Theory and Theology

Paula M. Cooey

ANALYSIS OF THE DESIGNATION of certain kinds of women as "bad" exposes serious limitations both in social theory and in theology for understanding human agency in Western culture.[1] Mainstream social and cultural theorists of the self have inadequately dealt with the significance of difference in gender for the formation of identity. Meanwhile, most feminist theory has not sufficiently included the voices of all women, particularly the voices of "bad women" and of witnesses on their behalf. Mainstream theological anthropology has universalized elite, white male experience to the exclusion and detriment of women, among others. At the same time, feminist Christian and post-Christian theological anthropologies have often overly simplified identity by tending toward optimism regarding women's agency and by addressing issues of violence almost exclusively from the perspective of women as victims or survivors of victimization.

These limitations result in several serious problems. The oversimplification of women's agency, whether theoretical or theological, perpetuates a polarization of images of women either as incapable of evil or as demonic. Within this polarity, both theorists and theologians alike tend to relegate women's transgressions to the realm of the demonic, rather than acknowledging women as highly complex agents interacting within their surrounding circumstances. This oversimplification further perpetuates the view of women as defined solely by their relations to others, particularly as actual or potential mothers or as nurturers. Moreover, theoretical and theological tendencies to overly simplify agency ultimately produce unnecessary closure on the meanings of the concepts woman and human.

137

Thus, recognition of women's full complexity as human persons or subjects remains at best inadequate and at worst denied. Likewise theoretical and theological concepts of what constitutes human either suffer masculinization masked as universal humanity, or they oversimplify women's agency by underestimating its moral ambiguity. Serious implications follow for theological doctrines of sin and grace, as well as for theological ethics.[2] In particular, social theory, especially as appropriated by theologians, plays no small role in the demonizing and romanticizing of women. Worse still, both theory and theology insufficiently recognize the role of class in the social construction of the concept woman.

I propose to look at the implications of the absence of bad women's voices in the construction of culture as a way of exposing the limitations of theoretical and theological conceptualizations of subjectivity or agency. Once I have addressed the issue of what constitutes "bad women," I shall analyze theoretical representations of bad women, particularly bad mothers, after which I shall discuss feminist Christian and post-Christian theological silence on this issue. The "data" against which I shall be assessing theory and theology alike consist of interpretations of what I am calling "actual bad mothers."[3] Following my analysis, I shall propose an alternative theoretical stance for theological anthropology.

Bad Women

"Bad women" is a conceptual fabrication that reflects a social construal of certain kinds of actions by women. In other words, designating women as "bad" is a discursive practice. "Bad women" refers here specifically to women whose actions violate or resist relations that have traditionally defined women in this society in ways that place them at odds with various cultural systems governing these relations, for example, legal and social services. This violation often occurs within a context of violence which women may have initiated or in which they may have actively or passively participated. Most of these relations occur within the family and assume heterosexuality as normative. In addition to bad mothers, bad women may include bad daughters, bad sisters, bad wives and lovers, female prostitutes,[4] and rebels, by which I mean specifically women who consciously resist or reject being defined in terms of these relations.

Bad women can be further distinguished as mythological or actual women. Mythological bad women are cultural icons produced by popular media and the arts. They are usually fictions, whether of religious origin, "great" literature, the visual arts, or popular culture. They may also be fictions of the humanities and the social sciences as well. By contrast, actual bad women are women whose actions make them vulnerable to being brought up on charges by social services, ending up in the courts charged with criminal activity, or being institutionalized or otherwise engaged in psychological therapy. In some cases, for example, Pattie Hearst and Madonna, actual women may take on mythological status. I shall focus my analysis predominantly on actual bad mothers for several reasons, not the least of which is scope.

I shall focus on bad mothers because mothering is at the very foundation of traditional views of women as distinguished from men, such that no woman escapes association with mothering in the form of nurturing as, in some sense, a measure of her social value and status. In other words, the central feature that historically distinguishes women from men in this culture is a woman's capacity to bear children. According to much of the rhetoric on motherhood, to be a bad mother is to defy the nature and essence of womanhood.

Bad mothers neglect, fail to protect, overtly abuse, or even kill their children. Medea and Agave from the plays of Euripides exemplify mythological bad mothers who killed their own children.[5] Susan Smith exemplifies an actual bad mother who killed her children. Politicians and jurists designate pregnant women addicted to crack cocaine bad mothers.[6] A woman from Woodstock, Georgia, was charged with cruelty to a child for slapping her son in the face in the grocery store because he was tormenting his sister. According to Georgia law cruelty to a child constitutes a felony for which punishment can include twenty years' imprisonment; if convicted, she will qualify as a bad mother such that she will lose custody of her children.[7] Thus cultural designation of a woman as a bad mother covers a wide range of possible behavior from apparent mistreatment and neglect during pregnancy to possible assault and murder.

Actual bad mothers in the most extreme cases do actual physical damage to children, either overtly or through neglect. What constitutes child neglect, however, is subject to historical fluctuation on the part of social services. Furthermore, the definitions are heavily tainted by race, class, and ethnic bias on the part of the authorities.[8]

A brief profile of mothers charged with or suspected of abusing children, who have interacted with civil authorities, is revelatory. In her study of family violence in Boston from 1880 to 1960, Linda Gordon found that child abuse is "the only form of family violence in which women's assaults are common" and that child-battering mothers were no less violent in assaulting their children than were child-battering fathers. Gordon also notes that social-service workers of this period perceived child-abusing mothers in terms of middle-class bias; that is, they assumed underclass women by definition of being poor were more likely to abuse their children. However, Gordon herself found that, contrary to social workers' assumptions regarding the relation between level of affluence and the treatment of children in the home, most poor parents did not abuse their children.[9]

Gordon further reports that when accounting for their actions to social-service staff, "though [the mothers] felt badly [sic] about hurting those they loved, they did not necessarily condemn violence against children; they more often condemned other women's failure to discipline children."[10] Lawyers who as public defenders represent substantial numbers of mothers charged with child abuse report that virtually all women whom they defend deny that they have abused their children; the lawyers attribute these denials to an inability on the part of the mothers to recognize themselves in the accounts of their actions presented to them by civil and criminal authorities.[11] Psychologists who work with bad mothers through the social-service and court systems often diagnose them as suffering from "borderline personality disorder," a diagnosis whose symptoms are increasingly linked to a history of having been abused as a child, though 80 percent of abused children do not themselves become abusers.[12]

Actual bad mothers are thus most likely to be exposed to the public if they are poor, regardless of race or ethnicity.[13] In addition, they may be quite violent, though they tend to perceive themselves as disciplining their children rather than damaging them. Furthermore, they themselves are likely to have suffered a past history of abuse.

In summary, "bad women" refers to a range of women whose ostensible immorality and criminality establish, by way of contrast, what this culture deems to be normative womanhood. Furthermore, the consequences of these constructions for all women can be devastating. I shall focus on what I consider the heart of the discursive practices that establish what is normative, namely, bad mothers, with the idea that my analysis has some application to bad women in general. Because bad mothers exemplify limit situations regarding what our culture claims to be willing to tolerate, they reveal the fractures within current discursive practices surrounding womanhood and thus provide some of the best instances for contesting meaning.

Questioning norms and contesting meaning notwithstanding, I want to make clear what I am not doing. I am not proposing a fully developed Christian theological anthropology. More important, however, I am also not arguing for the domestication or the mystification of women who damage others. Quite the contrary, I am arguing in part that the discursive practice of demonizing women who damage others mystifies the moral agency of some women for the purpose of domesticating the rest. The question is not whether these acts are morally acceptable; rather, I am asking: What do the culturally authoritative construals of the agency of such women, in the absence of their own voices, tell us about the limitations of how we conceive what it means to be human, especially with respect to what it means to be a woman? Do such acts and their wider context expose limitations to how we, particularly as feminists, think about selves either in social theory or in a theological context? Do such acts and their wider context provide a helpful critique for assessing what we as theologians, particularly as feminists, construct when we envision not only women's agency as women, but human agency? Christian and post-Christian feminist theology, like other liberation theologies, has in many respects been written by relative outsiders. To what extent do "bad women" as outsiders to the outsiders challenge the very distinctions good and bad, inside and outside, center and margin?[14]

Theoretical Representations

Because mothering has received perhaps the most attention of all the roles defining women, representations of the bad mother abound in theoretical literature. Legal theorists Marie Ashe and Naomi Cahn include a review of these representations in their work; their analysis, taken in conjunction with Gordon's social history of family violence, makes clear the ahistorical nature of most theory, feminist as well as nonfeminist, and raises several issues of relevance to theological discussions of what it means to be a woman or a human being. These discussions include the issue of class, the contradiction between what is considered normative adult subjectivity and the expectations placed on the good mother, and the theoretical construction of motherhood as exemplifying exclusively the perspective of the child.

Bad Mothers

In respect to class, though mythological bad mothers cross all class lines, as evidenced by Medea and Agave from the aristocratic classes, actual bad mothers, that is, women who enter into the social-service and judicial systems, come disproportionately from the underclasses. This gap may reflect differences in economic resources that might go to child care or to therapeutic treatments of any perceived problems rather than criminal procedures. I suggest, however, the gap also reflects a tendency on the part of those who report neglect and abuse, as well as those in the legal and social systems who deal with the mothers directly, to perceive neglect and abuse as more characteristic of mothering in the underclasses, in other words to expect abuse in the context of poverty.[15]

The element of class bias reflected in this gap plays a crucial role in both feminist and nonfeminist theoretical silence on the issue as well. This silence masks the extent to which theoretical expectations surrounding mothering, including both the good and the bad mother, differ greatly according to class. Whereas many professionals tacitly assume that affluent women are less likely to abuse their children because they are more affluent, theoretical constructs of good mothering reflect or idealize conventional expectations placed on middle-class mothers and assume middle-class economic structures. In other words, professional expectations and theoretical representations are mutually reinforcing. This kind of class bias not only falsely assumes that underclass women by definition are more likely to act violently toward their children, but it also masks middle-class women's vulnerability to frustration, rage, and subsequent guilt in respect to their child rearing. Whereas the culture expects bad mothers to be a product of poverty and ignorance, an expectation that may be "read in" when poverty-stricken mothers encounter professionals, it expects mothers from affluent environments to fulfill successfully the needs of their children without ever losing control, and furthermore to enjoy doing so.[16] Thus we commit injustices against both underclass and middle-class mothers.

In the case of mothers from affluent contexts, class bias sets up a contradiction between normative subjectivity and normative mothering. While mothering by affluent women may be less subject to direct social control compared with mothering by poor women, the lack of "reading in" on the part of professional authorities regarding middle-class mothers implies that the agency of ostensibly good mothers is not vulnerable either to emotional complexity or to moral ambiguity, traits normally associated with mature adult subjectivity in the abstract. For example, as Ashe and Cahn point out, according to Freudian theory, good mothering requires of women a suppression of aggression, sexual sensuality, and nonmaternal creativity; and, according to object-relations theory, even "good enough" mothering nevertheless demands masochistic self-sacrifice, as well as total, exclusive involvement with the child for an extended period of time.[17] This contradiction ultimately presents a no-win situation for all actual mothers. In short, being a good mother by definition precludes one from acting like a mature adult subject to moral and emotional complexity.

This contradiction pervades the lives of all women insofar as we are vulnerable to being perceived as potential mothers. All women are vulnerable to the denial of our status as subjects, whenever we are expected by men and women alike to fulfill nurturing roles that we may be reluctant at the time to fulfill. To the extent that women reject such roles as centrally determining of our identities, we are further subject to being stereotyped as bad or inadequate.

Theory plays no small role in this transaction. For example, Susan Suleiman suggests that psychoanalytic theory is a theory of childhood, a concept picked up by Ashe and Cahn and applied as a category of analysis to feminist critiques of theories of mothering as well, notably the work of Dorothy Dinnerstein and Nancy Chodorow.[18] Indeed, Ashe and Cahn argue at length that almost all theoretical representations of mothering, feminist or otherwise, are intentionally or unintentionally views from the perspective of the child. By "perspective of a child" they mean from the perspective of unmet childhood needs and expectations. Not only is this perspective in its theoretical forms ahistorical, it also excludes any representation of mothering or childhood from the perspective of actual mothers (or for that matter, from the perspective of any adult). Such theoretical representations explicitly propose or at the least imply an essentialism definitive of what constitutes the human, namely, an inner child, continuous throughout one's existence as part of one's identity; in fact, rather than describing or explaining what it means to be a human subject, such theoretical discourse is producing certain kinds of human beings—

namely, ones who fancy themselves entitled to have all their infantile needs met.[19]

This theoretical elision reflects and in turn influences social attitudes, values, and power arrangements. In ordinary human interaction, a child's perspective is not necessarily restricted to children; rather, adult humans of both genders frequently view reality through the lenses of their experiences of unmet needs as children and carry childhood memories, conscious or unconscious, of these unmet needs into their personal and professional relations in ways that make life extremely difficult for women who resist nurturing them. Ashe and Cahn pose, as an alternative theoretical discourse on mothering, an incorporation of multiple perspectives or voices, including the voices of bad mothers and those who advocate on their behalf.

Women's Subjectivity and Violence

Critique of theoretical literature thus suggests an important feature concerning the significance of bad women for the construction of women's subjectivity. The perception of adult women by men and women alike through the lens of the unmet needs of a child appears to lie at the heart of demonizing and romanticizing women through mythological projection. In any case, theoretical construals of the subject are at best troubling and at worst profoundly flawed, particularly with respect to gender and especially as theoretical constructions of gender difference presuppose class bias. Though Gordon does not pursue race and ethnicity at great length in her studies, her analysis nevertheless also indicates that issues concerning the significance of racial and ethnic difference are at least as problematic.[20] As Ashe and Cahn point out, virtually no theoretical framework places gender difference in historical context, nor do theories of subjectivity take into account the perspectives of actual mothers.

I have tried to build on their critiques by arguing that prevailing theories of subjectivity are further inadequate in that they assume conflicting expectations for adult women in contrast to human subjects in the abstract; thus, as prescription for what is normative, theoretical discourse also perpetuates serious conflicts in the formation of actual women's identities.[21] I suggest that understanding these conflicts as rooted in the exclusion of women's voices helps to understand better the mythological construction of bad women. Much more importantly, I suggest that both the contradictions involving class bias and the conflict between what constitutes normative human subjectivity and normative motherhood may themselves contribute to actual women's violence as mothers, daughters, sisters, sexual partners, and social rebels. Given the inadequacy of theory, it is no surprise that theological formulations of what it means to be a subject share many of the same problems.

Theological Implications

As in the case of theory, so it is in the case of feminist theology.[22] Though significant and necessary critical and constructive work has been done that relates child abuse and male abuse of adult women to Christology, to church teaching, and to moral agency, mothers' voices, particularly the voices of abusive mothers and witnesses on their behalf, remain absent.[23] The absence of theological attention to these voices reinforces a view of women as essentially not capable of violence, a view that denies women's rage once it occurs outside the boundaries of women's victimization. This denial constitutes a romanticizing of women, albeit motivated by the understandable desire not to further blame victims. It is a denial to which I certainly confess being vulnerable, but a luxury which I think we cannot as feminists afford without vastly undermining the very complexity of women's subjectivity that we seek to convey.

Thus, for feminist Christian and post-Christian theological anthropology, a reconstruction of subjectivity that would take seriously the moral ambiguity of women's agency, as exemplified by the actions of women who run afoul of legal and social-service systems, would in certain respects have to begin from scratch. Such reconstruction would minimally involve three related tasks. The first task requires theologians to pay attention to the accounts of bad women in their own words, insofar as they are available, and in the words of witnesses on their behalf. Distinguishing as moral critic between bad women as historical phenomena, that is, women who damage others, and the ascription of evil to women as a discursive practice, the aim of which is production of certain types of subjectivity, serves as a second step.[24] Representing bad women as complex subjects, reducible neither solely to victims nor solely to agents of violence, constitutes a third task.

Paying Attention

There are a variety of resources available to which theologians need to pay attention. Court cases, transcripts of trials, and media accounts are public events and public records. Data also include social-service cases no longer open, provided confidentiality is maintained. In addition, there is a growing body of feminist legal theory. All of these resources are empirical as in historical, though they are also representations of bad women that must be read critically. To read them critically requires, in addition to a consideration of one's own social location and an attunement to gender bias, a keen awareness of racial, ethnic, and class bias potentially present in all genres, not to mention a skepticism regarding media accuracy and motivation. Reading also requires becoming literate in the literature on abused women and children. Reading critically moreover entails struggles with one's self-awareness—awareness of an element of voyeurism as well as a sense of invading the privacy of another. One example will suffice:

A recent newspaper account covers a nineteen-year-old, poverty-stricken Latina mother charged with capital murder for beating her twenty-one-month-old daughter to death and awaiting trial in a Dallas jail. The headline runs, "Mom accused in daughter's killing notes cycle of abuse."[25] The mother was herself beaten and sexually abused by her stepfather from the time she was seven until she ran away from home at the age of fourteen. In the interim, at the age of twelve, she bore him a child. Of this time in her life she is quoted as saying, "I didn't have anyone to listen to me. My mother knew what was going on, but she wouldn't do anything about it. I left home when I was fourteen because I couldn't stand it anymore. It was disgusting." The reporter remarks that she spoke these words in a "low, timid voice." Of her abuse to the point of killing her own daughter she says, "I did spank her every day. But it's because she has a mind of her own and she won't listen to me." She is also quoted as saying, "I didn't mean to hit her hard enough to kill her. I didn't mean for her to die. I feel like the world hates me." According to the reporter the police said that the child "suffered more extensive injuries than any other child-abuse victim in recent memory." A Dallas policeman describes the child's body as "severely beaten over her entire body. It was obvious that she had been severely battered over a period of days." The reporter notes, though does not quote directly, that the mother admits that the memory of her own abuse should have prevented her from doing the same to her child, that the mother feels remorse, and that the mother misses the child. The reporter also remarks that, according to an expert interviewed, the mother's behavior is typical of abused children and quotes the expert as claiming, "This is a classic case of abuse going on for generations. It becomes a cycle. We tend to parent the way we were parented." The mother has also given birth to two other children. Her first child, the one fathered by her stepfather, she gave up for adoption. A second child lives with a different father in another location, and a third child, a ten-month-old daughter, will likely be placed in the custody of Child Protective Services.

This newspaper account can and must be read from at least two over-lapping yet contending perspectives, namely, one on behalf of the dead child and one on behalf of her mother. On behalf of the child a baby has not only died, but from the police officer's description of the baby's body, she has lived a very short life marked by repeated beatings, a life of sus-tained pain. There can be no compensation either for her death or for the pain endured throughout her life. Beyond this recognition the child's life is surrounded by silence; we do not even know her name. The mother, also once a child, has likewise endured a life of hideous suffering, in which her own mother appears to be passively complicit, the brutality of which she unsuccessfully resisted by fleeing her home. She escaped abuse only to become an abuser. Her words, contrasted with the quotations from the expert who sees her as a fatalistically determined victim-become-victimizer and the police officer who describes the child's body, reflect a view of her-self as disciplinarian, remorseful and grieving, and filled with self-loathing. Alone as a child ("I didn't have anyone to listen to me"), she becomes a very young adult whose intentions are not commensurate with her actions ("I didn't mean to hit her hard enough to kill her; I didn't mean for her to die"). The article implies that she connects her past victimization with her present victimizing for it begins, "[The mother] says she knows the pain of fists pummeling a little girl's body"; the reporter goes on to add that the mother admits that her own experience should have been enough to stop her from doing the same thing to her daughter.

What are we to make of this event? The main focus of the article is on "cycles of abuse," though it reflects some ambivalence on the part of the reporter. The reporter appears to be struggling with a conflict between sympathy for the mother, given her past, and repulsion for the mother on behalf of the daughter.

On the one hand, the reporter cites the experts on child abuse who claim that the mother's behavior is typical of battered children who reach adulthood. Note the inaccuracy here; that four out of five victims of abuse do not go on to become abusers seems to have escaped the expert's attention.[26] Furthermore, the expert conflates the kind of abuse suffered by the mother with her abuse of her daughter as if the neglect and incest suffered by the mother were the same thing as the battering she inflicted on her daughter. Note especially the portrayed inevitability of the mother's actions which she as victim is helpless to escape. The mother's words about her own intentions seem to support this view.

On the other hand, the reporter also represents the mother as agent, as one who knew she should have treated her daughter differently, the implication being that knowledge of what should and should not happen entails responsibility to make it so. The reporter's account of the mother's self-loathing, projected on the world she perceives as hating her, along with her admission that she should have known better, further supports this view of her as agent. That the two views of the subject here are at odds goes unnoticed by the reporter and could be easily missed by the reader as well. If the mother is doomed by her victimization to become a victimizer, how can knowing better make any difference whatsoever? If knowing better means a genuine opportunity to act differently, then why should the mother's past be of any relevance whatsoever?

This contradiction illustrates a deep fracture in conventional, theoretical, and theological ways of talking about human identity in this culture. It points to the inadequacy of talking about subjects as agents and victims as if the two stood in dichotomous relation, an inadequacy which has serious implications for what it means to be a subject from a Christian theological perspective. I shall return to this issue shortly. This contradiction should further alert the reader to the ideological implications of such an article appearing in a major newspaper in one of the largest cities in the country as well. Given the horrible, monotonous frequency of domestic abuse, what makes this case or any other case merit special attention? The issue of selection brings me to my second point—the task of distinguishing between phenomenal bad women and their ideological use to enforce social control.

The Discursive Uses of Bad Women
in the Production of Normative Female Subjectivity

The reporter's ambivalence toward the mother charged with beating her daughter to death marks serious progress in media reporting of such events. Typical media coverage of domestic violence ranges from highly sensational to feigned neutrality to the demonization of alleged perpetrators. However, such coverage should be placed in conjunction with the class, ethnic, and racial bias that runs through social-service and judicial records, as well as a tendency to identify exclusively with victims—if the victims are children and the alleged perpetrators are women. All of these forces work together with mythological constructions of bad women to produce certain normative types of female subjectivity.

While the actual events of violence by women are in themselves morally troubling, their selection and appropriation into popular culture are disturbing as well. Witness the disproportionate fascination with the case of John Wayne and Lorena Bobbitt or the obsession with Tonya Harding. Consider the bashing of working mothers engaged in by the politicized fundamentalist Christian Right. In this particular news article, the reporter's sometime-sympathy toward the mother notwithstanding, the reader quickly picks up on the poverty, ethnicity, youth, and single status of a mother who has had multiple sexual partners fathering several children, all details that reinforce prevailing political polemic directed toward young single mothers on welfare. While it would be paranoid to suggest a well-organized plot hatched by a specific person or group of persons to "get" women, ongoing cultural representation of women as bad nonetheless works to preserve a culture that is not only profoundly antifemale, but ironically antichild as well. Poor women of all races and ethnicities, particularly but not exclusively those who mother children and rear them alone, tend to figure heaviest as cultural representatives for vilification, but any transgression of what are largely middle-class moral conventions and piety make women vulnerable to cultural representation as bad, unless they have strategies for looking acceptable.

The threat of being perceived as a bad woman works very effectively to keep us as women in our place, or at least looking like we are in our place. The threat is effective because it is all-pervasive, from media coverage of women's violence to our own successful internalization of guilt and fear of failure, tied directly to nurture, as mothers, daughters, sisters, sexual partners, and workers in the public arena. And so we nurture beyond the point of exhaustion and otherwise try to look nurturing. We associate violence with anger and then suppress anger. Indeed internalization of the fear of being perceived as bad women runs so deep that we may project our anger onto the women whose violence becomes public. Recognition of guilt, fear, and anger as an internalization of patriarchy, particularly regarding sexual behavior, lay at the heart of consciousness-raising early in the Second Wave of feminism. However, we have yet to explore what this internalization means, not only in terms of women's actual violence toward others, but also in terms of its continuing cultural uses to reproduce female caretakers, as well as the effects of this reproduction on relations among women.

Christian teaching, practice, and theology play a direct role in the production of a culture that not only produces violent women but uses them ideologically in support of existing arrangements of power. More often than not, what the culture, including its religious traditions, calls "good" depends for its very existence on guaranteeing the perpetuation of what it calls "evil." Nevertheless, systems of injustice that sustain the status quo do not exist in the abstract as if human beings were merely pawns. Whenever Christian theologians interpret and construct the life of the church in ways that support conventional views of good and evil or remain silent on the ideological use of women's violence, we perpetuate the suffering of all women. In the long run both conventional theology and theological silence fail the very communities theologians seek to serve by failing to challenge all cultural forms of idolatry.

Women as Complex Subjects
Who Differ from One Another

It is not enough to challenge the idolatry involved in demonizing women, however. Feminist Christian theologians need to provide strong representations of women as complex subjects as an alternative to prevailing views of women either as victims or as agents. We need to capture the full tragedy of what it means for women to resist circumstances only to be destroyed by them, as in the case of the nineteen-year-old mother who rebelled by running away from home to escape the abuse of her father, only to end up charged with murdering her own daughter, just as we attend to the grace of what it means to survive and to transcend the damage others have done. As feminist Christian theologians, we need to acknowledge on theological grounds that no human being, including and especially anyone vulnerable to cultural demonization, is simply reducible to the damage she has done, just as we stand in support of those who have suffered the damage.

Fiction provides a major resource in addition to the more empirical sources, though I caution that, taken by itself, fiction is no substitute. Contemporary novels written by women of color particularly capture the intersection of racism with sexism, whereas contemporary Anglo-American novelists often reflect the conjunction of class interest with sexism.

For example, Toni Morrison and Gloria Naylor represent the complexities of mothering and mother-child relations in the context of violence exceptionally well, all against a backdrop of white racism. Pauline Breedlove of Morrison's *The Bluest Eye* lovingly mothers the white children whose parents pay her, but she is emotionally cold to her own African American daughter, Pecola, who is ultimately driven mad by her desire for blue eyes.[27] Sethe, the main character of Morrison's *Beloved,* seeks to save her children from slavery by killing them; she succeeds in killing one of her daughters only to be haunted by her.[28] Ceil of Naylor's *The Women of Brewster Place* loses her daughter Serena to a hideous accident when Serena is left alone in their racially segregated housing project.[29]

Fictional representations of adult women as complex in their relations with their parents as well as with their children are relatively recent phenomena. Jane Smiley's retelling of *King Lear* provides an outstanding example of retelling Shakespeare's tragedy of father-daughter relations from the perspective of the two daughters originally demonized in Lear.[30] Recast in the context of contemporary middle-class, Midwestern farm life, the narrative not only presents highly complex daughters who also become mothers, but women whose relations as sisters provide an important study in conflict among female siblings as well.

Agnes Smedley's fictionalized autobiography *Daughter of Earth* and, more recently, Joyce Carol Oates's novel *Foxfire: Confessions of a Girl Gang* provide two of the best examples of fictional narrative from the perspective of women who reject relationships that have traditionally defined women, through prostitution and through political rebellion that includes violence.[31] The main characters of both works are working class, though *Daughter of Earth*'s characters are rural as well. In both books the central characters are political rebels whose choices, motivated by the best of intentions, result in violence and tragedy even as their political commitments are nevertheless affirmed. Both books explore the cost of a woman's being defined by her relations to others, though both reflect a more explicitly Marxist stance than a feminist one.

In spite of significant differences among them, all of these fictional characters share the quality of being subjects—their violence notwithstanding—who are women about whose well-being a reader cannot help but care deeply. They are furthermore highly particularized subjects who reflect the conditions that produced them, even as they modify those conditions by their responses to them. Reducible neither to victims nor to demons, these characters provide lenses through which to view differently the actual women who have run afoul of various social systems, conventional morality, and self-righteous piety. As fictional characters they are convincing in part because many of them appear to choose to speak for themselves or to remain silent. Where this choice is not available within the narrative structure, their interactions with others nevertheless communicate a resistance to oversimplification. Neither romanticized nor demonized, these subjects sometimes briefly defy subversion into demons by the culture, even as they transgress cultural norms.

Religious in some cases, antireligious in others, such characters and their authors have much to teach us about sin and grace, about the capacity to care deeply for another, however strange, as one who shares certain affinities with another, if not her circumstances—to care deeply without denying or trivializing genuine social evil. In short, such characters, precisely because of their status as social pariahs who as such are after all complex persons, call for a reconstruction of agency that interrelates multiple voices and their surrounding, often conflicting, worlds without eliding difference.

Reconsidering Theory and Christian Theology

Assuming as I do that Christian theological anthropology and social theory are interactive artifacts of culture, I have proposed here to explore the limitations of both endeavors in their efforts to conceptualize the self by examining the role played by the cultural designation of certain kinds or types of women as "bad." In fact, my analysis pushed all the way results in a loss of theological innocence. Analysis of both the cultural practices of demonizing women (often performed in specifically religious contexts) and the damage that some women actually do explodes any notion of closure on all of the concepts that constitute Christian theological anthropology, namely: self, human, nature, woman, man, and deity, whether one's perspective is feminist or otherwise; it explodes the theories on which theological anthropology depends as well.

The events that surround women designated bad stand as surds in relation to grand narratives of what it means to be human, definitive statements of what it means to be a woman, and, most of all, any academic presumption to identify with a demonized other as if we immediately shared or fully understood her circumstances. Women who run afoul of the law are denied their voices. Not only do they lose their voices, assuming their voices were acknowledged to begin with, they also lose all rights to privacy or to discretion. If jailed, even their bodies are no longer their own. Every interaction with civil authority works to reinforce the denial of any right to claim their own authority. This is no less true in the case of theological authority. In the last analysis, even to those who seek to bear witness to them, bad women remain other, and this otherness stands in judgment on all theoretical and theological attempts to proclaim, construct, explain, or describe what it means to be human, convicting theoretician and theologian alike.[32]

CHAPTER 9

BECOMING AN AMERICAN
JEWISH FEMINIST

Laura Levitt

Identity is not the goal but rather the point of departure of the process of
self-consciousness, a process by which one begins to know that and how the
personal is political, that and how the subject is specifically and materially
en-gendered in its social conditions and possibilities of existence.
—Teresa de Lauretis

IN THIS ARTICLE I take as my starting point the idea that identity is a point
of departure, part of a process of self-consciousness. I do not offer an
abstract argument for turning to feminist theory. I take that move as a
given and instead offer an enactment of such theory. More specifically I try
to show what such a process of self-consciousness might look like in practice. In this way, I take issue with liberal constructions of identity in terms
of a unified self.[1] By offering a Jewish feminist position that is both multiple and contradictory, I question the normative status of the unified self
even within much of contemporary Jewish feminist writing.[2]

In other words, this article offers *self-consciousness* as a different kind
of Jewish feminist critical practice.[3] Here the self is de- and reconstructed
in relation to specific texts, Minnie Bruce Pratt's "Identity: Skin Blood
Heart"[4] and Biddy Martin and Chandra Mohanty's "Feminist Politics:
What's Home Got to Do with It?"[5] Through a reading of these texts, this
paper shows how Jewishness and feminism are specifically and materially
en-gendered in the social conditions and possibilities open to Jews,
women, and Jewish women in United States at the end of the twentieth
century. By engaging with these particular texts, the instability within
American Jewish feminist positions becomes increasingly evident. Critical

assumptions about what it has meant to be at home in America are called into question. In this respect, these texts allow this Jewish feminist to interrogate her faith in America, its liberal emancipatory vision of Jews and women, as well as its promises of justice and protection.[6] As I will argue, it is precisely these kinds of local beliefs that continue to shape our consciousness in specific material ways that need to be called into question.[7]

Thus, unlike previous Jewish feminist works, especially in the fields of Jewish studies and religion, this article explicitly challenges some of the material and discursive legacies of American liberalism as they continue to define Jewish women.[8]

Reading and Writing the Self in Relation

Further research will, I hope, flesh out the domestic space in such a way that this postcolonial feminist will no longer need to revisit French feminism as a way in, although it might remain an exigency in academic Cultural Studies. . . .

The way in through French feminism defines the third world as Other. Not to need that way in is, paradoxically, to recognize that indigenous global feminism must still reckon with the bitter legacy of imperialism transformed in decolonization.[9]

Like the postcolonial feminist critic Gayatri Chakravorty Spivak, I too have found that there are specific, in my case, American, feminist texts, texts somewhat removed from my own material situation which have, nevertheless, enabled me to claim my various subject positions or identities specifically in terms of home. In what follows I will now demonstrate how Minnie Bruce Pratt's essay in particular has become a critical part of my self-consciousness.

For me the process of self-consciousness is textual. To read and write about identity is relational. It demands a critical engagement with the texts of others within which the narratives of self and other become intertwined. Thus, it has been through my reading of Pratt's "Identity" that I have found, like Spivak, "a way in" to articulate my fluid position.

"Home" as Identity

Since this article is about the connections between home and identity or identity as a kind of home, I now want to start my reading with the concrete space, the house where I began writing about identity and home, the first floor of 317 Ninth Street in Atlanta.[10] I lived at this address from August 1987 through December 1991. It was my only home in Atlanta. It was large and sunny. The yard was extremely well taken care of by my landlord, an elderly woman living alone on the second floor. The building was about sixty years old, unrenovated but clean and neat. When I moved in all it needed was a new coat of bright white paint which my parents and I applied during three scorching summer days in August. When I moved in the apartment echoed. I had little furniture. I liked the emptiness of the space. For the first two years I had no soft furniture. I enjoyed the stark beauty of my home. Although it was often difficult to entertain, I was able to do my work. Among the first purchases I made were a computer and a desk. In the summer of 1989, I bought a futon couch and chair. They felt big and bulky but I got used to them. My home became more livable. It was easier to invite friends over, to share my space. In September 1989, I fell in love with a man who lived just a block away. He visited often. My home was filled with the promises of a new relationship. In November 1989 I was raped in my home by a stranger. After that I considered moving but could not imagine another home. I was angry at having to give up a place that was so much mine, a place where I had a history. I refused to move and chose instead to reconfigure my home. I painted the walls of my bedroom, the site of my rape. There were now two bruised purple walls and green trim. They matched a Botticelli poster on the wall, although, in truth, even the poster did not fully bring the room together again. I also moved the furniture. Since no walls felt safe, the bed floated in the middle of this room until I left Atlanta for good. The futon couch came in very handy as I could no longer stay at home alone. Friends became a constant presence in this home. I also got a dog who remains my constant companion. The house was never as neat or stark as it had once been. In the fall of 1990, as I began writing, I also tried briefly to stay at home alone. I was not comfortable. In October a friend moved in. I moved my office from the second bedroom into a breakfast nook. It was small, bright, and sunny. Nestled in between a file cabinet and a window, I felt safe and secure at my desk, writing. It was here where I began writing about home. The house filled up. There were lots of plants and lots of people. Another friend also spent much of this time living with us. With the dog that made four. Of course there is much more to tell.

This home was the site of a great many conflicting desires. It was a place of both comfort and terror. Nevertheless, it was my home. The knowledge that home could be both de- and reconstructed was visceral. It lived in the walls of this place I called my home in Atlanta. It was here that I began a process of self-consciousness that would allow me to reconfigure home on many fronts.

I began writing about identity and home in this place in 1990, a year after I was raped and just months before I was to end an important relationship. Between then and now the physical places I have called home have changed. The relationships that offered safety and protection have also shifted. "Home" has become something quite different, and yet some things have also remained constant. I continue to interrogate what it means to claim and configure a Jewish feminist identity in the midst of conflicting visions of home, making explicit how and in what ways it is crucial to theorize out of the contingent places we call home. I now want to demonstrate how reading and writing as a form of self-consciousness can help explain in nuanced and powerful ways the complexities of our lives, how it can enable us to explore the seams in the construction of our identities within the constraints of various social, cultural, and political configurations of power and desire.

What's Identity Got to Do with All of This?

In order to answer this question fully I want to bring the pieces of my story together now in a slightly different way through my reading of Minnie Bruce Pratt's "Identity."

Although my rape is not the only motivation for this article, it has been constitutive. It perhaps more than anything else has called into question so many of my beliefs about what constitutes home. These include my construction of my heterosexuality, my notions of family, of domesticity, of agency, and of personal safety and protection. To say I am a Jewish feminist in light of all that has happened to me, in light of all that I have done, and to make some sense of these disparate experiences is at the heart of this reading. To be honest about the complexity and contradictions of my experiences is the challenge I have posed for myself. As part of coming to terms with all of this, I have engaged with many traditions and many texts but, as I have already explained, Pratt's essay offered me a particularly meaningful place to begin this work on identity as home. Because she

interrogates her own commitments to being at home in America, her essay
has allowed me to explore my own place within an American dream of
home. Her narrative has held me up. It has provided weight and authority
for me to claim the specificity of my own position, a position that ironically both connects and separates me from Pratt.

I started thinking about home and identity in the spring of 1988 in
my first course on feminist theory.[11] It was here that I was introduced to
Martin and Mohanty's "Feminist Politics: What's Home Got to Do with
It?" and Pratt's "Identity: Skin Blood Heart."[12] Although my understanding of these essays and other works in feminist theory continues to evolve,
these particular essays have haunted me, informing my thinking about the
intersection of politics, identity, and home. I have remained especially
attached to Pratt's personal narrative. Martin and Mohanty raise cautions
about the applicability of Pratt's approach for other feminists, warning,
"We do not intend to suggest that Pratt's essay, or any single autobiographical narrative, offers 'an answer.'"[13] Nevertheless, I have remained
tied to her text. For me it is not so much "an answer" but a partial strategy
for putting together a life. For me, Pratt's narrative has operated as an invitation, giving me permission to speak honestly about the complexities of
my own position in America, especially after the disruption of my rape.

Not long after I was raped a series of letter bombs were sent to liberal
judges across the South. Some of these judges were killed. Accounts of
these incidents were all over the Atlanta news. White supremacists claimed
credit for these attacks, claiming to have acted on behalf of white women
who had been raped by black men. I had been raped by a young black
man. These claims spoke to me in direct ways. These men claimed to act
on my behalf. They committed acts of violence and used my experience as
justification. In a previously published essay about my rape, I chose not to
write about race. As a part of the final edit I was convinced by an editor
that simply writing that I had been raped by a black man, with a note that
briefly addressed some of my ambivalences about relaying this information, was not a sufficient way of addressing the complexity of these issues.
I would simply be reinscribing the kind of racist assumptions my note was
attempting to avoid.[14] Since complexity is so much a part of what I am
interested in addressing here, I return to this question. My race is an issue
especially in light of these bombings. My initial reaction was shame and
anger. How could these white supremacists act on my behalf? Who gave

them permission to invoke my experience? Rereading Pratt, I have had to think again about this construction of events in terms of what she describes as "that soundless blow, which changes forever one's map of the world."[15] My being raped had done this for me.[16]

What Pratt says about the event that shattered her vision of safety caused me to pause once again in trying to come to terms with my rape. Pratt writes:

> For me the blow was literal, the sound was rifle-fire. In broad daylight, in Greensboro, North Carolina, about 50 miles from where I lived, Klansmen and Nazis drove into an anti-Klan demonstration, shouting "Nigger! Kike! Commie bastard!" They opened fire, killing five people: four white men, two of them Jews, one Black woman; labor union organizers, affiliated with the Communist Workers Party. The next day I saw in the newspaper an interview with Nancy Matthews, wife of one of the Klansmen. She said, "I knew he was a Klan member, but I don't know what he did when he left home. I was surprised and shocked. . . ." But the Klansmen defended their getting out of their cars at the rally, rifles in hand, by saying they saw the car holding some Klanswomen being attacked and were "rushing to their rescue."[17]

I quote Pratt at length here in order to make clear the issues at stake. Not unlike the letter bombers, the Klan invoked the notion of protection to justify its acts of violence. In Greensboro, blacks, Jews, and communists were all at risk together. In my case these alliances were less clear. I was a white Jewish woman raped by a black man. How or in what ways did those letter bombs relate to my experience? Pratt reminded me that my Jewishness could be an issue, especially in the South. Am I a white woman or not? How and in what ways did this matter either to my attacker or to the white men who sent those bombs?

In my struggles to figure out who could protect me and at what costs, like Pratt I looked to the traditions and physical places I had called home for some answers.

Between November 1989 and November 1990, I learned a great deal about who and what could offer me protection. I learned not to be surprised that the same white men who claimed to act violently in the name of the violation of "their" women were, more often than not, also deeply implicated in the abuse of these same women. I learned that American women are most at risk when they are at home. Not only are they more likely to be beaten, raped, or killed in their homes than elsewhere, those who commit these acts are rarely strangers. Perpetrators are most often husbands, boyfriends, fathers, and uncles—the men we live with.[18]

Since my rape, I have learned about the connection between pledges of protection on the one hand, and acts of violence on the other. When I went to the legal system for help, I discovered just how little justice liberalism had to offer me. Through a combination of frustrating interactions with the police and a great deal of reading on rape laws and feminist political and social theory, I learned that rape has been constructed within the parameters of proper sexuality—heterosexuality. In this system rape and marriage are paired in binary opposition. Marriage is the positive term which is defined over and against the negation of rape. Marriage is legally sanctioned heterosexuality which is scripted as protective and consensual, while its other, rape, is defined as illegal, threatening, and nonconsensual. This economy of proper hetero/sexuality is naturalized through the institution of marriage within the liberal American state. In exchange for protection, a man acquires sexual access to his wife's body, a right protected within the boundaries of his home.[19]

In a man's home in America, the dynamic of threat and protection is replicated in relation to children. They are also defined in terms of "needing protection." This need forms the basis of a man's legal relationship to his wife and children within the liberal state. Under this logic he both controls and protects his family. The problem is, as I have argued elsewhere,[20] that the liberal construct presumes that home has been a safe place for women and children. What happens to women and children inside their homes is rarely questioned. Protection is simply assumed. In other words, under this system, the liberal state has no compelling interest in what goes on within a man's home. This so-called private sphere remains off limits to the state, making it difficult for those of us whose bodies have been violated at home to seek justice.

Even in cases like mine in which women are raped by strangers, cases which presumably reinforce this logic of protection, the legal system rarely offers resolution. In my case this meant that the man who raped me was never pursued. Despite the fact that I had immediately reported the crime, made a statement to the police, and even had evidence from a rape exam done the night of my rape, there was no follow-up. Like thousands of other reported rape cases in Fulton County, Georgia, and throughout the United States, my case was simply dropped. There was no follow-up.

Until this happened to me, I had not fully understood how much I had trusted in the state's promise of protection. What I came to realize was just how much I had believed in the state's version of liberal justice. Perhaps because my case never even went to court, I learned just how illusory these promises of protection and justice actually are.

When I first read Pratt's essay in 1988, I seemed to skip over these passages. I had not yet had a blow that would change forever my map of the world. At that time, I focused on Martin and Mohanty's reading of Pratt. I was especially interested in their enthusiasm for her notion of identity as ever shifting. I had ambivalent feelings about such claims. The passage from Martin and Mohanty's text that disturbed me most at that time idealized this notion of identity. The passage presented Pratt's fluid account in opposition to her father's more rigid position. These seemed to be the only options. Either identity was stable and constant or it was in perpetual motion. They wrote:

> What she has gained . . . is a way of looking, a capacity for seeing the world in overlapping circles, "like movements on the millpond after a fish has jumped, instead of the courthouse square with me at the middle, even if I am on the ground.". . . [H]er difference and "need" . . . emerges as the contrast between images of constriction, of entrapment, or ever-narrowing circles with a bounded self at the center . . . and . . . the images of the millpond with its ever-shifting centers.[21]

As a Jew, I felt uncomfortable with these sharp distinctions between what is fixed and what is able to change. In 1988 I was keenly aware of how history had marked Jews in ways that were not negotiable. In other words, I experienced some aspects of my Jewishness as fixed. In many ways, I understood my being Jewish as a given. It was not simply a matter of choice. My Jewishness meant that my story was different than Pratt's. My narrative was not so mobile and, yet, I also identified with her. I shared much of her privilege—her class position, education, cultural capital, and white skin. I also had other privilege—my heterosexual desire. Thus, from the beginning, my identification with Pratt was complicated by difference. I knew this in 1988, but was not sure what to do with it.

When I returned to Pratt's text later I made new connections. This time I was struck by her discussion of the interplay between violence and protection. I found new links between our narratives and wrote about the following passage from Martin and Mohanty's text:

> During the height of the civil rights demonstrations in Alabama . . . her
> father called her in to read her an article in which Martin Luther King Jr.
> was accused of sexually abusing young teenaged girls. "I can only guess that
> he wanted me to feel that my danger, my physical danger, sexual danger,
> would be the result of the release of others from containment. I felt fright-
> ened and profoundly endangered, by King, by my father: I could not
> answer him. It was the first, the only time, he spoke of sex, in any way, to
> me.[22]

I used this statement to make connections between my interrogations of
rape and marriage laws in rabbinic, liberal, and liberal Jewish theological
sources and Pratt's relationship with her father.[23] At that time these links
were inferred. They were not spelled out. I was unable to articulate fully
these connections.

In returning to Pratt's essay, I have become more able to spell out
these lingering connections as well as new distinctions. Pratt's response to
the incident in Greensboro was to return home, to see what the places and
traditions that she had been raised in had to teach her, not only about this
tragedy, but about her own violation—the loss of her children when she
came out as a lesbian and left her husband.[24] Like me, Pratt too returned
home to work through her disappointments with American liberal justice.
Like me, she has not let go of these places. Even as she reconfigures her
relationship to them, they remain a part of her.

The passage about Martin Luther King Jr. that Martin and Mohanty
referred to comes as part of Pratt's discussion of her sense of what change
would entail. After Greensboro she begins to realize that she is not only a
victim of injustice, but that she, too, is implicated in histories of injustice
done to others. As she writes, "I felt myself in a struggle with myself,
against myself. This breaking through did not feel like liberation but like
destruction."[25] Pratt connects this double message to a childhood memory
of staying up late at night reading Edgar Allen Poe. "I was scared but fas-
cinated by the catastrophic ending; when the walls of a house split, zigzag
along a once barely noticeable crack, and the house of Usher crumbled
with 'a long tumultuous shouting sound like the voice of a thousand
waters.'"[26] Pratt uses Edgar Allen Poe's story, a story about a woman who
is buried alive and whose confinement has everything to do with the
demise of a southern home, as a way of talking about her own complicated
feelings about her childhood home in Alabama.[27]

Recalling the historical moment in which Poe wrote, "the 1840's [as]
a time of intensifying Southern justification of slavery,"[28] Pratt makes con-

nections to her experience of growing up in Alabama in the 1950s. She continues, "Poe's description of the dread, nervousness, fear of the brother, pacing through the house from 'whence for many years, he had not ventured forth' could have been a description of my father, trapped inside his beliefs in white supremacy, the purity of (white) women, the conspiracy of Jews and Blacks to take over the world" (36). Like the woman who is entombed in Poe's story, Pratt sees her own place in her father's home as similarly constricted. Protection comes at the cost of confinement. To live in her father's house meant "physical, spiritual, sexual containment." The only way out was, therefore, necessarily destructive.

It is at this point in her narrative that Pratt writes about Martin Luther King Jr. and her father. The discussion of King is framed by a critical reading of the "protection" which men in her culture used to keep "their women" pure. She writes: "It was this protection that I felt one evening during the height of the civil rights demonstrations in Alabama, *as the walls that had contained too many were cracking*" (emphasis mine).

Like Poe, Pratt is aware of the end of a certain way of life. A new order is being ushered in that will offer both liberation and destruction. What she loses as she breaks out of her father's house is her own once-romantic reading of the protection he had offered. She eloquently ties together the tale of a romantic knight, which Poe's characters read to each other on that stormy night when the house of Usher falls, and the Southern knights who continue to fight for "the sanctity of the home," and who struggle to "protect . . . the homes and women of the South" even as these edifices are crumbling (37).

After enumerating the various kinds of violence that kept the walls of her father's home intact, Pratt's narrative returns to Greensboro. By exploring this history, she lets go of "the fear of others' release from containment" that her father had tried to frighten her with in talking about King. Still, these passages are characterized by a deep sense of loss. Liberation has required an end to her father's way of life. His is a home that has fallen. In its wake, Pratt begins to see new possibilities for making a life that is different. She remakes a series of homes that she can live in, at least for a time.

Remaking Home

Some things are lost while others are gained in the process of remaking home. There is no "simple escape from constraint to liberation . . . no reaching a final realm of freedom."[29] Do I hope, like Spivak, that "further research will . . . flesh out the domestic space in a such a way that this . . . feminist will no longer need to revisit [American feminist texts] as a way in"?[30] I am not so sure. The "bitter legacies" linger and, as paradoxical as that might seem, we continue to need to find "ways in." The task of writing the self requires an ongoing critical engagement with others, an exploration of similarities as well as differences. By reading and writing about Pratt's "Identity" as myself, I have tried to demonstrate how selves change. At discrete moments in my reading of Pratt's essay, I have claimed certain positions, but these have been contingent. I have made this clear by calling attention to how my readings have changed. What I have offered are multiple and, at times, even contradictory Jewish feminist positions in relation to Pratt. By claiming all of these positions, at least for a time, I have attempted to show how I continue to claim America as my home. By making explicit the interplay between similarity and difference in my reading of Pratt's essay, I have tried to show how my Jewish feminist self has been "specifically and materially en-gendered" within the social conditions and possibilities of existence open to me at the end of the twentieth century in liberal America.

CHAPTER 10

A History of Our Own
What Would a Feminist History
of Theology Look Like?

Sheila Briggs

In Search of a Theory

I want to make clear the starting point of this article and its relation to the general theme of this conference with two initial remarks. First, the scope of feminist theology is not only the whole field of theology but all of its problems and issues. The question of what would a feminist history of theology look like is no different than that of what would a history of theology look like. To argue this in substance requires claims about the pervasiveness of the construction of gender in Western and in most human societies and about the feminist subjectivity which the feminist theologian would bring to any theological inquiry. More obviously, however, feminist theology is no longer marginal to the discipline except in the eyes of a patriarchal ostrich with its head in the sand. Never before have so many women been professional theologians. This is not to discount theological reflection by women at the grassroots, but to point out a significant index of women's social power in the academy and in the churches—namely, we get paid for what we do. After a quarter of a century no one could reasonably dismiss feminist theology as a passing fad. It is the largest and most enduring movement in the theology of the Western world in the late twentieth century. Feminists are in the position to determine what theology will look like.

Second, if we feel daunted by the awesome development and opportunities, which I have just outlined, then there are no lack of theories to offer a helping hand. In the eighties we saw a turn to theory among feminists in every academic discipline, including theology. The many varieties of postmodernism predominated in the explosive growth of feminist theory, but it would be an inadequate explanation to say that postmodernism brought about this feminist hunger for theory. One might look for the reason for the feminist turn to theory in the dismal prospects for feminist politics during the Reagan-Bush era. Yet this is also only a partial explanation. Throughout the Western world the eighties saw a conservative political shift, and this demanded that feminists analyze their goals and visions in the hope of creating a more effective politics. Nevertheless, the eighties were far from a time of political defeat for feminism, nor were the paradigms of feminist thought inherited from the sixties and seventies exhausted. The feminist turn to theory was occasioned by more than political failure or perceived deficits in the theories that had hitherto informed feminist praxis.

Laying claim to our half of humanity, our half of history, many feminists felt unsatisfied with what they got. The feminist turn to theory sought ways of articulating this dissatisfaction. The attraction of postmodernism lay in its ability to give a systematic account of why feminist thought and action remained effective and plausible and yet had already, after a brief and spectacular period of growth, run up against the limitations of its discourse. These were in fact not only the boundaries of its own discourse but of all discourses. The irony of the feminist subject and agent of history was that she would be the bearer of the knowledge that these categories—subject, agent, history, knowledge—were indeed not empty but arbitrary, not false but malleable. History itself was reconceived; no longer was it to be seen as a process of transformation in which groups and individuals could attempt to change the conditions of human life, but as the localized and disparate contestations for power through which the identities and subjectivities of groups and individuals first were created.

A feminist history of theology must begin by taking account of the historical situation in which feminist theology has, like other feminist studies, come to prominence in its discipline. Yet its theoretically sophisticated discourse tends to undercut the claims to truth which one might expect that it was now in a position to raise. In discussing the nature and status of the past in feminist theology and therefore in defining the tasks and methods of a feminist history of theology, I believe we must take a double track. We must, on the one hand, ask how the theoretical constraints of our own context can be productive of new insights into and new meanings for theology's past. On the other hand, we must be willing to question these theoretical constraints themselves. The postmodern view of a history without closure is in many ways the mirror image of the neo-conservative proclamation of the end of history. In both cases, despite the eschewing of all absolutes, one sets one's own theoretical model as absolute in the sense that one de facto assumes that there will be no theoretical model of conceiving history that will surpass one's own.

The Politics of a History of Theology

Over the past decade the most controversial political and intellectual topic in feminist theory has been its approach to women's experience. Put in the simplest terms, we have seen a shift from talking about women's experience to representations of women, from talking about women to talking about gender. At the same time, the inclusivity of a concept of women's experience has been questioned. A unitary category of women's experience tends to privilege and universalize the experiences of only some women. Yet as one attempted to diversify and particularize the understanding of women's experience along multiple axes of race, class, sexual orientation, age, physical ability, and so forth, one noticed how elusive became a representative experience of all women or of any group of women, however well specified. I do not intend to rehearse these debates here, but want to point out some of the ramifications for the original central tenet of feminist theology.

Women's experience is normative for feminist theology. With this declaration feminists engaged the field of theology, intending to dismantle its patriarchal foundations, to recover women's past, and to transform their present and future in the religious traditions of our culture. Nevertheless, the notion of women's experience, which grounded feminist theology, is open to the sorts of challenge I have just outlined. I do not think one can deny that feminist theology began as a modernist discourse. Although it mounted a critique of all previous, male-defined theology, it nonetheless retained one of the central assumptions of modern theology since Schleiermacher—that theology proceeds out of experience. Initially, at least, keeping this basic premise of modern theology served feminist theology very well. It allowed feminists to connect theological formulations to male interests and therefore unmasked their ideological posture of being disinterested attempts to attain universal truth. In doing so feminist theology had immediate political repercussions on the Western Christian churches where it began. Mainstream Christianity in the West prided itself on its inclusivity and its openness to the changing demands of its society. Feminists hit Christianity ideologically where it hurts.

Like other forms of women's history, committed to the recovery of women's experience, feminists began the retrieval of women's actions and words in the past of Christianity, Judaism, and other religions, and began to reinterpret this past by moving women's experience from the margins to the center of religious history. Again the political effects were immediate; in the sixties and seventies the ordination of women was hotly debated in the mainstream Protestant churches and in the Reformed and Conservative synagogues. Demonstrating that women held positions of leadership in earlier periods of a religious tradition—in some cases the same offices which were now denied them—provided the theologically powerful weapon of precedent for the ordination of women. The task of situating women in the historical record continues. So does the interpretative agenda of showing how the history of women leads to the reconceptualization of the past of any religious tradition. But the historical work of feminist theology is not limited to these tasks.

I subtitled my article, "What Would a Feminist History of Theology Look Like?" not, "What Would a Feminist History of Christianity Look Like?"—my own tradition and the tradition I study. The distinction I am making here is analogous to that between the history of science and the history of technology, between a discourse's theoretical constitution and its effects in the social realm. It is not an indication that I am thoroughly skeptical of women's experience as an analytical category and therefore doubt the value of a history of women that relies heavily on it. In fact, experience is an extremely useful concept because of its fluidity, which allows us to talk about an inherently ambiguous and indeterminate set of connections. It allows us to join the *inside* with the *outside,* our mental worlds with the external universe, our personal meanings with the socially constructed universe which confronts us. Obviously, the interest in making such connections is a modern one, where there is no single divinely ordained order that can legislate with absolute authority these connections as a given. Since feminist theologians neither want to nor accept that they live in such an authoritarian universe, they necessarily have had recourse to the category of experience. Talking about experience is not in itself naive, and we do not become more theoretically sophisticated by reducing experience to language. It is true in the form of a tautology that we can only talk about experience by talking, that is, through the medium of language. But this is a long way from saying that all connections of the inside and the outside can be meaningfully described as primarily and necessarily linguistic events. In short, we are not always saying more when we talk about discourses of gender instead of women's experience.

The problem with experience is the same one which besets its postmodern successor, language. Their fluidity, their ability to perform a vast array of functions and provide explanatory models across disciplines leads to them becoming indistinguishable from that which they describe. Hence, *women's experience* becomes synonymous with *women's lives* and with *women's reality.* Reality is seen as contained either within human experience or within human language. I am not going to discuss further whether there is reality beyond human experience or language because, as I have indicated above, this resolves nothing. We construct reality as human beings, whether we conceive human beings as centers of experience or as implied within processes of signification. I am not saying there is no difference between these two conceptions, but that it is undecidable which is the better model.

Most of us, in fact, increasingly operate out of both models. This is evident in the work of two of the first American feminists to engage seriously postmodern theories, Sharon Welch and Alice Jardine. Welch, who in *Communities of Resistance and Solidarity* had powerfully demonstrated how Foucault could contribute to a feminist liberation theology, states in her later book (*A Feminist Ethic of Risk*) the need for feminists to draw on critical social theory produced on both sides of the modern/postmodern divide. In contrast to Foucault's claim that it is the discourse that counts, not who (arbitrarily) is speaking in it, Welch insists "that what matters is precisely who is speaking" and "the explosion of new speakers and writers," drawn from the marginalized throughout the world. She believes that Foucault provides better reasons for a communicative ethic than its original "modernist" proponent, Habermas! Our accountability to others and others' struggles requires us to be constituted, not only by the recognition of difference in a Foucauldian sense, but also in a more Habermasian sense by our work with others.[1]

Alice Jardine resists any attempt to naturalize experience or women's experience as reactionary politics. Women's experience is not a given truth that is available to us by any reference to it. Yet precisely because she celebrates the "demise of Truth-in-Experience" she can, with a postmodern sensibility, want to reconstruct modernity's category of experience.

> As long as we do not explore the boundaries of and possible common spaces between modernity and feminism; as long as we do not recognize new kinds of artificial, symbolic constructions of the subject, representation, and (especially) experience, we will be engaging in what are ultimately conservative and dated polemics, not radical theory and practice.[2]

In proposing a feminist history of theology I am arguing for a feminist theological approach to history that is not limited to the category of women's experience, but also does not discard it. Women's experience and discourses of gender will remain asymmetrical (to a greater extent than I think Jardine allows). But the asymmetry of the categories does not entail that they will be deployed incoherently within a feminist history of theology. Rather, their asymmetry reflects the discontinuities in our social construction of reality which cannot be banished by preferring one category to the other.

Two analytical limitations of women's experience have often been noted and bear directly on the project of a feminist history of theology. First, women end up doing all the work of gender. Women become the bearers and markers of gender difference; we search for their particularity under the ideological shroud of male universalizations. With this approach feminist theory comes too close to the reproduction of patriarchal discourse with its oppositions of male/female, self/other, universal/particular. Second, the history of women is also the history of the exclusion of women. Does that mean where men were successful in banishing women, feminists have no interest other than noting their exclusion?

If one is going to write a feminist history of theology, then even expanding the definition of theology to include a broader range of women's writings cannot conceal that there are expanses of theology's past where women are absent. This is especially the case in the history of doctrine, in which women were excluded from the male elites who attended the councils, who taught in the universities where Christian doctrine was formulated. Although the history of doctrine is a peculiarly Christian way of conceptualizing its intellectual development, a similar process of exclusion occurred in Judaism with the rabbinical schools. Now one can always write the social history of Christianity behind the formulation of doctrine, and in this wider social space women will be present. Nevertheless, this approach is restricted to explaining what is behind the doctrinal text rather than what is in it. Unless one takes a simplistic model of ideological super-structure and material base and reduces the former to the latter, doctrine to its social background, then the actual formulation of the doctrine remains residual in the feminist interpretation. I am not saying that the study of the social background of doctrine is without value. Quite the con-trary, the social correlates of a doctrine are as significant as its contents, but the two are not identical.

What one requires here is a feminist interpretative strategy which can operate even where women are absent and which can demonstrate how this absence is crucial for the production of the doctrinal text. For this task the analysis of gender is as indispensable as it is distinguishable from the study of women's experience. Joan Scott in *Gender and the Politics of History* deals with a similar situation confronting the feminist scholar in the field of political history. In many ways the development of political history and that of the history of doctrine have been parallel. Just as the history of doctrine, along with ecclesiastical history (the study of the evolution of normative church institutions), have concerned themselves with the thought and action of male clerical elites, so political history has as its sub-ject matter the discursive practices of male political elites. In many cases, of course, the male clerical and political elites were related by kinship ties and in some cases were drawn from each other's ranks, a state of affairs which has also been common among male ecclesiastical and political his-torians.

Scott does not try and solve the dilemma of the feminist scholar of political history by expanding its definition. She takes political history as the study of "politics and power in their most traditionally construed sense, that is, as they pertain to government and the nation-state." Her reasons for retaining the traditional definition are twofold. First, she wants to confront directly the claim of traditional political historians that gender is "antithetical to the real business of politics." Second, in her view, polit-ical history still dominates historical study despite the explosive growth of social history since the sixties.[3] I think the same can be said for the history of doctrine. Doctrine, like God, has been held to be free of gender. The study of doctrine and of the doctrinally orthodox churches still is pre-dominant in departments and journals of church history and historical theology.

Scott points out how gender is the metaphor of power. She examines three ways in which gender operates in the construction of the political. First, in political theory gender is the currency of the legitimation of political sovereignty—and not only where women rulers are concerned. As codes of masculinity and femininity, the forms of marriage are applied analogically to the political order to describe what are the proper relations of sovereign and subjects or the proper character of the nation-state. Next, Scott rejects the idea that "political theory simply reflects social organization." She alludes to several instances in which state power has been consolidated through the state imposing its gender and sexual politics on the society. Policies, such as preventing women's paid labor or banning abortion, are not dictated by material needs or current social dynamics. Instead, they are the literal rendering of the claims of (usually new or contested) government to legitimate power through the symbolic authority of the masculine. Third, gender is at work even where gender is not explicit. Scott emphasizes that gender as "a crucial part of the organization of equality and inequality" lies behind hierarchies, which depend on naturalized differences for their justification. Social relations and social groups are gender coded even where the appropriate social and sexual behavior for women and men is not at issue. Challenges to social hierarchies do not necessarily entail a rejection of naturalized, gender-dependent difference, they can involve the repudiation of one's ascribed feminine position and the adoption of a masculine one.[4]

This description of the gendered and gendering construction of the political can be transposed to the theological realm. The relationship of the formulation of doctrine to the legitimation of ecclesiastical power is especially intimate. The traditional masculine imagery for God and the traditional feminine imagery for the church have justified clerical authority, have been translated into church policies of women's subordination and exclusion, and have naturalized the hierarchy between clergy and laity (the sacrament of ordination confers an ontological distinction in Roman Catholic teaching). Scott makes a further point of crucial relevance to a feminist history of theology: the more removed from gender the political is taken to be, the more gendered it actually is. She writes:

> The subject of war, diplomacy, and high politics frequently comes up when traditional political historians question the utility of gender in their work. But here, too, we need to look beyond the actors and the literal import of their words. . . . High politics itself is a gendered con-

cept, for it establishes its crucial importance and public power, the reasons for and the fact of its highest authority, precisely in its exclusion of women from its work.[5]

In patriarchal political and ecclesiastical orders in which women are most absent, gender is most present. So the assumption that it is women who introduce the question of gender when they enter into the scholar's view is in a fundamental aspect false. The effects of gender are most intense where women's exclusion is most complete.

Let me illustrate this last point by a discussion of the Christology of the early church as it was formulated by the councils, which achieved recognition for their orthodoxy. Women were certainly in the historical background of the councils that defined the doctrine of Christ. The Council of Chalcedon in 451 could not have taken place without the political support of Pulcheria, sister of Theodosius II, who after his death succeeded to the throne of the Eastern Roman Empire in 450. Yet the bishops who attended the council were all men, and the Chalcedonian Definition, which they wrote, has absolutely no explicit concern with gender. If, however, we look more closely at what is considered the culmination of christological doctrine in the early church and the standard of later orthodoxy, then we see how gender constructed christological formulas and through them legitimated ecclesiastical power. It is so unquestioned an assumption that Christology was fundamental to the definition of Christian identity in antiquity that one does not seek the reasons for this. The passion, not to speak of the violence, which christological controversies inspired is taken as an indication that, in the later ancient world, the well-being of individuals and societies was seen as dependent on holding correct theological beliefs. Hence, the "inwardness" of late antiquity is often noted. When one analyzes christological formulations in terms of gender, then one realizes that the debates over the nature of Christ enact codes of masculinity and femininity, which had far-reaching consequences for the ecclesiastical, political, and social order of late antiquity. The Chalcedonian Definition states that Christ exists

> in two natures, without confusion, without change, without division, without separation; the distinction of natures being in no way abolished because of the union but rather the characteristic property of each nature being preserved and concurring into one Person and one subsistence [hypostasis] not as if Christ were parted or divided into two per-

sons, but one and the same Son and Only-begotten God, Word, Lord, Jesus Christ.[6]

Gender operates at multiple levels in this text. Christ represents normative masculinity; for in the Greco-Roman world masculinity was the form of reason, of the logos. Reason is eternally one and identical with itself, not subject to change, indivisible, neither separated from itself nor confused with anything else. Christ's manhood was what the church fathers at Chalcedon sought to emulate. But the pure masculinity of reason was unattainable for ordinary men, even for holy and orthodox bishops, even with the severest of ascetic practices. Ordinary men also possessed two natures—a masculine rationality and a feminine nature of the senses, which disposed men to passion (epithymia), the antithesis of reason. Christ's humanity was pure masculinity, but in relation to his divinity it was a lesser nature and occupied the position of the feminine. The order of Christ's two natures was the prototype of proper order, anthropologically, socially, politically, and ecclesiastically. In it the feminine was subordinated to the masculine as reason should rule the senses, men should rule women, the emperor should rule his subjects, and the clergy the laity. In Christ this order was perfect; there was no confusion of the natures, no contamination of the masculine by the feminine. As such it was the mirror of an ideal world where the senses did not infect reason, where women were not insubordinate, where subjects were obedient, and the laity did not meddle in the church's affairs. How was this perfect order of Christ's natures achieved? Through there only being one hypostasis, that is, one subject, and that subject was his divinity. There can be no disobedience, no revolt of Christ's humanity against his divinity, because it is devoid of subjectivity. For the dominant male discourse of antiquity, female subjectivity was an inherently ambiguous and contradictory notion, fraught with anomalies and dangers. When they encountered holy women or sympathetic aristocratic women, the church fathers followed ancient patriarchal custom and attributed these women's virtue to a virile mind. Although authentic subjectivity could never be found in the feminine, because this was not the form of reason, the feminine might, nonetheless, harbor pretensions to subjectivity, and here lay danger, not only for men's rule over women, but for all other hierarchical relations that were founded on the opposition of masculine to feminine. Christ's humanity could hold no such pretensions; no inferior and defective subjectivity threatened the divine subject in Christ. Again subjectivity of the kind of Christ's divinity was beyond the reach of ordinary men; it was a divine prerogative. Divinity was transcendent masculinity which might condescend to join itself to the feminine, and yet even in such union it remained a unitary and autonomous subjectivity against which the feminine could make no subversive claims to subjectivity.

Traditional historians of doctrine might object that I am reducing Christology to gender codes. On the contrary, I am not arguing that the Chalcedonian Definition is only superficially about the ontological status of Christ and really about gender. Rather, I am saying that the Council of Chalcedon deployed gender codes to articulate their understanding of Christ. These gender codes were as essential to the patristic discursive apparatus as ancient philosophy, to which they also belonged. Feminist historians of ancient Christianity as well as of other periods and other religious traditions are investigating discourses of gender. However, there is still no recognition that the construction of gender is coextensive with the history of theology itself, that behind the most rigorous and successful expunging of female presence, of feminine symbolism, even of gender and the difference it interjects, gender becomes most virulent in its effects, transmuting itself into every currency of human thought. Thus the task of a feminist history of theology is not only to write about the social construction of gender in whatever religious tradition and period is being studied, that is, about the discourses of gender, but also about the gendering of discourse. A feminist history of theology must retrieve the gender codes which underlie all of theological discourse and are not limited to when women and gender are the explicit topics.

Gender and Time

So far I have pursued a track which extends the perspective and methods of postmodern historiography into the history of theology. I believe it has been productive, but I do not think that it supplies all the theoretical needs of such an inquiry. Disciplines are not only constituted by their particular history; they also constitute their histories as implications of their present discourse. This is most clearly the case in science. History and philosophy of science are frequently pursued in conjunction, and one is faced with the question of the relationship of social world and physical universe. The production of scientific knowledge is no less socially constructed than any other discourse, but does this entirely explain why scientific paradigms change? Even the most ardent social constructionist will not deny the existence of a physical universe, but will insist that our knowledge of it is always mediated through the social activity of discourse. Yet this view betrays a surprising faith in or indifference to the stability and dependability of the physical universe. Surely there are conditions pertaining to human beings as inhabitants of the physical universe that can neither be taken for granted nor reduced to a particular social world or the sum of particular social worlds. Theologians and historians of theology have it much harder because of the widespread doubt that the subject matter of our discipline exists independently of the sociocultural constructs of particular religions. One of the problems of modern theologies of experience is that all the eggs of the theological basket are in a transcendental ground of human experience. This has progressively collapsed into the social construction of all human experience. Any feminist theology needs to be clear on whether it wants a God which also exists independently of human experiences in the social worlds we inhabit. How one decides this issue determines what sort of history of theology one will develop.

Historians of theology, like historians of science in their discipline, need to advance some argument about what verifies or falsifies theological claims. Here I expect to find no consensus even among feminists. In all cases, however, the history of theology will be internal to and intrinsic to the current discourse of theology. That historians of theology and historians of science write histories internal to their disciplines does not mean that theologians and scientists inhabit separate social worlds with separate pasts. It indicates, rather, that both groups of historians have to take a position on whether the social construction of knowledge fully explains every aspect of how truth claims are proposed, tested, accepted, or rejected in their discipline. The other implication of my description of history as internal and intrinsic to a particular discourse in its current state is that all forms of history cannot actually or potentially share exactly the same set of theoretical models. Obviously, there are going to be large degrees of overlap, because what we study in the historical inquiry of any particular discourse is going to coincide in the social world with inquiries of other discourses. Part of my point is that history is always reconstruction of the past in the light of the interests of a particular perspective, a particular discursive practice. Additionally, I would argue that an understanding of human temporality resides implicitly or explicitly in every form of historical inquiry and that the conception of time provides the link between the past or antecedents of the particular discourse and its present. I realize that here the distinction between a history of theology and a theology of history becomes blurred. Such ideas as divine providence, a succession of covenants, and salvation history have attempted through their respective conceptions of time to link current theological discourse with what originated and shaped it in the past. That these ideas fail to convince most feminists is not an indication that the bracketing of the past and antecedents of a discourse with its present, through the medium of temporality, is a fundamentally flawed endeavor, but that we find these particular theological discourses neither attractive nor persuasive.

I am going to conclude with some remarks on the connections among gender, temporality, and the history of theology. There has not been a large feminist literature on temporality. What does exist often poses the question of *women's time,* and is therefore open to criticism by some feminists as essentialist in its view of women and separatist in its politics.[7] Whatever status one attributes to women's time, one has to admit that some women, at least, perceive themselves as experiencing temporality in a specifically female way. Moreover, if gender is a shifting and contested social construct, why should not time be the same? The qualities of women's time, which distinguish it from male or patriarchal time, are understood as circularity as opposed to linearity, as internal and unbounded time as opposed to an externally imposed and quantifiable time. Interestingly, many advocates of women's time find an ally in modern physics.[8] Other strands of feminism have an underdeveloped view of time partly in reaction to the perceived essentialism of women's time and to de Beauvoirian existentialism, but largely due to the fact that they take time for granted. The postmodern rejection of metaphysics forecloses the discussion of temporality. Certainly, there is an interest in taxonomies of time, in calendars, in the discontinuous and localized meanings given to time. But as for the topology of time, that is, the characteristics inherent in time as distinct from the sociocultural meanings given to time, this is considered to belong to the futility of metaphysics. So discourse is enacted on the inert medium of time. Time, for instance, is the seemingly undifferentiated and unproblematic expanse on which Foucault's epistemes deploy themselves. Or time is narrative time and therefore, perforce, malleable and arbitrary. The advocates of women's time have at least raised the question of the topology of time and what feminists might have at stake in this issue.

The topology of time should also not be an indifferent matter to a history of theology. Many truth claims in Christianity and in Judaism have been claims about temporality. Feminist theologians may not want to accept all or any of these truth claims, but such claims make us aware that how we conceptualize time has consequences for our theological projects and how we write their history. Like the advocates of women's time, we need to pay attention to discussions of time in the contemporary physical sciences. What we can learn there is not so much data, but theoretical models that can sharpen our own conceptual means of thinking about time. At present, my own conclusion on temporality is that it is neither socially constructed nor a property of the physical universe. It seems, in my view, that temporality is an ontogenetic ability to construct the physical universe and to connect it to our constructions of self; that is, we develop as individuals and as a species a capacity to situate ourselves in the physical universe. In this you may have correctly surmised my indebtedness to Kant's doctrine of time, which has, on the whole, not enjoyed great favor among later philosophers. "Time is nothing," Kant wrote, "but the form of inner sense, that is, of the intuition of ourselves and of our inner state."[9]

There is little to suggest that across historical periods or cultures the constitutive features of time in this sense, what I will call ordinary time, vary. Even the advocates of women's time do not claim that for women time ordinarily flows backwards. However, I would leave open the possibility that human beings may be capable of multiple temporalities, and access to these may be culturally and historically variable as well as affected by class, ethnic, and gender status. Whether human beings have access to multiple temporalities or not is for me not as interesting as the question of the relationship of the social construction of reality, especially of gender, to the ontogenetically given construction of temporality. Human beings are always simultaneously social and temporal beings, so ordinary time always coexists with the social time of gender. The social meanings we give to time, I have argued, should not be conflated with or seen as making the topology of time superfluous. Nonetheless, in lived experience the two are connected. Although feminist historians of theology may not want to concur with my conclusions on temporality or with those of the proponents of women's time, all of us engaged in the project need to expand our theoretical models to include the discussion of temporality and to articulate its relationship to the construction of gender.

Social Theory concerning the "New Social Movements" and the Practice of Feminist Theology

Kathryn Tanner

The last several decades have seen the emergence of social theories that are designed to account for the so-called new social movements such as feminism, environmentalism, and movements for ethnic and minority empowerment. Incorporating insights from both Marxism and poststructuralism, these social theories offer a political understanding of the workings of culture. This new understanding of cultural process has great importance, I believe, for the practice of feminist theology. The tasks of feminist theology, strategies for promoting the influence of a feminist theological agenda, and the significance of the past for constructive feminist theological work can all be reconceived in light of an understanding of culture informed by the writings of Antonio Gramsci and Michel Foucault. By helping feminist theologians become more self-conscious about the nature of their enterprise, these new theories of culture enhance the political effectiveness of the struggles in which feminist theologians are engaged.

A Political Understanding of Culture

Definition

The social theories that I employ in this article understand culture as one important—increasingly important—site of political struggle in the modern West.[1] Political struggle of a cultural sort takes place in fights over both the meaning and the articulation of a society's cultural stakes or symbolic resources. The meaning of politically significant cultural stakes is at issue, for instance, in contemporary contests in the United States over the definition of *family* or in controversies over the character of the rights that gay people claim for themselves—should the rights they claim be designated special rights? Articulation of cultural items has to do with the way chains of association are formed among cultural items, as well as between these chains of cultural items themselves and social forces; *articulation* refers both to the interlinking of cultural elements in discourse and to the manner in which those chains of cultural items are interwoven into the social field. Articulation in these senses is at issue in current struggles in the United States over whether to associate or dissociate gay liberation and the black civil rights movement: Does the fight for gay rights belittle, even hamper, efforts to improve the situation of African Americans, or are the two movements allies in a common struggle? An issue of articulation common in continental social theory concerns whether democracy is to be allied with socialism or with a liberal state that supports a competitive market economy.

Questions of meaning and articulation such as these amount to political questions; they concern power relations. Following Roberto Unger's definition of politics in its broadest sense, one could say that these questions are part and parcel of "the conflict over the terms of our practical and passionate relations to one another and over all the resources and assumptions that may influence those terms."[2] They are political questions according to an expanded understanding of politics which views it not as a separate institutional sphere—say, the realm of government—but as a pervasive dimension of social relations generally. Cultural questions are part of political struggle because, as Joan Cocks succinctly puts it, what one can think establishes what one can think to *do*—acquiesce or object, conform or resist.[3] Cultural questions are political questions because institutionalized relations among people do not proceed apart from people's interpretations of those relations. Finally, these questions are political because the meaning of cultural items and their articulation one with another, and with certain social forces and institutional structures, help establish hegemony, the solidification of particular arrangements of power by virtue of "the complex interlocking of political, social, and cultural forces."[4] Hegemony results when the symbolic reserves of a society and its institutions reinforce one another in such a way that those social arrangements seem fitting or natural, a matter of common sense. This common sense, the practical consciousness of people that saturates their social existence, is at stake in fights over the meaning and articulation of cultural forms.

Theoretical Underpinnings

Although a variety of other theoretical paths may lead to it—for example, symbolic or interpretive anthropology is another avenue of approach[5]—the political understanding of culture that I employ here brings together the work of Gramsci and Foucault. More broadly, the approach on which I draw represents a confluence of Marxism and post-structuralism in contemporary social theory.[6]

The Marxist contribution is partly theoretical: the notion of hegemony originates with Gramsci;[7] Louis Althusser's nonperjorative notion of ideology also marks an important point in the development of a political understanding of culture.[8] Most generally, the theoretical influence of nonreductive Marxisms, of those Marxisms that highlight the political importance of ideology, is being felt here. But in great part the significance of Marxism for a political understanding of culture is normative. Marxism provides the normative motor for a politics of culture; it gives poststructuralist theory a clear emancipatory edge. When the contribution of Marxism to a politics of culture is understood in this way, "Marxism" stands in for the emancipatory interests of the cultural analyst.

The theoretical work in a politics of culture is largely done by poststructuralism.[9] The power-knowledge relation assumed here is found in Foucault, although the less monolithic side of his account of these relations is highlighted; these relations do not come in the internally consistent, periodized blocs suggested, for example, by *The Order of Things*.[10] Ideas, symbolic resources, are produced, reproduced, and conveyed in concrete institutions; institutionalized social relations require, and are therefore productive of, certain objects and subjects of knowledge and techniques and criteria for their specification. The floating signifier of poststructuralism is also presupposed in a political understanding of culture. It makes sense to think that the meaning and articulation of symbolic elements are up for grabs in a political contest only if a number of typically poststructuralist assumptions are made: (1) cultural forms are only loosely referential, and meanings are fluid and shifting rather than fixed; (2) coherence is the always temporary and contingent distillate of a lot of hard and ultimately futile rhetorical work; and (3) social and cultural relations are fields of forces which are "normally," that is, apart from efforts to have things otherwise, dispersed, discontinuous, and unsynchronized.[11]

Theorizing the "New Social Movements"

Besides clarifying the normative agenda of the analyst, the Marxist contribution to a political understanding of culture helps demonstrate its relevance, as a theory, to particular forms of liberative practice. Political understandings of culture with a Marxist heritage developed in reaction to the failure of traditional social theory to account for the so-called new social movements, which burgeoned in the late sixties in both the United States and Europe—student antiwar movements, the prison reform movement in France, civil rights activism in the United States, the women's movement, antinuclear and ecological movements, and protest movements by ethnic and social minorities. Political theories of culture are an attempt to rethink the categories of social theory in order to make sense of these new social movements.

Traditional Marxism was inadequate to the task for a number of reasons having to do with the peculiar characteristics of these new social movements, their defining features. First, the new social movements are not class based; they are not propelled by working-class interests, more specifically. The movements are organized instead around identifications that are cultural and experiential; allegiances are formed across class lines by virtue of gender, or ethnic and racial background, or because of a shared experience of oppression, for instance, as prisoners of the state. Because they are not class based, the new social movements do not conform to a Marxist understanding of broad-based struggles: struggles that break down along lines of the proletariat versus the capitalists. Second, the new social movements are not oriented around questions of state power—politics in the more usual, narrow sense of the word. Instead, they are more local, more tactical in orientation, and often limited in their range of issues. Those issues, moreover, have a strong cultural component; they concern the way oppression is built into the normal processes of everyday life by way of stereotypes and unquestioned norms, assumptions, and symbols.[12] Assumptions about men and women, and about ethnic and racial minorities; standards of proper behavior, dress, and beauty; the meaning of democracy and its implications for full citizenship and economic opportunity; patriotism and its associations with war policy; the conduct of family life and its impact on economic opportunity for women—all sorts of cultural assumptions like these come into question within the new social movements as a way of furthering social, political, and economic change.

Political understandings of culture in social theories with a Marxist bent attempt to theorize this way in which culture is politicized in the new social movements. According to these theories, the political struggles of the new social movements can be understood most generally as struggles over the meaning and articulation of those symbolic resources in which the operations of social institutions are highly invested. Because the organization of society is highly invested in them, symbolic resources of society become highly charged sites of controversy over how society should be run.

This sort of analysis of the new social movements forms the basis for a general social theory. An understanding of culture as the site of political contest becomes, for example, the basis for an analysis of party politics in the work of Stuart Hall.[13] It turns into a general theory for analyzing how power is consolidated in the social and political life of society overall.[14] Theorists extend the implications of an analysis of the new social movements by asking what modern society as a whole must be like if it can spawn new social movements as instigators of fundamental sociopolitical change.[15]

Relevance to Feminist Theology

Feminist theology can profitably employ this body of cultural theory since this theory was designed to make sense of the social movement of which feminist theology is a part—the feminist movement. Feminist theology is part of the feminist movement; theories that account for the political workings of the feminist movement should be of interest, then, to feminist theologians trying to understand the sort of feminist advocacy in which they are engaged. Feminist theorists across the board appropriate and produce these theories of culture.[16] Why shouldn't feminist theologians do the same?

One might answer this question in the negative by doubting whether these theories of culture have anything to add to what feminists know in practice. My account of the way a political understanding of culture emerged from an attempt to make sense of the new social movements might suggest that theory learns from practice, but not the other way around. Supposing a political theory of culture accurately accounts for the political impact of social movements such as feminism, attending to such a theory would seem just a circuitous route back to what feminists already know in practice: culture matters. Why make the detour?

For two reasons. First, even if a political understanding of culture is only describing in more general terms what feminists are already doing, the self-consciousness that such theories provide retains a strategic value. Theory becomes an aid to better political calculation; it helps one do better, more consistently, with fewer missteps, what one is otherwise already trying to do. Second, theory is not redundant here because feminist practice—in religious contexts or elsewhere—is not monolithic or uniform. Such diversity of practice means that these theories of culture, when accurate, are not describing what all feminists are always doing. These theories amount, therefore, to a specific recommendation from among alternative existing practices, with the object of bringing about more effective struggles for emancipation.

This aspect of normative recommendation in the theories is evident in the literature, with reference to leftist politics generally. For example, Stuart Hall develops his understanding of cultural politics to better arm British leftists against Thatcherism; the left is not adequately prepared, Hall argues, if it does not understand the kind of cultural warfare necessary to defeat Thatcherism. Ernesto Laclau develops his theoretical position to help socialists combat the emergence of fascistic mass movements. He supposes that socialists in Europe failed in such a struggle before because, again, they did not understand the kind of cultural warfare in which it was necessary to engage, cultural warfare to ally nationalism and populism with democracy and to wrest them away from displays of autocratic tyranny.[17]

Implications for the Practice of Feminist Theology

Reconceptualizing the Tasks of Feminist Theology

In order to see the contributions that a political understanding of culture might make to feminist theology, it is first necessary to see how the tasks of feminist theology can be reconceptualized in its terms. To understand this, one must understand how the tasks of theology generally would be conceived along the lines of a politics of culture. The tasks of feminist theology become a specification of the tasks that characterize theology generally.

The first thing to see when theology is understood in terms of a politics of culture is that theology becomes a subset of a wider sphere of cultural struggle that is not specifically theological. Although theologians have available to them the whole of the wider society's symbolic resources, they are preoccupied with a narrower, more specific pool of socially circulating symbolic resources. This pool is nevertheless enormously complex. Limiting myself to the Christian case, these circulating symbolic resources include:

1. Biblical materials: birth, passion, and resurrection narratives in their various gospel renditions, parables, Jesus sayings, tales of the mighty acts of God in the Hebrew Bible, songs of praise, and so forth

2. Theological materials: creedal and confessional statements, and the historical traces of theological developments and controversies, with the losing positions never finally pushed from the discursive field and therefore usually retrievable in the present

3. The cultural materials of lived Christian experience: the symbolic resources of liturgical practices, prayer life, and the whole practical ideology of Christian activity in the world, which also includes the wider cultural baggage that Christians carry with them as participants in institutions and communities that are not specifically Christian—for example, the public schools, military, and government offices of societies that enforce a separation of church and state

Following the poststructuralist assumptions of a politics of culture, one would presume that the meaning and organization of these heterogeneous cultural materials are not fixed. Cultural elements are indeed found with meanings and organizations already assigned. Meanings and organizations of these symbolic materials are part of what circulates. Creedal statements, for example, often order cultural elements from the Bible or Christian liturgies, and specify the meanings of those elements to some extent. Insofar as they help constitute the practical consciousness of lived experience, certain understandings of and connections among cultural elements are already found articulated within the social practices of Christians in church settings and in the wider society at large. These securings of meaning and of inferential and associational networks are not generally, however, set in stone. Alternative meanings and alliances of the same elements are also often circulating, with the potential, therefore, to dislodge the currently pervasive ones. Any secured meaning or articulation is only relatively secure, since it is the product of ongoing struggle with contending forces. Furthermore, no one meaning or organization exhausts the discursive field. The discursive field extends beyond any set meaning of a cultural element, in the sense that every cultural element is susceptible to reinterpretation by being placed in new discursive alignments. For example, the power of God will take on a new meaning when it is associated, not with the destruction of the enemies of Christianity, but with the death of God on the cross. The discursive field is wider than any one organization of cultural elements, since no organization of elements is ever inclusive of all available elements to the same degree; organization by definition requires selection and selective emphasis, and therefore always leaves a potentially destablizing remainder in its wake.

If, for these reasons, meaning and organization are not already established once and for all, the production of meaning and organization is the ongoing, never finally completed responsibility of the theologian. The theologian always has before him or her the tasks of (1) elucidating the meaning of cultural elements, (2) forming an order among them by selecting and selectively emphasizing elements out of the available, socially circulating pool of symbolic resources, and by creating inferential or associative networks among them, and (3) determining the way in which social practices are part of those inferential and associative networks, the way certain social practices are to be interwoven with the meanings and organization of cultural elements which the theologian produces. In the most general terms, this is how the tasks of the theologian are conceived according to a political understanding of culture.

Feminist theologians are doing the same sorts of things; they are performing the usual theological tasks. They do so, however, with the specific intent of allying or articulating the elucidations and inferential or associative networks they produce with a feminist politics, and with the social relations that feminists hope to bring about in the church and the wider society. This is creative, constructive theological work, but it has clear negative moments. Feminist theologians work to counter the interpretations and organizational foci of Christian articulations that serve the interests of men at the expense of women, inside or outside the church; they interrupt the inferential and associative links of theological discourse that supports sexist institutional structures of those sorts; they disarticulate certain highly charged cultural elements and their networks from association with social practices that demean and exclude women. In short, by doing what

theologians usually do—rethinking for themselves the meaning and organization of the cultural materials with which Christian theologians
work—feminist theologians contest the cultural hegemony of patriarchal
forms of theological discourse on the way to constructing new theologies
for a new set of interpersonal relations, in which women are finally to be
granted their full humanity.

Making the Strategies of Feminist Theology More Effective

My description of the tasks of feminist theology bears a strong resem-
blance to the usual methodological self-understanding of feminist theologians. A political theory of culture just elaborates into a coherent
theoretical package what feminist theologians have commonly thought
their own enterprise to involve: (1) a critical consideration of the political
alignments of theological discourse, a rethinking of theological commitments in light of their effects on women and other oppressed minorities;
(2) a reworking of theology that highlights or moves into a central place
the previously marginalized theological voices of women; and (3) a refusal
to believe that given theological constructions are as incontrovertible or as
monolithic as their self-presentation often makes them out to be; according to feminist theologians, dominant theological conceptions are the
product of controversy and therefore fail to exhaust the domain of theological possibility. Such a convergence is not unexpected given the prove-
nance of feminist theology and a politics of culture that I recounted earlier:
feminist theology emerged out of the feminist movement, one of the new
social movements that a political understanding of culture was itself
designed to render intelligible. One might conclude, therefore, that a
political understanding of culture more fundamentally reconceptualizes
theology in general than it does feminist theology. Indeed, my general
description of the tasks of theology will probably strike readers as the more
surprising. A contribution is nevertheless made thereby to feminist theology. This reconceptualization of the nature of theology in general is at least
of strategic importance for feminist theology. A political theory of culture
makes the self-description of feminist theology the rule for rather than the
exception to the usual practices of theologians, and thereby obviates the
charge that feminist theology is an unfortunate and unnecessary politiciz-
ing of the theological enterprise.

For the reasons outlined in the first part of this article (see section
titled "Relevance to Feminist Theology"), it is also true that an account of

the tasks of feminist theology, according to a political understanding of culture, revises substantially the strategy that feminist theologians themselves should take in order to implement changes in theological and social practices. On a number of fronts, this redescription of the tasks of feminist theology amounts to a recommendation for an improved politics.

First, this redescription alleviates the naivete and despair that may sometimes result when feminist theology takes a purely oppositional stance toward patriarchal theological discourse, that is, toward the discourse of male-dominated theological circles that appears bound up with the devaluation of women and with institutional structures that stand in the way of their full flourishing. Feminist theology, to the detriment of its own desire for change, often assumes that feminist consciousness will necessarily flower, simply as a matter of course, once such patriarchal theological discourse is successfully pushed out of feminist theological construction. When those magical hopes are disappointed in fact, feminist theology that relies on this sort of oppositional strategy for instituting change is at a loss as to what to do. Understanding the tasks of feminist theology according to a politics of culture suggests, to the contrary, that resistance needs to be actively constructed; it also points to the general shape of the discursive means to be taken toward that end.

Second, understanding feminist theology according to a politics of culture widens the terrain of feminist tactics, and in a sense makes a feminist theological strategy easier. Feminist theologians are not forced to produce a feminist discourse from the bottom up; they do not have to try to replace patriarchal theological discourse with another form of theological discourse having as little as possible to do with the first. That kind of enterprise would be quite difficult to maintain in its purity. Such an enterprise, moreover, is unnecessary. It presumes that the cultural elements employed in patriarchal theological discourse are intrinsically and irremediably patriarchal. According to the political understanding of culture that I have sketched, however, such a presumption is false. These elements do not in themselves express patriarchal interests; their service to patriarchy, or to male-dominated social structures, is a function of their articulation to such interests by way of particular discursive formations. Since this is so, every element in service to a patriarchal cause has at least some potential for alignment with a feminist one.

This sort of realignment of cultural items—their disarticulation from service to patriarchy and their rearticulation for feminist purposes—will not necessarily be easy. The patriarchal meanings and associations of theological elements have already been secured to some extent. Because these meanings and articulations are already on the ground they operate as a relative constraint on the sort of feminist activity that is being recommended. Patriarchal meanings and associations are to some extent taken for granted—they already have a prominent position in the theological discursive field—and they are included within and reproduced by the relevant institutions—for example, they make up regular Sunday worship services and seminary curricula. In sum, they constitute the practical consciousness of existing patriarchal social relations in Christian contexts. One has to remember, however, that this prior securing of meanings and articulations is vulnerable. It is a contingent historical development, and, if a political understanding of culture is to be believed, it requires active maintenance; the struggle to secure these meanings and articulations is never over. It is therefore possible for feminist theologians to enter the fray with some effect.

Entering the fray at these points is necessary, moreover, if feminist theology is to be effective as an emancipatory strategy. The cultural elements that are already articulated with patriarchy in the form of common sense or practical thinking are highly cathected with political significance. For that reason, they are the primary stakes in a political struggle. Whoever manages to align them with their own political agenda and vision for social relations gains the advantage; the political stakes of theological controversy are highest exactly at these points.

What I have just said does not imply that every element prominent in patriarchal theological discourse has to have the same prominence in a feminist articulation. Some elements might even be too closely associated with patriarchy to be worth the effort of reinterpretion and disarticulation. Some elements of patriarchal discourse should be suppressed and de-emphasized, particularly insofar as they operate as organizing principles for patriarchal discourse (say, the idea of God as a repressive power). Hitherto marginalized or subordinated elements in the discursive field should be emphasized instead, particularly as organizing principles—say, the idea of God as helper found among some *mujerista* theologians.

It is still the case, however, that as many elements as possible from patriarchal discourse should be rearticulated to a feminist purpose. That is the only way to keep feminist theology from being classified as a marginal, fringe movement. The more that feminist theologians use for their own purposes the cultural elements that have been appropriated by patriarchal interests, the greater the feminist claim on theological credibility, and the harder it is for a feminist agenda to be dismissed by those committed to the dominant patriarchal organization of theological discourse. Such a procedure establishes feminists as serious participants in theological discourse; it establishes their right to be talked to rather than about.[18]

The tactic of disarticulating as many elements as possible from patriarchal discourse and rearticulating them for feminist purposes is also the only way to further a feminist transformation of theological and social practices. The more theological elements that feminist theology can articulate to its own interests, the greater the effectiveness of feminist theology in mobilizing support for change and for a new organization of culture and society in which women are valued. The hegemony of patriarchy is gained by enlisting popular support through discursive means, that is, by articulating to its own social vision as many as possible of the values, beliefs, and cultural assumptions that have some resonance for the majority of people. Feminist theologians should not let the present patriarchal alignment of those cultural elements discourage them from discursive incorporation of comparable breadth. Trying to avoid altogether the theological elements that patriarchy appropriates is a recipe for isolation in a ghetto of feminist purism.[19] It unduly restricts the scope of feminist efficacy; it sharply curtails the influence of feminist cultural and social projects. A feminist theology will gain wide support for its cultural and social vision only where it succeeds in organizing as many as possible of the elements incorporated in patriarchal discourse, according to a different logic—that is, according to different organizing principles and a different value system and set of objectives.

In recommending this strategy for consolidating support, I am assuming that a feminist agenda is not exhausted by a simple anti-hegemonic impulse. Feminist theology, like the feminist movement of which it is a part, does not merely attack patriarchy; it hopes to further an alternative social vision. A new social order, one respectful of the full humanity of all its members, including women, and dedicated to their flourishing, is to be established not at a remove from a patriarchal society of exploitation and domination, but as its replacement. A legitimate worry about inequities in power that might attend the successful implementation of a feminist social and cultural order should not lead feminist theologians to renege on their moral responsibilities to transform patriarchy according to a distinctive alternative vision. No doubt the new feminist social and cultural order will not be perfect; power imbalances will remain. The exploitation and domination of patriarchy need not return in full force, however—one system of domination and exploitation merely replacing another—so long as the feminist vision that is implemented includes an openness to criticism and resistance. For that openness to occur, the ideals of feminism have to take precedence over concern for its own institutional forms at any particular time. This is a possibility in a feminist social order, but something that the rigidity of patriarchal power imbalances forbids; in contrast to a feminist social vision, the point of patriarchy is simply to consolidate power inequities.

One could say, then, that feminist theology aims toward the hegemony of its social and cultural vision: theological and social practices in which the full humanity of women is taken for granted; theological and social practices of which feminist assumptions constitute the practical consciousness. A feminist social order that was hegemonic in this way—by virtue of the mutual reinforcement of cultural and social dimensions of life—need not mirror the exploitative and dominating characteristics of patriarchal hegemony. Because it is exploitative and oppressive of women, minorities, and the poor, patriarchal hegemony consolidates popular support by incorporating popular values and beliefs without fully addressing popular needs, without real concern for the interests of the people. A feminist social order would be hegemonic without domination and exploitation to the extent it genuinely addressed the needs of all by way of democratic processes of decision making. Arguably, this is just what a feminist social vision amounts to, at the most general and formal level. The institution of such a social vision would involve hegemony in its purest sense: popular support for a social order that is based entirely on informed consent and not on imposition, coercion, and deception. As such, it would be the most stable sort of hegemonic formation; because its institutions can genuinely respond to the needs of all, a feminist social order would be unlikely to lose popular support.[20]

Finally, I raise a more minor point about effective feminist strategy. A political understanding of culture contributes to the effectiveness of a feminist theological agenda by making feminist theologians more wary of the way patriarchal discourse can incorporate feminist theology. What feminist theology is supposed to do to patriarchal theological discourse, patriarchal discourse can do to it: disorganize and reorganize it, or trivialize it as a mere matter of fashion or political correctness. It is not enough, therefore, for feminist theologians to produce a feminist articulation of theological elements; that articulation requires continual struggle against patriarchal reappropriations if its effectiveness is to be maintained.

Reevaluating Appeals to Tradition in Feminist Theology

One might paraphrase the above recommendations by saying they suggest the strategic importance for feminist theology of remaining traditional. The influence of feminist theology is strengthened to the extent it wrestles constructively with the theological claims that have traditionally been important in Christian theology; the more traditional the material with which it works, the greater the influence of feminist theology. This reference to tradition still needs to be thematized, however. What is the nature and status of the past according to a political understanding of culture, and what authorizing force can appeals to the past retain?

Since we are suggesting that feminist theology incorporate a politics of culture within its own self-understanding, it might help to begin by discussing the way appeals to the past enter into the method of a politics of culture, before exploring the way a politics of culture interprets appeals to the past in discursive formations such as Christian theology. The *past* is not an especially prominent category within the politics of culture as a method of interpretation: a politics of culture is not interested in the past qua past but in circulating symbolic resources in the present, and notions of what might be done with them. The past use of cultural elements does not determine present or future interpretations or articulations of those elements; a politics of culture therefore has little interest in establishing the origins or sources of a cultural element. The past use of cultural elements is, however, of interest insofar as it constitutes a relative constraint on new interpretations and articulations. Past uses constitute the starting point for efforts of disarticulation and therefore are a measure of the difficulties involved in proposing new interpretations and articulations of those elements. Within the method of a politics of culture, the past, then, refers to those meanings and organizations of cultural elements in the present that are already secured. Although circulating at the present time, the work that secured them took place in the past. Although circulating in the present, these already secured meanings and articulations are also designated the past so as to contrast them with emerging efforts of interpretation and organization that work to destabilize them.

Of more direct relevance for the shape of a feminist theological agenda is the question of how a politics of culture interprets appeals to the past within the struggles over culture that it studies.[21] If feminist theology incorporates a politics of culture within its own self-understanding, what should it make, for example, of appeals to an authorizing past within the patriarchal theological traditions it intends to subvert? What form should the fight against patriarchy take with respect to such appeals?

According to a politics of culture, the past in such cultural fights is a category assigned to certain presently circulating cultural elements; it is a way of labeling, a way of singling out or marking certain presently circulating symbolic resources. Such labeling establishes a negative or positive value for the elements so marked: a negative value—"oh, that is an old idea"—or a positive value—"this is a part of our venerable heritage." Whether the designation of the past has a positive or negative value is determined by the importance of the place the marked element occupies within a presently secured discursive formation or articulation. The past becomes merely archaic, dismissible, and irrelevant to the extent the cultural elements or elements so labeled have a minor role within such a discursive formation. The past is valued—it becomes tradition in a positive sense of a valued heritage—to the extent the cultural element or elements so labeled have a central function within a presently secured discursive formation. Appeals to the past become in this way the justification for a particular discursive formation, one organized with reference to or with a heavy inferential or associative dependence on the items so labeled. Those cultural elements establish the boundaries of authenticity or identity, the boundaries of acceptable discourse; cultural elements that are not part of, or that have no inferential or associative connections with this valued past, are marked off as alien or inconsequential. The appeal to the past to explain present discursive practice—the claim that present practice is traditional—helps, in short, establish the hegemony of a particular discursive formation; it "offers a historical and cultural ratification of a contemporary order."[22]

Because of what is riding on them, it is appropriate that the cultural elements that are marked as a valued past in patriarchal forms of theology become the site of political contest by feminist theologians. Whoever controls the interpretation and designation of the past that authorizes present practice gains the power to establish the boundaries of religious identity, the power to delimit what is authentically Christian, what is appropriate for a Christian to say and do. Feminist theologians can contest the authorizing past of patriarchal theological discourse in a variety of ways: by reinterpreting and rearticulating the cultural elements so designated, by disputing their purported continuity with what has gone before, and/or by transforming the archaic into a rival authorizing past by establishing its own connections with present practices and future possibilities.

Contrary to the Enlightenment association of tradition with the stultification of creativity and human agency, tradition becomes in this way the material and context for innovation and change. Within a political understanding of culture, the meaning of tradition expands, one could say, to include diversity and novelty as essential constituting moments. The explanation given for this is very different from the one offered by the other major theory of culture that disputes an Enlightenment opposition between tradition and novelty of interpretation: a Gadamerian hermeneutics. The explanation does not involve an account of tradition as a process in which temporal distance and changes of situation draw out the inherent richness in meaning of certain cultural forms—for example, classic texts. Changes in time and place, while clearly relevant to diversity in the interpretation of tradition, are not necessary to explain the phenomena. Highlighting them as an explanation occludes, moreover, the potential for diversity of interpretation within the same time and place; it suggests an already unified cultural inheritance adapting as a block to changing exigencies of time and place. A politics of culture breaks open the potential for interpretative diversity in appeals to tradition by questioning just this assumption of a unified cultural block at any one time and place. As is true of any cultural formation, the body of cultural elements marked *traditional* at any one time and place is the product of an ongoing struggle over a diversity of interpretations that can never finally or thoroughly be held in check: the meaning of such elements floats, points of tension and inconsistency among them are never fully excised, and the designation *traditional* and organization of elements so marked remain contingent.

The account of appeals to the past that is given by a politics of culture has the capacity, however, to undercut all by itself the hegemonic force of such appeals. Publicizing that account can therefore be a major part of the effort by feminist theologians to counteract the hegemony of patriarchal theology. Feminists need not try to play on their own terms the same game of authorizing present practice with reference to the past; they can simply make it a major part of their counterhegemonic strategy to spread the kind of authority-deflating interpretation of such appeals that a politics of culture offers.

The reader may already have noticed how circular appeals to an authorizing past seem to have become, according to the interpretation of them offered by a politics of culture. The elements that constitute an authorizing past are just those elements that play a major role in the discursive formation they are to justify. The appeal to an authorizing past seems to be simply a way of privileging the cultural elements that are emphasized within a presently secured discursive organization. This impression of circularity in the account that a politics of culture gives of appeals to an authorizing past seems to vitiate the force of such appeals as a way of justifying present discursive practices.

This suggestion of circularity does not come about because a politics of culture denies the existence of the past; it does not depend on the assumption that the past is nothing but a present cultural designation. A politics of culture does not assume that the past is a fiction and, for that reason, a merely self-justifying designation of discursive formations; the past is not the mere self-projection of a discursive formation that justifies itself through the creation of its own past. According to a politics of culture, the elements that a discursive formation designates as past may really be so. What a politics of culture points out is that, in any case, such a designation is selective; the selectivity in appeals to an authorizing past is what supports a charge of circularity.

The past is far larger than the designated past of a particular cultural formation; many more presently circulating cultural items could legitimately be so labeled. Almost all the cultural elements in present circulation are carryovers from the past; most of what circulates now also circulated in the past. The continuous nature of human practices over time and the inevitability with which human memory drags the happenings of the past into present and future are enough to ensure this.

The authorizing force of an appeal to the past increases to the extent a presently secured discursive formation can disguise that a selection has been made from this more widely available past. The work of selection is disguised by giving the impression that the past is a natural, already given, found object, to which the presently secured discursive formation, qua tradition, has merely been true. The presently secured discursive formation has legitimacy as a traditional form of discourse, in other words, to the extent it can claim to have done nothing but carry over without alteration a past deposit of beliefs, values, and practices, which it found with contours and shape already determined. A politics of culture contests this way of giving appeals to the past an authorizing force by suggesting that an authorizing past is always the result of a selective activity of interpretation in the present; the cultural items that are designated as an authorizing past could have been different and, therefore, the presently secured discursive formation cannot make appeals to tradition a way of reneging on its responsibility for how present discursive formations are organized.

A political understanding of culture does not make feminist appeals to an authorizing past pointless. It remains legitimate to argue for a particular organization of Christian cultural and social practice on the grounds that it has some continuities with what Christians have said and done in the past. Feminist theologians who incorporate a politics of culture in their own self-understanding can still, in other words, make respect for tradition a precondition for appropriate Christian discourse and practice in the present. Respect for tradition cannot, however, be a sufficient condition for Christian appropriateness, because the possibility of alternative significant pasts exists. Respect for tradition does not, in other words, answer the question, "Which tradition, which part of the extant or recoverable past, should be designated an authorizing past?" Continuity with the past is not sufficient to answer that question; further argument about the respective merits of alternative proposals of an authorizing past is necessary. Such arguments would have to concentrate on the content of the proposals and not on the claim of continuity with past practice per se. It would be appropriate to ask, for example: Does this account of an authorizing past make better sense of the complex, variegated history of Christian practice, which a politics of culture itself helps to highlight? What are the moral, intellectual, and spiritual benefits of the organization of Christian theology and practice that such a past authorizes? Would, for instance, this particular theological organization prove more illuminating of present human experience than other possible organizations?

In sum, a political understanding of culture prohibits any appeal to an authorizing past that merely serves to block further discussion and argument over the shape that Christian theology and social practices should take. One can no longer say, no further argument is appropriate since this is simply what the Christian tradition demands. An appeal to the past may remain a way of authorizing present practice, but it cannot be used to deflect responsibility for the shape that current practice takes. A politics of culture, by pointing out that the extant and recoverable past is wider and more diverse than any particular identification of an authorizing past, makes clear that things could always be different. The way they are therefore remains a matter of human responsibility; it is not dictated by the past as some sort of incontrovertible deposit of hard fact, some immovable object to which human beings can only make obeisance. Should Christian feminists make appeals to an authorizing past part of their strategy for furthering the transformation of cultural and social practices, a political understanding of culture helps open up the available past for feminist appropriation. According to a political understanding of culture, there is no reason to think that the sort of contests over meaning and articulation that have led to the present diversity of theological positions were not always a feature of history. By widening in this way expectations about the multiform richness of the past to which feminist theologians can refer, a political understanding of culture actively encourages the idea that appeals to an authorizing past, when properly qualified, may be an effective strategy for feminist theologians to pursue.

CHAPTER 12

CONTINUING THE STORY, BUT DEPARTING THE TEXT

A Historicist Interpretation of Feminist Norms in Theology

Sheila Greeve Davaney

INTELLECTUAL MOVEMENTS THAT ARE VITAL and viable over long periods of time are ones that have both the capacity for internal critique and the ability to respond to external challenges and developments. Feminist theology has struggled in its still-young history to be such a dynamic enterprise, dedicating itself to ongoing self-examination, encouraging a multiplicity of views, altering emphases, and even significantly changing its direction. The result has been the emergence of a theological perspective marked by diversity and lively differences. Yet despite the fact that, ever since its inception, feminist theology has been plural in nature, comprised of a variety of voices, there have been characteristic assumptions, themes, and commitments that typified most theological reflection labeled feminist. These have included omnipresent appeals to women's experience, the use of gender as the central analytical tool, a theoretical and political commitment to the emancipation of women understood as a distinct group, and the location of criteria for evaluation in the critical consciousness and experience of women. Thus while differences certainly always existed among feminist theologians, it was still possible to speak of feminist theology as a more or less unified theological perspective, distinguishable from other theological movements, and located in a specifiable site on the theological landscape.

A number of developments have occurred in recent years that have significantly altered this situation. First of all, there have arisen widespread theoretical shifts, both in theology generally and in the broader reaches of current intellectual disciplines, that have contributed to the dismantling of long-held assumptions within theological reflection, including feminist theology. These shifts have been termed variously the move to postmodernism or poststructuralism, the emergence of a new historicism, the rehabilitation of the material and the concrete, the celebration of difference and heterogeneity, the rise of subjugated knowledges, and so forth. Such developments have not, however, resulted in any newly fashioned theological unity, but in the articulation of very distinctive, even contradictory, responses to this novel theoretical environment. Feminist theology is less and less a singular identifiable site on the theological spectrum and more and more a characteristic or version of varying methodological and substantive theological agendas.

Concurrently, new challenges and constructive proposals have taken shape within feminist theological reflection itself that have opened up and indeed mandated new directions in feminist theology. These changes are both particular to feminist reflection and reflective of those broader discussions. The result is that feminist theologians now find ourselves at varied theoretical locations along the theological spectrum, expressing our feminist commitments using different and differing theoretical frameworks.

This article will examine several of the significant theoretical shifts that are occurring which are having special impact within feminist theology. In particular, it will focus on the complex of issues concerning normative criteria and the questions of how we choose among competing visions of reality and differing conceptions of human life and meaning. But before delving into the current issues around criteria, it is necessary first to look at how feminist theology has been construed in the past and to examine the theoretical changes that, in turn, are reshaping the debate around norms.

Perhaps, over time, the most consequential debates in feminist theory, especially in its theological form, have revolved around the nature and status of the female subject. Until recently, most feminist theologies centered their claims around women's experience. On the most elementary level, feminist theologians noted that women's lives and experiences had been absent from theological reflection, considered either insignificant on their own or subsumed under the male-defined category of human experience, and thereby rendered invisible. Any theology that adequately accounted for human life had to contend, feminist theologians declared, not only with the lives and thoughts of males but also those of females.

But feminist theologians employed the category of women's experience in more complex and important ways than simply to argue that the data for theological reflection needed to be enlarged. Four related claims were also articulated in much feminist theological reflection.[1] The first was the assumption that women's experience, for all its variety and specificity, had a common character. Sometimes this commonality was attributed to an underlying female nature, while at other times it was said to emerge from the historical reality of women's oppression; in still other instances, it was linked to the structure of critical feminist consciousness that developed out of the struggle against oppression. Thus to appeal to women's experience was certainly to turn attention to the concrete particularity of female lives, but it was also to assert a universal and common essence that somehow defined women as women, and that laid the basis for feminist solidarity as well as providing the content for feminist reflection.[2]

The second claim that followed from these understandings of femaleness was that women's experience was also seen as the normative site against which theological assertions were tested. Whether in the form of Rosemary Radford Ruether's "full humanity of women" or Elisabeth Schüssler Fiorenza's "self-affirmation, power and liberation" of women, theological positions were to be assayed in terms of how they embodied and contributed to women's critical consciousness and transformed experience.[3] Moreover, for most feminist theologians, these notions of normativity reflected not only the historically contingent option of women on behalf of women, but the more far-reaching assumption that the appropriateness of this evaluative criterion arose from the privileged character of women's experience. For certain feminist thinkers, such as Mary Daly, this privilege arose from claims about women's ontological nature and status; for others it emerged from the conviction that women's historical experience of and transformative struggle against oppression provided a uniquely authoritative vantage point from which to render critical judgment.[4] But whether historically derived or ontologically given, feminist theological reflection widely bestowed on women's experience a weight it assumed was missing elsewhere.

A third implicit and sometimes explicit move that was made in much feminist theology concerned how religious traditions, especially Christianity, were construed. Often there was present, among Christian feminist theologians, an essentialist notion of tradition that paralleled the essentialist notion of the female self. Now this was no simple parallelism and it took a variety of forms. Some feminists, especially more conservative and evangelical women, argued that the biblical tradition was a unified whole that was liberating if correctly understood.[5] More commonly it was suggested that the real essence, often located in a biblical core, was liberating; while the entirety of the tradition might not be life-giving, indeed perhaps the opposite, nonetheless the heart of the tradition was thought to have an emancipatory character. Moreover, and very importantly, many feminists posited that there was a resonance or correspondence between feminist consciousness and the biblical core. Thus Ruether normatively referenced the prophetic-liberating strand within the Hebraic and Christian traditions, Letty Russell distinguished the liberating center of the traditions, and Sallie McFague called for the correlation between contemporary positions and the basic Christian paradigm.[6] In each of these cases, Christianity, whether in part or as a whole, was assumed to have some identifiable center which could be established and which was interpreted as lending authoritative weight to the vision articulated by feminist thinkers.

Finally, in most feminist theologies there has been the further tendency to equate a feminist critical perspective with claims about the divine in such a manner that a strong correspondence was suggested between feminist norms and the purposes of divine reality. Thus thinkers such as Elisabeth Schüssler Fiorenza predicated that the "spiritual authority of women-church rests on this experience of divine grace in our midst" and Rosemary Radford Ruether argued that the feminist principle of the full humanity of women corresponded, albeit imperfectly, to the divine matrix.[7] Such an association by feminist theology enhanced the credence of its norms by providing them with an ontological or divine foundation. Thus while virtually always acknowledging that these criteria were humanly created and socially circumscribed, feminist theologians have also posited grounds beyond the contingencies of human argument for validating their claims.

Together these theoretical assumptions and moves have issued forth in a particular line of argument that until recently has structured much feminist theology, especially its Christian versions, for all its internal variety. Centered in a common female nature or authoritative experience that, on the one hand, corresponded to the essence of religious traditions and, on the other hand, to the constitutive purposes of divine reality, feminist theology argued for the unique validity of its perspective. Thus, as Elsa Tamez suggests, feminists' and liberationists' reading of the Bible from the perspective of oppressed poor women resonates with the hermeneutical key "offered by the Scriptures themselves" and with the parallel assumption that "God is on the side of the oppressed."[8] While often simultaneously granting the contingency of its arguments and the plurality and diversity of its referents, feminist theology pleaded its normative case on the felicitous coincidence of female nature or experience, tradition and divine purpose.

There were assuredly good reasons for feminist theologians to take this general direction of argument. It gave expression to the profound awareness of the condition of women's existence and a desire for solidarity for the cause of all women. It embodied a strong recognition of the traditioned character of life and of the necessity of contending with the past. And it was clearly cognizant of the power of religious symbols and the need to deconstruct and reconstruct them in ways that contributed to women's survival and flourishing.

As feminist theology developed there were certainly modifications of these claims as more voices entered the theological debate. Analysis increasingly emphasized diversity and conceptualities were sought to account for that diversity along with the assumed commonality. The liberating center of religious traditions became more difficult to identify, and the varied and conflicting ways religious symbols were appropriated became more clear.

Recent developments, however, within feminist theology and theory as well as in the broader intellectual milieu have greatly intensified these departures from earlier positions, casting radical doubts on many of feminist theology's most significant claims. While often concurring with the emancipatory intentions of these earlier theologies, feminist thinkers, including some of the authors of those earlier claims, are engaging in a critique of the assumptions that have grounded the normative vision presented by feminist theology. Central to this reevaluation is what I will term the historicizing of the female subject and, with it, the questioning of essentialist notions of subjectivity and the arguments that flowed from those notions, including arguments about the normativity of feminist positions.

With particular force, women of color have stressed that feminist theology's emphasis on commonality, its essentialist undercurrent, and its prioritizing of gender as an analytical tool all conspired to conceal the racial and class differences among women, and hence allowed white feminists to avoid responsibility for our complicity in the oppression of other women. As Jacquelyn Grant put it so bluntly: "Feminist theology is inadequate for two reasons: it is White and racist."[9] In particular, the additive approaches of much white feminist thought, wherein gender is the fundamental oppression and other forms of oppression become addenda to that, without significant analytical recognition that the experience of gender is affected by such things as race, class, and sexual orientation, have seemed singularly inadequate to many theorists of color. Womanist, *mujerista,* and Asian feminists, among others, have thus argued for a more localized interpretation of experience that traces the historically particular situations of women, and resists all attempts to homogenize that experience into the abstract category of all women. Moreover, they have undertaken the analysis of religious traditions and theological interpretations of reality along the same lines, mapping the unique developments and configuration of different communities as well as their conflict-filled interrelations. Thus Katie Cannon has utilized literature to enter the distinctive sphere of black women's lives; Delores Williams has traced the rise of the Universal Hagar's Spiritual Church; Kwok Pui-lan and Chung Hyun Kyung have turned to autobiographical reflections; and Ada María Isasi-Díaz has appropriated ethnographic methodologies, all in the attempt to give specificity to the lives of the women and communities that have previously been absorbed and rendered invisible by white feminist thought.[10]

Concurrently, feminists, including both white women and women of color, who work explicitly out of historicist theoretical perspectives, including what is widely termed postmodernism, have also strongly challenged essentialist notions of the self. Across wide ranges of feminist theory, it is now argued that there is neither an unchanging core that characterizes individual humans nor some transpersonal nature that is constitutive of humans or, in our case, females as such. In a vein similar to and, among certain thinkers, overlapping with the above argument, these theorists conclude as well that there are no universal forms of experience shared by everyone across temporal and historical boundaries. These appeals to commonality, be they to ontological nature or historical experience, increasingly appear as illusory abstractions obscuring particularity and the contentious differences that characterize human experience. Thus there has been a move away from humans or females in general toward the particular, the concrete, the local, and the specific.

This denial of a universal female nature, or common experience, and the drive toward particularity has not, however, issued forth in notions of hyperindividualism. Instead, much current feminist theorizing has stressed the contextual and communal character of female identity, pointing to its dependence on the discursive fields from which it emerges and within which it dwells.[11] Hence while there are no women in general, neither are there autonomous, isolated individuals, interpretable apart from their historical, cultural, and social location.

If much credence is given to the importance of contextuality and tradition, a growing number of feminist thinkers, including a significant number outside the dominant intellectual and geographical North Atlantic context, are giving this argument an interesting twist. For they are insisting first that the traditions and contexts that shape female subjectivity and identity are internally pluralistic, conflictual, and unstable. While subjectivity and identity are always situated and those contexts are always part of larger historical traditions, neither contexts nor traditions are homogenous or monolithic, but are full of diverse and contending possibilities and limitations. Moreover, they are further suggesting that women do not reside only in one cultural or discursive tradition, plural though it may be, but are situated at junctures of multiple influences and are, therefore, not only traditioned but multitraditioned. Women, especially those with more than one ethnic and religious heritage, are, as Chinese theologian Kwok Pui-lan and Korean Chung Hyun Kyung have suggested, syncretistic selves,[12] born, in the words of Latina writers Aurora Levins Morales and Rosario Morales, "at a crossroads."[13] Finally, it is asserted that these plural sites or junctures within which female subjectivity is constructed are continually undergoing change; it is not only that women's selves are constructed in response to multiple influences but that, as Linda Alcoff puts it, female identity is always relative to a "(constantly shifting) context."[14]

Hence, in sum, feminist thinkers are engaged in a significant reinterpretation of female subjectivity and identity. In contrast to earlier interpretations of a common female nature, persisting within and despite real differences among women or appeals to universal forms of women's experience, there is the turn to particular, concrete identities of women constructed within differing material locales and out of varied linguistic and cultural systems. Moreover, the understanding of identity taking shape is not that of a historically and culturally particular, but still unified and stable, self. Instead there is emerging, in the words of feminist theorist Teresa de Lauretis, the concept "of identity as multiple, and even self-contradictory."[15]

Just as with the earlier feminist interpretations of women's nature, there are good reasons for these theoretical moves, and many positive repercussions are developing out of them. Feminist scholars, including theologians, are better able, both on a theoretical level and in terms of the concrete deployment of our analytical tools, to account for and trace the differences among women. Moreover, previously ignored and suppressed voices are claiming with greater force what bell hooks calls "counter-hegemonic" space, thus altering the direction and content of feminist thought and creating new forms of reflection altogether.[16] While feminist reflection in all disciplines has changed, feminist theology has been particularly affected as feminist theologians have cultivated new conversation partners such as the social sciences, literary criticism, and cultural studies, and have adopted new methodologies such as ethnography, cultural discourse, and literary analysis.

But if these theoretical shifts have brought clear benefits, they have also raised significant questions and problems for feminist reflection and especially for feminist theology. One question is whether feminists have bought into a notion of subjectivity that empties female agency of any meaning. As many representatives of groups historically denied the status of selfhood have commented, it seems that at the precise historical moment when such oppressed persons are demanding recognition as human selves, that self is declared illusory and nonexistent, or so thoroughly constituted by its environment that notions of freedom and self-determination become highly problematized.[17] Thus feminist theorists now have the task of articulating understandings of female subjectivity that weave a middle path between earlier essentialist notions and the deleterious postmodern dispersal of the self that renders notions of agency and identity meaningless.

Another issue concerns just how far down difference goes for women. The focus on diversity and particularity has revealed the uniqueness of individuals and communities as well as the conflicts within and between different groups. But it has also posed the problem of whether individuals and communities can relate in anything other than superficial show-and-tell or contentious power struggles. Put bluntly, what now are the grounds for solidarity among women?

Also flowing from this recognition of the centrality of context and tradition is the issue of how multiple traditions are integrated, even momentarily, in the formation of individual female identity. As earlier assumptions of common nature or universal experience were shed, the emphasis initially fell on women's location within singular historical traditions. But increasingly there has been a shift toward the plural locations of women. With this move the question not only arises of how these contexts relate to one another, but further of how to describe what might be termed the hyphenated identities or synthetic selves that emerge from the confluence of multiple, often conflicting sources of influence.

All of these interrelated issues might be seen to culminate in the question of feminist norms. Feminist reflection, and most certainly feminist theology, has always sought not only to interpret women's experience and condition, but also to present a normative vision that claimed greater adequacy than dominant, usually male interpretations of reality and human life. For all feminist theory, but most especially for feminist theology, the grounds for claiming such superior validity are now less clear. As stated above, much feminist theology predicated its normative appeal on the argument for the unique collaboration among a common female nature or women's experience, the liberating center or core of particular religious traditions (usually Christianity or Judaism), and the emancipatory purposes of divine reality. The result of this resonance of history, God, and female experience was that feminist theology could— and did—assert that its norms and constructive proposals were not merely contingent historical possibilities vying with other equally contingent options, but instead had a cosmic or ontological grounding, or at the very least the backing of an authoritative tradition that supported feminist claims to validity.

The current theoretical shifts now being developed and embraced by many feminist theorists are contributing, however, to the dismantling of this complex of normative assertions. If there is no common women's experience, but only the pluralistic, myriad, and conflicting experience of the multitudes of women, the appeal to such commonality loses its authoritative force. Or again, if the privileged vanguard of critical consciousness elevates one group's experience while covertly denigrating other groups, then its justificatory power is greatly diminished. Moreover, if religious traditions are also pluralistic, dynamic, and conflictual without clearly identifiable cores or unvarying essences, then resonance with strands in those traditions may provide historical antecedents, but no longer unique authority predicated on those associations. Finally, the feminist assertion of a correspondence between God's purposes and feminist visions also has become far more problematized. In particular, the humanly constructed character of religious symbols has become more evident, and with that recognition the issue of what role such symbols play in validating our normative criteria and proposals has emerged. If our ideas of the divine are not grounded in a universal experience or a uniquely authoritative consciousness or tradition, but emerge out of the messier processes of dynamic and conflictual history, bearing always a more localized character, then the claim of resonance between those notions of God and feminist visions may demonstrate conceptual unity and clarity in feminist proposals, but it does not provide an independent source of validation for those positions.

Feminist theology, like its analogues in other disciplines, has been contending with the repercussions of these new theoretical directions. Questions concerning female subjectivity and identity, the basis for solidarity among women, and women's relation to specific communities dominate much current discussion. There has been a general move toward particular communities and the concomitant acknowledgment of the historical character of criteria and normative visions. Yet in these moves there has not yet been in feminist theology a thorough grappling with the dismantling of the edifice on which feminist theology had built its claims to validity. Are feminist theologians content now to say that, not only are all normative visions human constructions, but that they are of equal value? Is it in fact the case, and should it be the case, that how these matters are decided is a question of, as Richard Rorty puts it, "weapons and luck"?[18] Or shall our claim be that norms and constructive proposals can indeed be evaluated and judged, but only within the

confines of particular communities and, hence, they can claim no validity beyond local borders?

At this juncture, I would like to begin to sketch out a response to
this question of norms. It is a proposal that reflects what I would term
the turn to historicity that broadly characterizes much of the current
intellectual scene. As such, this proposal is obviously predicated on
assumptions about subjectivity as embedded in and constructive of intri-
cate historical processes, assumptions that have only been hinted at and
which deserve fuller amplification. Moreover, it is offered not as a thorough venting of these issues, but as an attempt to encourage further
debate about the ramifications of our theoretical shifts and what these
changes portend, especially for constructive feminist theology. I do this
by indicating one direction a historicist form of feminist theology might
take, in order to avoid the twin dangers of ahistorical appeals to validity
on the one hand, and, on the other hand, the surrender of assertions of
greater adequacy. In particular, I want to articulate a position that closely
aligns the historicist sensibilities that this article has been setting forth
with a self-conscious pragmatism as one way to maintain the normative
dimension so characteristic of feminist theology.[19]

This approach is predicated on the assumption that, whatever arguments feminists make for our proposals, these must not renege on historicist insights. Such insights were what allowed feminist theologians
originally to raise critical questions about the pseudo-universal claims of
much traditional male theology, and to recognize that theological claims
were deeply value-laden and normative in character. We must, therefore,
resist the temptation to reintroduce, covertly or explicitly, ahistorical
essentialist appeals, be they about female nature and experience or religious traditions. Put positively, we must provide a historicist interpretation of these issues, which can support our quest for more adequate
visions of reality. The weakness of earlier feminist arguments is not that
they sought to articulate a coherent, internally connected set of theological claims or that they appealed to experience, tradition, and God. It is
rather that they did so in a manner that was in tension with their own
strong historicist tendencies and that finds less and less support in our
present theoretical milieu.

Beginning with this commitment and recognizing that there are
certainly other lines of argument that locate feminists at other places in

the theological landscape, I would like to suggest the following elements for a feminist reinterpretation of norms. These elements suggest the direction in which a fuller feminist pragmatic historicism would go and thus represent a future agenda to be explored.

First, feminist theologians need to return to women's experience, selfhood, and identity, but in historicist terms. This means, to begin with, that we must elaborate notions of subjectivity that recognize the contextual, traditioned, and hence concrete and particular character of our identity. In such an approach human subjectivity is a historical product, emergent within and dependent on the complex possibilities and limitations that have emerged within particular strands of history. There are, therefore, only concrete women and men who cannot be described or understood apart from the particularities of their historical location and the traditions out of which those locations emerged.

Second, the complex and plural character of these locations requires acknowledgment and theoretical expression. That is, feminist theology must also develop theories of traditions that point to the internally dynamic and pluralistic nature of those traditions, and that further recognize that identity is constructed not within the stable confines of one tradition but at the juncture of multiple traditions. These two points are important to hold together. The first indicates that existence within any historical strand or context is never existence within a seamless and uniform setting. Every cultural, religious, or political context or tradition is really, as Delwin Brown has stated, multilithic, not monolithic, a conglomeration of multiple contending traditions, not singular hegemonic ones.[20] Thus, for feminist theology to claim that female identities emerge in and out of concrete historical traditions and contexts is to locate them within the ever-present struggle for cultural and historical resources, products of and contributors to, not settled givens, but ongoing contests for power, meaning, and value.

The second point stresses that it is no longer adequate to assert the internal diversity of single traditions. Instead we must acknowledge that individuals and, indeed, new traditions emerge out of multiple strands of influence. Identity is the product not of purity but of the functional confluence of the myriad materials at our disposal.

These claims suggest that the rehabilitation of the concrete, contextual, and traditioned aspects of identity must avoid notions of isolated, impermeable, and utterly incommensurable traditions. Without open boundaries between communities, traditions, and individuals we cannot account for the fact that women continually weave our identities out of varied, sometimes contradictory, and always plural influences. We are synthetic selves, wrought through the combining of disparate elements to form coherent, if only for the moment, wholes that are ourselves. Notions of singular locations within bounded communities do not adequately express this reality. Neither do they allow an account of or encourage acts of solidarity across divisions of race, class, or national, ethnic, or religious borders, nor do they hold us accountable for the damage our supposedly local perspective wreaks on others. Nominalism, whether in reference to individuals or communities, will not do.

Third, our notions of subjectivity, while acknowledging our situatedness, must not only give expression to this conditioned character of our identity, but also maintain our hard-fought sense of female agency. The recognition of historicity certainly entails an acknowledgment that we are historical products, constituted in some real way by what we have inherited and by the limitations and resources of our given contexts. But historicity entails not only receptivity; it also has an agential side. If we are not autonomous ahistorical superagents, neither are we merely constituted by our environments or histories. Instead, precisely as historical beings, we are also constructive historical agents, creating new identities and visions out of the disparate inheritances from our pasts and from the multiple, if not infinite, options of our various locations. It is because we not only inherit plural histories but also forge new identities out of them that we can speak both of responsibility and of hope.

Out of these conceptions of a historicized subjectivity, a move toward a new argument concerning norms as primarily pragmatic is taking shape. It is not possible, I think, to return to earlier arguments for the validity of feminist visions of reality. The neat circle of women's experience, God, and authoritative tradition, while compelling for a time, has been broken. Nor is it possible simply to historicize those arguments, acknowledging the historical nature of both feminist claims and religious traditions, but still insisting that there is a felicitous coherence between the feminist visions and the normative core of a tradition. The force of this article has been to suggest that traditions have no such identifiable essence, but rather are composed of diverse, plural, and contradictory strands linked by their historical contiguousness, not by a stability of meaning or a unity of value. Thus the values and normative claims that emerge within them are multiple and not reducible to some common center with which feminists might identify.

To say that there is no essence of religious traditions is, as the arguments above indicate, not to assert that we do not inherit values, visions, interpretations of reality. Clearly, in a historicist perspective we do. In such a view, new possibilities never emerge out of nothing but always out of the creative reconstruals of our plural inheritances. But those inheritances are multiple; they are historically contingent; they are the residue of earlier human reconstruals. While we may trace the resonance between our current claims and past ones, doing so tells us about our lineage but not about the validity or adequacy of our claims. It may help us, like the tracing of a family tree or the work of good therapy, to have a sense of where we have come from, but it is not adequate for determining who we can or should be.

Those judgments, I would suggest, while influenced by the past, are finally our responsibility in every contemporary moment and context. It is we who need to articulate norms for our time, recognizing their location in the present, though acknowledging their debt to what has gone before. We must accept the responsibility for, as Berkeley Breathed states in the children's book, *Goodnight Opus,* continuing the story but departing the text. Knowing that we are continuing a story—really, many stories—will remind us that we are not isolated but historically connected with what went before. Departing the text will focus our attention on the call not merely to repeat or conform to the past, which is as fully contingent as any present, but to self-consciously engage in constructing practices and interpretations that are viable for today.

We must, as we depart the text, also grant the fallible and ambiguous character of our visions, pleading neither a privileged epistemological nor an ontological status for them. Feminist interpretations of reality and proposals for human action and relationships are always, like those they seek to replace, quite thoroughly historical; they emerge out of varied pasts and current contexts; they reflect the struggle for power and survival; they include certain persons and realities and always leave others out; they hold out the vision of certain goods and values but are always incomplete, contingent, fallible, and hence vulnerable to challenge and open to revision or replacement. Moreover, acknowledging the historical character of our own feminist proposals entails that there will be no one set of feminist norms or visions, but numerous sets, each offering possibilities to be tested in the arena of history. Just as there is no essential female nature, neither is there a singular feminist vision. Feminists are not monolingual but speak in multiple tongues. In a historicist and pragmatic perspective this multiplicity is not a sign of failure or a danger to be overcome, but the inevitable expression of our historicity, providing us with varied possibilities to be engaged.

Admitting both the contingency and the multiplicity of our visions does not lead, however, to a sense that all visions or proposals or practices are equal. Feminists, from our varied locations, need to argue for the greater adequacy of our visions both in conversation with one another and in the arena of wider theological debate. The question is on what grounds we should do so. I would suggest that, as this analysis clearly implies, we forego the invocation of ahistorical experience or tradition as grounds for assaying theological claims and adjudicating among competing proposals. Instead, I believe we should assess the adequacy of our constructive proposals primarily in terms of the pragmatic repercussions that we anticipate might result from adopting one set of values and visions rather than another. In lieu of asking whether our visions cohere with a universal nature or offer "demonstrable continuities" with an authoritative past, we should ask what difference they make to real lives in differing circumstances. If women and men are not humans in general but always concretely, then we need to ask ourselves what might result from living one way rather than another, out of one set of values and one imaginative rendering of life instead of different ones. What difference do these questions make to our bodies, to our communities, to the communities and persons affected by our more specific locale, to the larger web of human life and nature? Recognizing the limited and partial nature of human values and norms, we must interrogate ourselves and others concerning who is left out, what new and often covert privileging is taking place. Realizing that our proposals foster and nourish certain goods while inhibiting other, often compelling, goods, we need to answer why we have chosen these values, why these goods, and not others that have been left aside. From the historicist perspective articulated here, reality is not easily divided into good and evil, but is far more ambiguous, demanding from us not self-righteous assertions of truth but more chastened calls for self-critical and open-ended proposals to improve our human condition. But that our visions and proposals will be, in a sense, more circumscribed does not alleviate the hard work of arguing on their behalf, or recognizing that they offer significant alternatives that compel our allegiances.

To propose that we invoke pragmatic norms does not, however, settle the question of how we should fill out those norms. What should count as a positive or life-giving repercussion versus a dangerous or life-denying one is not clear. Some theologians can only answer those questions by referencing the historically derived norms found in local communities. But if the analysis offered in this paper has any validity, to return to such communities is not to return to environments providing clear and stable criteria, but multiple and conflicting criteria. While I would agree that we must engage those varying norms in order to determine what has counted historically as valid, true, and adequate, I would venture that we also test our visions in terms of how they contribute to what we now understand to be a historicized subjectivity. That is, I think, we must evaluate our proposals according to how they nurture the emergence of selves able to creatively constitute themselves and their worlds out of the welter of plural and contradictory influences, how they facilitate the creation of communities that support and defend the development and extension of this subjectivity, and finally how they enhance the larger web of communities and the natural world on which all subjectivity is based. For feminist visions to be judged more adequate than competing visions, we need to explicate how they will, indeed, further this historical process.

Giving this content to our pragmatic norms is only a beginning. It leaves undetermined whether subjectivity and selfhood are primarily to be rendered in individualistic terms or more communal ones, to say nothing of questions concerning what kind of political, economic, cultural, and religious communities deserve our allegiance when these are our norms. These questions cannot be answered, I think, in general or for all time. Instead they require ongoing exploration in which differing proposals are aired; what makes sense for one historical moment or one particular locale may not make sense in another time or place. What appears to be liberating or inclusive to its proponents may well entail hidden privileging or exclusions that deal death to others.

Precisely because the content of pragmatic norms is not given but continually forged, it is imperative that full and open debate concerning them is pursued. These debates around the pragmatic adequacy of our visions will certainly take place within the boundaries of particular communities. However, I do not think that this should be the only locale for such discussion. The recognition that humans are multitraditioned and, hence, don't reside neatly within those confines, that traditions are not utterly impermeable to each other, and finally the growing awareness that our more local judgments reverberate for good or ill across an interconnected world—all suggest that wider debate, with all its problems, must also be developed.

This article has argued that essentialist notions of women's experience and nature, and of religious and secular traditions alike, have been unraveling. In their place have emerged historicist interpretations of subjectivity, identity, and traditions, including religious traditions. These historicist moves undercut any claims to privilege or easy assumptions of solidarity. In many ways they herald the loss of innocence, or more accurately an illusory innocence, as we confront the limited and ambiguous character of even our best efforts. But they have not, thereby, removed from us the possibility or responsibility of constructing and judging our visions and our practices. Freed from the quest for timeless truth, privileged experience, or even correlation with an authoritative past, this historicist turn has released feminist thought for the pragmatic task of forging new visions that we openly test in the widest arena possible. Finally, however, the form of feminist historicism taking shape here must acknowledge that, for either our more localized debates or these wider arenas of critical consideration to be sites of anything other than Rorty's choice between weapons and luck, feminists must recommit ourselves, not to a solidarity that is given, but one that is hoped and worked for; we must, from all our varied positions, renew our commitment to a radically democratic engagement that continually attends to and redresses historical and present inequalities of power, that seeks coalitions across lines of difference, and that sees our future, not as the repetition of the past, but in the bold if utterly fallible envisioning of new possibilities.

CHAPTER 13

Theorizing Feminist Theology

Rebecca S. Chopp

The preceding articles incorporate contemporary issues of feminist theory into feminist theology. In so doing these articles call into question the nature of feminist theology from within the contours of "feminism" itself. That these feminist theologians have incorporated the debates of feminist theory into feminist theology is important and promising. The importance of theory consists of its staging the problems and possibilities of politics, culture, and subjectivity. As Laura Levitt's article "Becoming an American Jewish Feminist" demonstrates, theory can help us to survive and transform ourselves and our contexts. Levitt's article constructs a narrative of remaking home after a rape and interplays this narrative with her own attempts to reconstruct the home of Jewish identity. As Levitt notes, theory "can enable us to explore the seams in the construction of our identities within the constraints of various social, cultural, and political configurations of power and desire." These articles self-consciously use theory for the sake of survival and transformation.

Following a debate on the problems of feminism and theory set forward in a book entitled *Feminist Contentions,* I will frequently invoke the notion of contentions in this article.[1] I use the term, as do the authors in the forenamed book, to indicate the intense debates around issues in current feminist theory. Like any good theory, feminist theory can be understood best through its sites of contentions, the fundamental principles around which debate centers. Feminist theory contains three major sites of contention: (1) the nature and status of the subject, (2) evaluative criteria and norms, and (3) the nature and status of the past.[2]

215

But I will also use the term in a way neither intended nor included in feminist theory. I want to employ the term *contentions* to challenge the contours of feminist theology done within the limits of feminist theory. This contentiousness will be invoked only in my conclusion and will seek to identify potential problems for theology if conceived within the limits of current feminist theory.

Before turning to the task of theorizing feminist theology, I want to be clear about the frame of reference of this article. Almost all of the articles in this book are written from the perspective of Christian feminist theology. There are two notable exceptions. The first is the article by Laura Levitt, and it is written from a Jewish perspective, among several other perspectives, or what Levitt will term identity/identities. The second is Janet Jakobsen's article, "The Body Politic vs. Lesbian Bodies," which is written from a feminist ethical perspective. I incorporate some of the points by both of these authors in my "mapping" of Christian feminist theology. But I do so aware, and with public acknowledgment, that Levitt and Jakobsen occupy decidedly distinct voices in this text.

The Need for a New Map

The history of feminist theology, at least in terms of theory, can be written in two distinct stages, or to use a spatial metaphor, by drawing two different maps. The temporal metaphor helps us identify a sense of historical frame, but the spatial metaphor allows us to see that quite different questions, issues, and ways of thinking define the two spaces of feminist theology. In the first stage or map, the theoretical assumptions of feminist theology were the ones shared by most "liberal" Protestant and Catholic theologians. These theoretical assumptions were also the assumptions of modern theory.

The modern theoretical assumptions, the ones that first-stage feminism largely shared, can be identified as operating through a three-point structure.[3] The first point entails the belief in a coherent self that has a fixed, essential structure. The second point contends that there is a true form of reason that can understand this essential structure of the subject as well as the essential structure of world. The third point in the modern theoretical structure combines the objective nature of reason and the fixed structure of existence to assert that history, culture, and language can be objectively explained and communicated clearly through language. Thus, modern theory understands itself as uncovering the foundations of existence, objectively stating them for the beneficial use of humankind, and communicating them through the translucent medium of language.

Sheila Davaney's article, "Continuing the Story, but Departing the Text," identifies how feminist theologians employed this modern theoretical structure. Davaney offers a four-point frame that includes the three points of the modern structure plus a fourth point linking the revelation of God's purpose to the purposes of feminist theology. The first point of this modern feminist theological frame assumes a common and universal character to women's experience. Though argued for in a variety of different ways by feminist theologians such as Rosemary Radford Ruether, Judith Plaskow, and Elisabeth Schüssler Fiorenza, the strategy was "to assert a universal and common essence that somehow defined women as women, and that laid the basis for feminist solidarity as well as providing the content for feminist reflection." The second point of modern feminist theology uses women's experience (the theoretical construction of experience) to provide a normative site for warrants and justifications. The third point interprets history, in this case Tradition, through an essential structure or core of meaning. So Rosemary Ruether could speak about a prophetic-liberating strand, while Letty Russell could find a liberating center, and Sallie McFague could seek a correlation between the contemporary situation and the core of Christianity. The fourth point of the modern theological frame, a point not found in feminist theory, identifies the feminist frame with God's revealed intent. (This divine foundationalism was common to all forms of modern theology!)

This map of feminist theology is rather identical, with one major addition, to the map of first-stage feminist theory and its correlation to modern theory. This three-point or four-point frame established the horizons and adjudicated the conflicts of modern thought, no matter what the discipline. In this stage, both feminist theory and feminist theology simply extended and stretched the modern frame to make it more equitable in its inclusion of women. In the horizon of how theology operated and adjudicated its claims, for example, Ruether's "foundational" moves were really no different than those of Karl Rahner, Paul Tillich, or H. Richard Niebuhr. The difference between Ruether and her male, modern counterparts had to do with whose experience became normative, whose forms of rationality provided the evaluative norm, and what material from the past got selected to form The Great Tradition. Neither Ruether nor Rahner differed from modern theorists in the framing of their theories, except in their insistence on resting the whole foundationalist enterprise in God's revelation as an epistemological correspondence between theory's aims and God's disclosure.

Some variations, of course, did occur within this modern frame. A radical intensification of this frame, say in a theologian such as Mary Daly, led to a kind of ontological-existential-political separatism. Another variation among feminist theologians consisted of the "romantic" feminists who followed feminist theorist Carol Gilligan and argued that women's different position contributed an important "balance" to the structures of church and world. Such variations would simply add more options to the same modern theoretical frame instead of calling its basic contours into question.

If the first stage or map of feminist theory and feminist theology covers the use of modern, foundationalist theory for the aims of feminism, the second stage or map plots the critique of modern theory and the ensuing journey between foundationalism and relativism. Questions about the contours of modern theory can be charted from many places, with the resulting sense that modern theory was displaced from all sides at once. African Americans, Hispanic Americans, lesbians, and others who could not or would not occupy the "subject" position of modern theory asked whose interests modern truth and power served. Those not represented in the dominant center questioned how their otherness had been constructed or rendered invisible. Poststructuralist theory uncovered the binary structure that regulated all meaning through oppositional thinking. The linguistic turn in many disciplines revealed that there is no transparency to language, that language itself is constantly changing, and that meaning has a rich plurivocity and, thus, ambiguity. In what thinkers such as Jane Flax and Seyla Benhabib call a "hard version" of postmodernism, modern theory was beset with the death of man, the death of metaphysics, and the death of history all at once. The feminist versions of these three deaths were the "Demystification of the Male Subject of Reason," the "Engendering of Historical Narrative," and "Feminist Skepticism toward the Claims of Transcendental Reason." Postmodern theologians added the death of God, and feminist theologians announced the "De-idolization of God as Sovereign Male."[4] These three (or four) deaths, so to speak, become the sites of contestation in feminist theory and feminist theology. What is contested is not so much the hard version of the end of the essential subject, universal criteria, and absolute history, but the ensuing possibilities for agency, emancipation, and the future. The second stage or map of feminist theory and feminist theology can be framed as a question: How can we avoid the problems of modern foundationalism without landing into a nihilistic state of relativism?

Site One: The Nature and Status of the Subject

Feminist theorists criticize from a variety of perspectives the notion of an essential, universal structure of the human subject. Feminism, as a cultural movement, had its initial impetus through a banner of women's equality that presumed a universal category of woman which included all women. But feminist theorists soon realized that there is no such thing as one structure of *woman*. Cross-culturally what is represented as woman can vary widely. And woman or gender cannot be separated from other constitutive factors such as race, class, and religion. All such representations of a common structure of woman inevitably reflect the experience and interests of those in power more than the experiences of all persons. Some feminist theorists may insist on the strategic importance of maintaining the category for political action, but very few feminist theorists espouse anything like an essential structure to the category of woman.

Though there is significant agreement in the opposition to the notion of a universal structure of woman, there is substantial disagreement about how to speak of the human *subject* in ways other than those implied in a universal structure. For the sake of this article, we can identify two foci of debate for the nature and status of the subject. The first focus raises the question: What is the subject? If the human subject is not secured behind or beyond history, then how is the subject constructed? How can one speak of her identity or what it means to be this particular person in this time or place? Is there an "I" that maintains some unity, be it an ontological "I" or a regulative idea? Or is the subject, to use Julia Kristeva's notion, a subject on trial, always in a process of conflict and contradiction?[5] Or do we speak of the subject in Judith Butler's sense, as performative, constituted through reiterated acts?[6] Joan Scott explains this particular focus on the subject: "It is not individuals who have experience, but subjects who are constituted through experience. Experience in this definition then becomes not the origin of our explanation, not the authoritative (because seen or felt) evidence that grounds that which is known, but rather that which we seek to explain, that about which knowledge is produced."[7]

The second focus asks about the usefulness of gender as a category for theory. How does the subject in gender or the gendered subject both deconstruct the universalizing of gender and work for change for women?

A related topic is the linkage of gender and body, and how various uses of gender privilege certain bodies and hide other bodies. The gendered body may relate to particular groups of women in quite different ways, so that a single theory of gender simply may not be accurate in even explanatory, let alone interpretive, power. Gender may be a quite problematic category if one is attempting to deconstruct the oppositional ordering of hetero-sexuality/homosexuality. But a theory of gender may be necessary if one is trying to understand current laws around rape in the United States. How do we employ the category to make sense of present structures of power and, at the same time, deconstruct the category so as to transform the way present structures require gender construction and regulation of gender?

To ask what is the subject and what is gender is to question the fun-damental terms of "feminist" theory and theology. It is, in some sense, to deconstruct the "natural" or commonsense categories on which feminism has been dependent. To employ Levitt's language, such questioning pushes at the seams. But push we must or the terms slip easily into hegemonic use; that is, the category of *women's experience* becomes a way to privilege white women, and the category of gender becomes a way to privilege heterosex-uality.

One of the difficulties of this site of contestation is how to be credible to human agency and social construction at the same time. How do we both recognize the social construction of subject and still respect the agency of the subject? Thus, Nancy Hartsock has wondered why at the time when women begin to assert themselves we question the notion of a subject.[8] We will return to this issue under the second site of evaluative cri-teria and the third site of history. For now, we can simply state the prob-lem in the following way: given the desire to turn to the historicized subject, how can we make normative claims of emancipation?

The debates around the subject, both in terms of the deconstruction of the modern subject, and the resultant problems and possibilities of the-orizing the subject and gender, comprise the major concern of our authors. In "Women's Experience between a Rock and a Hard Place," Serene Jones maps the various positions on the subject in contemporary Christian fem-inist theology. Jones divides feminist theologians in two groups: those that occupy the space of a rock and those that find themselves in a hard place. The rock signifies those feminist theologians utilizing universalist or ahis-torical claims to argue for an essential structure of woman's experience. The hard place identifies those employing some form of poststructuralism to argue for descriptions of historically localized and culturally specific groups of women. Jones adeptly demonstrates that there are a variety of ways to argue for or rely on the notion of some essential structure to woman's experience, referring to the works of Elizabeth Johnson, Catherine LaCugna, Catherine Keller, Delores Williams, and Sallie McFague. The hard place is represented both by cultural-anthropological accounts (Kathryn Tanner, Ada María Isasi-Díaz) and by poststructuralist accounts (Rebecca Chopp). The feminist theologians caught in this hard place use various historicized methods to emphasize the cultural construction of identity and language.

Now this map is quite odd for cartographers: who has heard of a map with only two places—especially those of a rock and a hard place? Does Jones not render the complexities by narrowing the positions on the map? Yet in so doing, she introduces a major concern of feminist theory into the center of nearly all feminist theologies: universal structures allow normative claims, while historicized methods provide a more credible view of reality but struggle to construct normative claims. Jones concludes that the way forward is the space her map has not explored, "the still-uncharted chasm which stretches between the rock and the hard place."

It is this territory that Linell Cady hopes to at least chart in her article, "Identity, Feminist Theory, and Theology." Cady identifies the debate around the nature and status of the subject as one in which modern (liberal) and postmodern feminism mirror each other. Modern feminism assumes a unified, homogenous subject while postmodernism accentuates the extreme of multiplicity and fragmentation. The destabilized subject of postmodern feminism cannot make normative judgments. Cady opts for a historicist perspective that rejects the "abstract, unified subject of modernism" by recognizing that identity is multiple, but limited in time. In Cady's words, "Identity is constituted by the subject's creative, agential negotiation of the intersecting currents and competing loyalties that run through her." Now Cady's definition of postmodernism is one, like Benhabib's, that many theorists will find an extreme version of relativism. Yet her historicist position, which in fact many would label postmodern, is an attempt to protect agency while it recognizes historical description.

Laura Levitt's article also draws a map beyond modern/postmodern, but this map is one of oceanic tides and changes rather than relatively fixed territory. Whereas Levitt is certainly sensitive to the agent's ability to continually construct identity, she is also acutely aware of how the subject is formed and determined through social structures, catastrophic events, and relationships. The language of interactive, intertwining, disparate experiences indicates the "strategy" of constructing a life. Levitt crafts a triple mirrored image of being raped in a liberal political state, being a feminist woman in Judaism, and being a Jew in the modern liberal state. Issues of race, theory, politics, furniture, friendships, Jewishness as a religion and culture, and sexism all refract against each other, allowing us to glimpse identity/ies as the "task of writing the self requires an ongoing critical engagement with others."

Mary McClintock Fulkerson offers yet a third way of interpreting the crisis of the subject. Rather than pose the discussion in terms of the modern/postmodern (objectivism versus relativism) problem of the subject, Fulkerson moves the question to focus on a way of thinking about gender that does not promote a hegemonic subject; in other words, a way of reconceiving the very *question* of the nature of the subject. Fulkerson relies on poststructuralism (distinguished from postmodernism), not as a constructive position in itself, but as a way to render problematic fundamental assumptions about gender, concluding that gender is a "moving category." Fulkerson then turns to linguistic theory to explore how language creates exclusions, including the exclusion that supports the binary logic of man and woman. For Fulkerson, the subject is neither an abstract universal nor a socially constructed self, but rather a function of a position within a system of differences.

By relocating the subject, and thus human agency, within the moving field of language, Fulkerson can explore the possibilities of the ongoing process of transformation.[9] For Fulkerson, transformation occurs in the process of knowing how to speak in contigual relations; that is, how to make the creative moves in a particular context of extending relations. In terms of the Christian narrative about the *imago Dei,* feminist theologians must continually explore who is being excluded, who is not included in the image of God.

Like Fulkerson, Paula Cooey is also concerned with how feminist theory and theology exclude certain subjects, in this case "bad" women. Cooey insists that we hear the voices of bad women, and through the process of including these voices, we understand the human subject as morally complex, as neither solely agent nor victim. Cooey demonstrates what Fulkerson argues: the gendered subject, from a theoretical and theological point of view, must perform the continually reflexive act of considering whom she is excluding.

Feminist theologians thus incorporate feminist theory's site of the subject in a variety of ways. Yet the "result," however one poses the prob-

lem, is that the subject will never be the universal, abstract subject by him-
self or her*self* again. The problem of how to find norms for emancipation
while being sensitive to historical context, a concern for almost all feminist theorists and, now, feminist theologians, moves us to the second site
of contestation.

Site Two : Evaluative Criteria and Norms

The second site of contestation in feminist theory covers the areas of
epistemology and rationality. Like other contemporary theorists, most
feminist theorists reject any kind of pure foundationalism. By foundationalism theorists mean the attempt to find a certain pure objective starting point and grounding point of all rationality and knowledge. Modern
rationality (in both its forms of empiricism and its rationalism) attempted
to provide an objective correlation of the order of consciousness and the
representations of the world outside of man's consciousness. In this model
reason is transcendental, language is transparent, and objective truth can
be guaranteed through indisputable norms and warrants. This foundationalism was criticized by the "masters of suspicion" such as Marx and
Freud who questioned the ideological and unconscious structures of
knowledge; by Nietzsche and others who criticized modern rationality as
domination; and by semioticians such as Charles Sanders Peirce and Ferdinand de Saussure who criticized the illusion that language is a translucent medium for truth. Feminist theorists tend to identify more with one
critique than the other, depending in part on their own theoretical tastes.
The debate among feminist theorists within this site of contention focuses
on how to avoid the specter of relativism once universal, abstract norms
and foundationalism are declared illusions and dominating practices. How
will evaluative criteria and norms be established? How can the emancipation of women, and of other persons, be both argued and guided?

Feminist theorists tend to respond to this threat of relativism in one
of three ways. First, some feminists return to the issue of universals and
seek to discover some regulative ideas not as certain, fixed truths but as
guiding practices, or quasi transcendentals, to mediate conversations. In
this position the focus on rationality provides a normative guide, especially
in intersubjective and public arenas. Seyla Benhabib, for instance, refor-
mulates Jürgen Habermas's theory to offer a kind of procedural analysis of
communicative interaction in order to provide validity claims.[10] This position, according to its critics, tends to overlook the particular and the

concrete in rationality, struggling to mediate particular embodied differences in situated contexts. Such theories with their universal claims tend to be used by those in dominant positions, raising again the question of power, interest, and knowledge.

A second type of response to the threat of relativism is offered by those theorists who opt for particular voices over any universal claim and concentrate on the ongoing exclusions of others. Judith Butler uses Foucault to construct a genealogical analysis of how common sense and norms are based on exclusion and oppression.[11] This position powerfully expresses how everyday life too often depends on repressive and oppressive practices. But this expression of the particular site of oppression and repression fails to provide adequate norms for the relations of power and interest in society. As Chandra Mohanty points out, this position fails to analyze the interconnections between various groups of persons.[12]

What I will call *pragmatism* comprises the third response to relativism. Within this position I locate those feminists seeking to find strategies of truth through either culturally situated communities or culturally complex traditions that can empower human flourishing. This position promises that we can combine theories for ultimate aims, but precisely because it is resistant to any metatheoretical frame it has difficulty describing specific criteria. Nancy Fraser, for instance, calls for an eclectic neo-pragmatism that is a tapestry of various theoretical perspectives.[13] This position reforms Theory into theories and hopes to use theories as successful tools for addressing particular conflicts.

Feminist theologians incorporate the critique of foundationalism not only from feminist theorists, but from other theologies as well. And, like feminist theorists, each feminist theologian articulates her critique from her own particular theoretical frame. In this volume, we see Cooey and Davaney utilize historicism and pragmatism, Jakobsen and Tanner employ poststructuralism, Fulkerson and Levitt engage linguistic theory, and Fulkerson and Tanner rely on neo-Marxist theory. Yet as our theologians envision ways to establish evaluative criteria and norms, there is an interesting agreement emerging in their position on the third option of pragmatism in feminist theory.[14] In the interest of space, I will treat only two articles in this volume, the two that directly address the site of evaluative criteria and norms, Janet Jakobsen's "The Body Politic vs. Lesbian Bodies" and Sheila Davaney's "Continuing the Story, but Departing the Text." In many ways these are different types of articles, but the strategy of how to deal with evaluative criteria can only be called pragmatic in both.

Jakobsen describes her article as not engaging in theology, but in the "associated discipline of ethics." Using her own narrative of being an out lesbian in a tenure-track position, Jakobsen introduces how the standard figuration of the body politic tokenizes and excludes the bodies of gays and lesbians. The category of sex carries an implicit norm regarding whose body is allowed in the body politic and how the body politic is represented. Against a position of universal norms such as Seyla Benhabib's, Jakobsen argues that the relation between the general and the specific must be called into question in cases where the general necessarily trumps or adjudicates the specific. Jakobsen locates norms in the networks among the different concrete representations. Since the general is an imagined site, Jakobsen asks, can we not reimagine a new way, a way of interconnections and interstices rather than a "general" that must necessarily exclude any concrete representation or group? Jakobsen combines a postmodern concern for exclusion with a pragmatic commitment to fallibility, engagement, and conversation. And, quite like Dewey, Jakobsen argues that the aesthetic is the basis of politics and logic, and the quest for reconstruction is, in part, a quest for new imagination, including a new imagination of the public.

Davaney's article, whose full title is "Continuing the Story, but Departing the Text: A Historicist Interpretation of Feminist Norms in Theology," is openly pragmatic in its conception of evaluative criteria and norms. Davaney argues that pragmatism "weaves a middle path between earlier essentialist notions and the deleterious postmodern dispersal of the self that renders notions of agency and identity meaningless." Or again in introducing her own constructive position, Davaney states that she hopes to indicate "one direction a historicist form of feminist theology might take, in order to avoid the twin dangers of ahistorical appeals to validity on the one hand, and, on the other hand, the surrender of assertions of greater adequacy." Signaling a pragmatic commitment to pluralism, experience, and reconstruction, Davaney argues for a return to experience but from a decidedly historicist perspective. Such a perspective must also apply to the multiplicity in and of traditions. Davaney argues for forming the norms in the present, "primarily in terms of the pragmatic repercussions that we anticipate might result from adopting one set of values and visions rather than another." Davaney concludes by arguing for the process of norm-making as an ongoing process.

The other articles follow, perhaps much more implicitly, a similar type of pragmatism. I should be clear that this is not Richard Rorty's pragmatism of easy conversation, but more the pragmatism of the classical American tradition of Peirce and Dewey, represented by contemporary thinkers such as Richard Bernstein and Nancy Fraser. By way of self-location, I inevitably see this through the lens of one who has rather consistently argued for pragmatism as the theory of evaluative criteria and norms in feminist theology.[15] Still, it is striking that given the variety of positions on the nature of the subject among our authors, there seems to be a quite productive agreement on evaluative criteria and norms. This productive agreement may well rest on a common struggle to live in, resist, and transform the metanarrative of history that informs Christian theology, that of The Tradition. This leads us to site three, which in feminist theory is the struggle over history and how to write history, and in feminist theology becomes the concern of how to live with and even use (T/t)radition.

Site Three: The Nature and Status of the Past

Feminist theorists have long resisted history as quite literally his-story. Where are women in the representations of history? Can we find women's history or her-story? In recent years the very notion of writing history has become a site of contestation. Can history ever be represented as a seamless whole, from a totally objective view?[16] Is history not always written in certain ways, to benefit those in power? The acceptance of Lyotard's observation about the loss of grand narratives underscores the recognition that the grand theories which account for everything from a God's-eye view are both oppressive and impossible. Neither liberalism nor Marxism nor Weberianism can ever really tell the full story of history!

One major implication of the end of writing history as a seamless whole, as a metanarrative, cannot be easily overlooked by feminist theorists. If the loss of metanarratives is true for theories such as liberalism and Marxism, it is also true for any grand theory of patriarchy. As a grand theory of history, patriarchy undergoes critique from at least two places. First, patriarchy as a grand theory privileges white women, since it interprets oppression through the lens of gender. Second, patriarchy as a grand theory represents a transhistorical category that cannot be sufficiently flexible or textured to account for historical particularities and differences in terms of gender.

The loss of a grand theory of patriarchy has led feminist theorists to consider what can hold feminism together for future political activity and how to construct views of the past in relation to gender. To this twofold question, feminists respond in a variety of ways. Some theorists call themselves postfeminists, arguing that feminism was itself a discursive effect of later modern liberalism. Some feminist theorists, such as Joan Scott, utilize poststructuralism to consider gender as a discursive construction, and utilize gender to understand how history is constructed and written through patterns of exclusion.[17] Still others focus on feminism as a strategic type of social history, analyzing how women in specific situations have resisted and subverted power. For feminist theologians this site of the nature and status of the past becomes focused on the construct of (T/t)radition. For Christian theologians, Tradition has long been accepted as authoritative because it is the recognized history of the past. Since this authoritative past has been handed down in the form of texts which construct some of the fundamental symbols of the religion through gender opposition and differences, feminist theologians have had to spend a great deal of energy and time on the (T/t)radition. As Laura Levitt's article indicates, there are other ways than a model of theology to conceive of one's history in religious terms, especially through the powerful metaphor of home.

It is important to consider the serious rethinking of (T/t)radition in Christian theology. For, as I have already indicated, the reliance on a common narrative or symbolic pattern may well be the reason feminist theologians turn to pragmatism as a resource to develop criteria and norms. Kathryn Tanner's article, "Social Theory concerning the 'New Social Movements' and the Practice of Feminist Theology," demonstrates how this site of contestation precipitates the issue of constructing tradition in light of the banishment of The Tradition. Tanner's way of constructing tradition, however, might be opposed by several of our other authors.

Rather than assuming any ahistorical narrative of Tradition, Tanner begins with a social theory of culture, derived from thinkers such as Gramsci and Foucault. Tanner explains that culture always involves power relations, and that cultural meanings and social institutions reinforce one another to form hegemonic relations. But as poststructuralist theories demonstrate, cultural forms are not fixed. Social movements such as feminism focus on struggles over "the meaning and articulations of those symbolic resources in which the operations of social institutions are highly invested." Located within the feminist movement, feminist theology participates in this broad social struggle over symbolic resources. This social theory allows Tanner to argue for the necessity of continued political struggle around the meaning and nature of Christian tradition. For Tanner all theology, as part of culture, is inevitably political, and thus every theology constructs "tradition" to argue for its own view in the politics of culture. Feminist theologians do not need to invent a new tradition, Tanner argues. Rather, feminist theologians must carefully judge what elements from all the past traditions will help the cause of their emancipatory struggle. For a construct of tradition to be authoritative, Tanner argues, it must not merely be *past* tradition, but it must be able to shape present Christian practice in appropriate ways. Though the tradition is necessary for giving an authorizing position, she multiplies tradition and grants it authority, not in itself, but in terms of its sufficient benefits for the present.

Tanner's position could, and I think would, be contested by other authors on two points. First, some theologians such as Linell Cady are not sure about the necessity, perhaps even priority, of a "traditions" model. Though Cady grants that a traditions model is legitimate for Christian theology, she is interested in the "look" of a theology that does not privilege a tradition. She grants that theologians are trained to be textualists and work within institutional constraints that often define a limit of "Christian," but she wonders about theology's attentiveness to multiple identities and social realities. As Cady maintains, "If the genre of theology were to be more reflective of the multiplicity that characterizes identity in contemporary, pluralistic cultures, then it must leave behind its rationalist mode that continues to reflect its authoritarian roots."

The second opposition to Tanner's position might come from Paula Cooey, who wonders if the "patriarchy" Tanner keeps referring to can be that easily separated from the rest of the elements of "tradition," even in the neotraditional way Tanner presents. Perhaps Tanner's belief that we can pick and choose doesn't take seriously enough the kind of fundamental good and evil structured into the very symbol system. Cooey would not have us read the texts of tradition to understand history, but the accounts of women, the silences of women, the news reports and interviews with women. In tradition, perhaps even multiplicatively understood, the silencing of moral ambiguity and the consistent effort to see women as evil may be too much a part of the story. Or to play on Davaney's title, perhaps we need to depart from the story, as well as the text.

To the notion that there must be a tradition, then, two objections might be made. First, do we need a Tradition to give us history? Second, does the Christian tradition need to radically deconstruct itself; is it just too intent on good and evil in morally simple ways? One might also ask if the reconstruction of tradition itself does not have certain symbolic limits?

Are there not certain limits to Christian narrative? Thinkers such as Tanner and Fulkerson would want to argue no; Cady and Cooey would answer yes.

Beyond Maps: Contesting Theory

While most of these articles by feminist theologians incorporate the perspectives and tools found within feminist theory, a few also raise caution about feminist theology defined within the limits of feminist theory. So I will conclude this article with an exception, an excess, and an exclusion in order to question theology within the limits of theory.

An exception. Catherine Keller's article, "Seeking and Sucking: On Relation and Essence in Feminist Theology," takes strong exception to how a great deal of feminist theory, especially that devoted to the critique of antiessentialism, gets used in feminist theology. Keller is not criticizing the use of theory per se; rather she is taking exception to how feminist theory is employed in theology. At one level Keller is asking the quite solid scholarly question: when we employ a theory to criticize one position, what unanticipated consequences come with the theory? On another level, Keller is taking a strong constructivist stance: feminism per se is about a global and earth-centered reality that is far beyond the anthropocentrism of much of current feminist theory. When epistemology becomes the fulcrum through which all theory and reality is read, Keller contends, far too much is excluded, including the important aspects of earlier feminist vision. Keller takes exception to how current feminist epistemological struggles threaten to sweep away both the real world in which we live and the real vision promised in feminism.[18] Perhaps rather than shrug off the global situation and the utopian vision of feminism, feminist theology might think even harder about the use of theory.

An excess. By excess I mean a use of theory that exceeds the three contentions outlined above and also exceeds, I think, the limits of current theory itself. This area has to do with the body, embodiment, and the relation of language and the body. In the Jakobsen article, we encounter the quest to reimagine the body politic differently, as composed of various bodies and diversity. Jakobsen's use of queer theory, including her critique of it, already exceeds much feminist theory in thinking about issues of the body. But Jakobsen's article must also be read as showing how body images and images of the body pervade theory itself. In Thandeka's article the turn to the embodied self is through historical resources, considering the different ways in which Winnicott, Kohut, and Schleiermacher argued for an embodied self. The article only suggests certain points that might be helpful for feminist theologians. Yet, as Thandeka indicates, the very need to recover an embodied self in feminist theology already reveals a major problem that current theory fails either to stage or to envision.[19] Feminist theory and feminist theology at present lack the necessary tools to address how the body moves into the imagination and into concepts, or as cognitive scientist and philosopher Mark Johnson puts it, the reality of the body in the mind.[20]

An exclusion (nearly). Perhaps this focus on the ambiguity, and yet obvious presence, of the body allows us to identify another issue within the body of Christian theology having to do with the symbolic language of God, Church, Christ, and so forth. Now in all fairness these authors were asked to bring feminist theory into theology. And feminist theory is almost carelessly atheological (in thinkers such as Kristeva, theology becomes the code insult for ill-informed and out-of-date modes of thought). To say it another way, feminist theory, in its modern and postmodern varieties, is quite devoted to the Enlightenment resistance to theology. To be fair, even some of the Christian feminist theologians in this volume indicate a similar disenchantment with or even resistance to theological symbols and theological doctrines.

Many of our authors are Christian theologians engaged, at some level, with the symbols of Christian practice and belief.[21] Yet the articles rarely mention the language or imagery of Christian symbols, let alone belief and practice. Where are any symbolic claims of God or constructive christological visions (even Keller's critique is, after all, a critique not of Christology per se, but of theories involved in Christology)?

In the dominant, even hegemonic stream of tradition, thinkers took theory into theology and addressed questions of norms, sources, and methods, but also used theory to transform theological symbols and visions. So God is transformed in Aquinas through Aristotle's doctrine of casuistry, even as Aquinas changes epistemological claims through Aristotle. Schleiermacher transforms not only how theology as theory is constructed in and through the nature of religious experience, but also the nature of Christology in and through God-consciousness as operative in a particular ecclesial community.

Sheila Briggs's article, "A History of Our Own: What Would a Feminist History of Theology Look Like?" can be read as offering resources for this theological task. Briggs contends that a feminist history of theology must not only represent voices of women, but ask about the gender coding of theology itself. Briggs argues that feminist history is a kind of archaeology of the gendering of doctrine, even when no mention of woman is apparent. Briggs employs the example of Chalcedon to demonstrate how Christ represents proper gender ordering of hierarchy between men and women, clerical and lay, the sovereign and his subjects, God and human. Now the article by Briggs does not indicate any kind of constructive theological stance but does indicate, I think, a way to use theory in the symbolics of theology both by examining how symbols are ordered through gender, or how they function, and by reinterpreting symbols through different gender codes, or as operating in symbolic systems other than gender. Mary McClintock Fulkerson's article, "Contesting the Gendered Subject: A Feminist Account of the *Imago Dei*," does use the theological symbol of *imago Dei* at least to suggest how theory might influence the substance as well as the form of a theological symbol.

I do not want to mount a strong critique against the theologians in this volume (including myself!), but simply to issue an invitation to take another step. Feminist theology need not merely accept the limits of feminist theory to define the sites of contestation and thus the substance of its reflection. How, for instance, can a feminist theory of multiple identities help us to transform a Christology from reflecting the essential structure of the subject to one constituting the diversity of bearing witness, a Christology perhaps more based in the multiplicity of the New Testament than in the unity of Chalcedon? Likewise, can rethinking how we imagine the body politic lead us also to imagine the body of Christ, not by focusing on and through the uniqueness of the individual or the romanticism of the community, but through the varied ways we embody difference and connection, past and present as well as future?

An exception, an excess, and an exclusion may well be interpreted as uncharted territories for the map of feminist theology to include, or around which it must be redrawn. These three questions of theology, falling within the limits of theory alone, are not the only questions, nor are they necessarily related as if providing together another stage or map for theology. Good theory should always open up new questions. As the articles in this volume amply demonstrate, feminist theory provokes important and enriching new questions for feminist theology.

NOTES

Chapter 1

1. The original group of scholars who committed themselves to participating in the conference and submitting articles for the volume was somewhat larger. Kwok Pui-lan, Shawn Copeland, and Susan Shapiro each had to withdraw close to the time of the conference. Jennifer Thompson participated in the meeting but was unable to contribute to the volume. These thinkers have offered significant contributions to current theoretical debates and were greatly missed.

2. The conference planners and participants were all exceedingly aware of the problematic nature of the category *feminist*. Many individuals and groups have chosen other self-designations. We continued to use the term because the thinkers represented in this volume still use it for themselves, even as they criticize its negative and problematic elements.

3. To say theoretical considerations have generally been missing from feminist theology is not to deny that some feminists have been engaging theory in other disciplines for some time. For example, see Elisabeth Schüssler Fiorenza, *But She Said: Feminist Practices of Biblical Interpretation* (Boston: Beacon Press, 1992). The recent formation of a group focused on feminist theology and theory in the American Academy of Religion is another indication of interest in these issues.

Chapter 2

1. Linda Alcoff, "Cultural Feminism versus Post-structuralism: The Identity Crisis in Feminist Theory," *Signs* 13, no. 3 (spring 1988): 407.

2. Iris Marion Young, *Justice and the Politics of Difference* (Princeton: Princeton University Press, 1990), 45.

3. The myth of liberalism construes the privatization of religion as an unambiguously positive emancipatory development essential to the establishment of a peaceful social order. This telling of the story, however, obscures the way in which this develop-

ment served the interests of the emerging modern state seeking to transfer ultimate loyalty from the church to the state. For an interesting exploration of this angle on the privatization of religion and the modern configuration of the public and private realm, see William T. Cavanaugh, "A Fire Strong Enough to Consume the House: The Wars of Religion and the Rise of the State," *Modern Theology* 11 (October 1995).

4. There is a growing body of literature that explores the gendered character of the public/private categorizations in liberalism. See, for example, Zillah Eisenstein, *The Radical Future of Liberal Feminism* (New York: Longman, 1981); Carol Pateman, "Feminist Critiques of the Public/Private Dichotomy," in *Public and Private in Social Life*, ed. S. I. Benn and G. F. Gaus (New York: St. Martin's Press, 1983), 281–303; and *Young, Justice and the Politics of Difference*.

5. Judith Grant, *Fundamental Feminism: Contesting the Core Concepts of Feminist Theory* (New York and London: Routledge, 1993).

6. See, for example, Carol Gilligan, *In a Different Voice: Psychological Theory and Women's Development* (Cambridge: Harvard University Press, 1982); Sara Ruddick, *Maternal Thinking: Toward a Politics of Peace* (Boston: Beacon Press, 1989); and Mary Field Belenky et al., *Women's Ways of Knowing: The Development of Self, Voice, and Mind* (New York: Basic Books, 1986).

7. Grant, *Fundamental Feminism*, 31.

8. bell hooks, *Feminist Theory: From Margin to Center* (Boston: South End Press, 1984), 18.

9. Ibid., 59.

10. Kenneth J. Gergen, *The Saturated Self: Dilemmas of Identity in Contemporary Life* (New York: Basic Books, 1991), xi.

11. E. Ann Kaplan, *Rocking around the Clock: Music Television, Postmodernism, and Consumer Culture* (New York: Methuen, 1987), 63.

12. Fredric Jameson, "Postmodernism and Consumer Society," in *The Anti-Aesthetic: Essays in Postmodern Culture*, ed. Hal Foster (Port Townsend, Wash.: Bay Press, 1983), 159, quoted in Kaplan, *Rocking around the Clock*, 146.

13. See, for example, Alcoff, "Cultural Feminism versus Post-structuralism"; bell hooks, *Yearning: Race, Gender, and Cultural Politics* (Boston: South End Press, 1990); Jane Flax, *Disputed Subjects* (New York: Routledge, 1993); Susan Bordo, "Feminism, Postmodernism, and Gender Scepticism," in *Feminism/Postmodernism*, ed. Linda Nicholson (New York: Routledge, 1990); Susan Bordo, *Unbearable Weight: Feminism, Western Culture, and the Body* (Berkeley: University of California Press, 1993); Biddy Martin and Chandra Talpade Mohanty, "Feminist Politics: What's Home Got to Do with It?" in *Feminist Studies, Critical Studies*, ed. Teresa de Lauretis (Bloomington: Indiana University Press, 1986); Teresa de Lauretis, *Alice Doesn't: Feminism, Semiotics, Cinema* (Bloomington: Indiana University Press, 1984); and Elly Bulkin, Minnie Bruce Pratt, and Barbara Smith, *Yours in Struggle* (New York: Long Haul Press, 1984).

14. Judith Butler, *Gender Trouble: Feminism and the Subversion of Identity* (New York and London: Routledge, 1990), 3.

15. Alcoff, "Cultural Feminism versus Post-structuralism," 420.

16. Cornel West, "Black Women and Men: Partnership in the 1990's: A Dialogue between bell hooks and Cornel West," in hooks, *Yearning*, 204.

17. B. Honig, "Arendt and the Politics of Identity," in *Feminists Theorize the Political*, ed. Judith Butler and Joan Scott (New York: Routledge, 1992), 220.

18. Ibid.

19. George Lipsitz, *Time Passages: Collective Memory and American Popular Culture* (Minneapolis: University of Minnesota Press, 1990), 34.

20. Hans Mol, *Identity and the Sacred* (New York: Free Press, 1986), 58. For an informative overview of the transformations in the formation of identity in the past few hundred years in the West, see Roy Baumeister, *Identity: Cultural Change and the Struggle for Self* (New York: Oxford University Press, 1986).

21. George Lindbeck, *The Nature of Doctrine: Religion and Theology in a Postliberal Age* (Philadelphia: Westminster Press, 1984), 21.

22. For a very readable account of the failure of feminism to speak for or to many women, see Elizabeth Fox-Genovese, *"Feminism Is Not the Story of My Life": How Today's Feminist Elite Has Lost Touch with the Real Concerns of Women* (New York: Doubleday, 1996).

23. Linell E. Cady, *Religion, Theology, and American Public Life* (Albany: State University of New York Press, 1993).

24. Delwin Brown, "Believing Traditions and the Academic Theologian," *Journal of the American Academy of Religion* 62 (winter 1994): 1169.

25. Van Harvey argues that the failure of theologians to attend to the lived world is a result of the professionalization of theological education and development of the seminary curriculum. See "On the Intellectual Marginality of American Theology," in *Religion and Twentieth-Century American Intellectual Life,* ed. Michael J. Lacey (New York: Cambridge University Press, 1989).

26. Seyla Benhabib, *Critique, Norm, and Utopia: A Study of the Foundations of Critical Theory* (New York: Columbia University Press, 1986), 9.

27. Ibid., 13.

28. Robert B. Reich, *The Work of Nations* (New York: Alfred A. Knopf, 1991).

29. Robert Booth Fowler, *Unconventional Partners: Religion and Liberal Culture in the United States* (Grand Rapids, Mich.: Eerdmans, 1989).

Chapter 3

1. Elizabeth Johnson, *She Who Is: The Mystery of God in Feminist Theological Discourse* (New York: Crossroad, 1992).

2. Catherine Mowry LaCugna, *God for Us: The Trinity and Christian Life* (New York: HarperCollins, 1991).

3. Johnson, *She Who Is,* 1–10.

4. Ibid.

5. LaCugna, *God for Us.*

6. Ibid., 288–92.

7. Rita Nakashima Brock, *Journeys by Heart: A Christology of Erotic Power* (New York: Crossroad, 1988).

8. Catherine Keller, *From a Broken Web: Separation, Sexism, and Self* (Boston: Beacon Press, 1986).

9. Delores Williams, *Sisters in the Wilderness: The Challenge of Womanist God-Talk* (Maryknoll, N.Y.: Orbis Books, 1993).

10. Sallie McFague, *The Body of God: An Ecological Theology* (Minneapolis: Fortress Press, 1991).

11. Kathryn Tanner, *The Politics of God: Christian Theologies and Social Justice* (Minneapolis: Fortress Press, 1992).

12. Ada María Isasi-Díaz, *En la Lucha: Elaborating a Mujerista Theology* (Minneapolis: Fortress Press, 1993).

13. Mary McClintock Fulkerson, *Changing the Subject: Women's Discourses and Feminist Theology* (Minneapolis: Fortress Press, 1994).

14. Susan Thistlethwaite, *Sex, Race, and God: Christian Feminism in Black and White* (New York: Crossroad, 1991).

15. Emilie Townes, *Womanist Justice, Womanist Hope* (Atlanta: Scholars Press, 1993).

16. Rebecca S. Chopp, *The Power to Speak: Feminism, Lanugage, God* (New York: Crossroad, 1991).

Chapter 4

1. Annewies Van De Bunt, "Milk and Honey in the Theology of Clement of Alexandria," in *Fides Sacramenti Sacramentum Fidei: Studies in Honour of Pieter Smulders* (Assen, the Netherlands: Van Gorcum, 1981), 27–30. I am indebted to my colleague Virginia Burrus for opening for me this textual tradition.

2. Clement of Alexandria, *The Instructor* (*Pedagogus*), vol. 2, bk. 1, chap. 6 in *The Ante-Nicene Fathers,* ed. Alexander Roberts and James Donaldson, reprint edition (Grand Rapids, Mich.: Eerdmans, 1983), 221. This translation reads: "Hence seeking is called sucking; for to those babes that seek the Word, the Father's breasts of love supply milk."

3. Hippolytus, *Trad. Apost.* 21, quoted in Van De Bunt, "Milk and Honey," 28.

4. Virginia Burrus has highlighted the significance of the fourth-century shift from a logos- to a Son-centered Christology. The emergence of a Son-centered Christology is closely linked with the "new" fourth-century emphasis on the Fatherhood of God, as traced by Peter Widdicome, *The Fatherhood of God from Origen to Athanasius* (Oxford: Clarendon Press, 1994); Virginia Burrus offers a feminist analysis of the same theme in "Fecund Fathers: Heresy, the Grotesque, and Male Generativity in Gregory of Nyssa's *Contra Eunomium I*" (unpublished essay).

5. Mary Daly, *Pure Lust: Elemental Feminist Philosophy* (New York: HarperCollins, 1984), 341 (see note at bottom of page).

6. Teresa de Lauretis, "Feminist Studies/Critical Studies: Issues, Terms, and Contexts," in *Feminist Studies, Critical Studies* (Bloomington: Indiana University Press, 1986), 9.

7. Judith Butler, *Gender Trouble: Feminism and the Subversion of Identity* (New York and London: Routledge, 1990).

8. Susan Bordo, "Feminism, Postmodernism and Gender-Skepticism," in *Feminism/Postmodernism,* ed. Linda J. Nicholson (New York and London: Routledge, 1990), 133-56.

9. Carol Gilligan, *In a Different Voice: Psychological Theory and Women's Development* (Cambridge: Harvard University Press, 1982).

10. Nancy Chodorow, *The Reproduction of Mothering: Psychoanalysis and the Sociology of Gender* (Berkeley: University of California Press, 1978).

11. Jean Baker Miller, *Women's Growth in Connection: Writings from the Stone Center,* with Judith V. Jordan, Alexandra Kaplan, Irene Stiver, and Janet Surrey (New York and London: Guilford Press, 1991).

12. Rita Nakashima Brock, *Journeys by Heart: A Christology of Erotic Power* (New York: Crossroad, 1994); and Catherine Keller, *From a Broken Web: Separation, Sexism, and the Self* (Boston: Beacon Press, 1986).

13. Bordo, "Feminism, Postmodernism," 146–53.

14. Iris Marion Young, *Justice and the Politics of Difference* (Princeton: Princeton University Press, 1990). See chap. 8, "City Life and Difference."

15. Seyla Benhabib, *Situating the Self: Gender, Community, and Postmodernism in Contemporary Ethics* (New York: Routledge, 1992).

16. John B. Cobb Jr. and Herman Daly, "Misplaced Concreteness: *Homo Economicus,*" chap. 4 in *For the Common Good: Redirecting the Economy toward Community, the Environment, and a Sustainable Future* (Boston: Beacon Press, 1989).

17. Julia Kristeva, interview by Alice Jardine, in *Discourses: Conversations in Postmodern Art and Culture,* ed. Russell Ferguson et al. (Cambridge: MIT Press, 1990), 84.

18. Catherine Keller, "The Breast, the Apocalypse, and the Colonial Journey," *Journal of Feminist Studies in Religion* 10 (spring 1994): 63.

19. David Harvey, *The Condition of Postmodernity* (Cambridge, Mass.: Blackwell, 1989); and Fredric Jameson, *Postmodernism, or, the Cultural Logic of Late Capitalism* (Durham, N.C.: Duke University Press, 1991).

20. Harvey, *Condition of Postmodernity,* 117.

21. Gayatri Spivak, *Outside in the Teaching Machine* (New York and London: Routledge, 1993), 57.

22. Gayatri Spivak, "In a Word: Interview," interview by Ellen Rooney, in *The Essential Difference,* ed. Naomi Schor and Elizabeth Weed (Bloomington: Indiana University Press, 1994), 155.

23. Since in the United States those receiving French theory were largely literary critics, generally innocent of other philosophical schemes, they tended to embrace it as the only "theory" and certainly the only meaningful antiessentialism. Thus they routinely perpetrate an odd essentialism themselves—identifying positions as essentialist, with no philosophical knowledge of what an essence is and therefore what it is not, and making a simplistic identification of any metaphysical description, ontology, cosmology, or epistemology as ipso facto "essentialist." Fortunately the development of a generation of poststructuralist feminist philosophers here has enabled a subtle and strong counter-critique, as evidenced by Schor and Weed, *The Essential Difference.*

24. Audre Lorde, *Sister Outsider* (Trumansburg, N.Y.: Crossing Press, 1984), 115.

25. Whitehead, Heidegger, and Sartre had each elaborated critiques of essentialism, and among antiessentialists today one can find relationalists as well as their opponents.

26. C. W. Maggie Kim, Susan M. St. Ville, and Susan M. Simonaitis, *Transfigurations: Theology and the French Feminists* (Minneapolis: Fortress Press, 1993).

27. Elisabeth Schüssler Fiorenza, *Jesus: Miriam's Child, Sophia's Prophet: Critical Issues in Feminist Christology* (New York: Continuum, 1994), 55.

28. Cathie Kelsey, "Feminist Reconstructions of Christology" (research paper, prepared for Harvard Divinity School colloquium, "Religion, Gender, and Culture," spring 1992), quoted in Schüssler Fiorenza, *Jesus*, 55.

29. Luce Irigaray, "Body against Body: In Relation to the Mother," in *Sexes and Genealogies*, trans. Gillian C. Gill (New York: Columbia University Press, 1993), 19.

30. Clement of Alexandria, "A Hymn to Christ the Saviour" (translation), bk. 3 of *The Instructor* (*Pedagogus*), in *The Ante-Nicene Fathers*, 296.

31. Ibid.

32. Ode 19, vv. 2–3, in *The Odes of Solomon*, edited and translated by James Charlesworth (Oxford: Clarendon Press, 1973), 82.

Chapter 5

1. Wilhelm Dilthey's phenomenological analysis of the human body has greatly influenced my own discussion of the human body in this article. See, for instance, *Wilhelm Dilthey: Selected Works*, vol. 1 (Princeton: Princeton University Press, 1989), 268.

2. I am in basic agreement with the claim made by Ann and Barry Ulanov in their book *Religion and the Unconscious* (Philadelphia: Westminster Press, 1975), that "primordial experience is the means by which we live and understand the primordial elements of being. In it we encounter directly the original strata of human life." Here, depth psychology and theology find common ground (14). As Jungians, they use Jung's theory, image, and theoretical construct of anima/animus as "maps to orient our lived experience" of this primordial ground (*Transforming Sexuality: The Archetypal World of Anima and Animus* [Boston: Shambhala, 1994], 4). For them, Jung's theory occupies a place on par with Heinz Kohut's self, which precedes experiences of instinctual drives. For them the Self is the center of the whole psyche, and the anima and animus are road maps to this center (*Transforming Sexuality*, 10). My investigation of the Self follows the contours of a different map. As this article will demonstrate, my work has been greatly influenced by the shift from instinct to affectivity in contemporary intersubjective psychoanalytic theory when explaining the basis for the dynamic unconscious.

Intersubjectivists Robert D. Stolorow and George E. Atwood, for instance, contend in their book, *Contexts of Being: The Intersubjective Foundations of Psychological Life* (Hillsdale, N.J.: Analytic Press, 1992), that this shift in explanations of the dynamic unconscious "is not merely a change in terminology." Rather, the very way in which the apparent boundary between conscious and unconscious is conceived must be changed. The boundary is always a product of a specific intersubjective context: "The regulation of affective experience is a property of the child-caregiver system of reciprocal mutual influence." In this article, I shall explore interaffectivity as the "dark core" of this mutual caregiver system from both a theoretical and a theological intersubjective perspective. One should note, however, that *both* the Jungian and intersubjective maps lead to the same place: our primordial experiences of the "inner other" (Ulanov, *Transforming Sexuality*, 9).

3. Maurice Merleau-Ponty, *Themes from the Lectures at the Collège de France, 1952–1960*, trans. John O'Neill (Evanston, Ill.: Northwestern University Press, 1970), 93. To elucidate this point, Merleau-Ponty refers to quantum physicist Niels Bohr's remark that "it is no accident that there is a harmony between descriptions of psychol-

ogy (we would say, of phenomenology) and the conceptions of contemporary physics. Moreover, the classical criticism of the perceived universe is bound to a mechanistic psycho-physiology which can no longer be retained as such at a time when scientists are throwing doubt upon mechanistic metaphysics" (93–94).

4. Sheila Greeve Davaney, "Problems with Feminist Theology: Historicity and the Search for Sure Foundations," in *Embodied Love: Sensuality and Relationship as Feminist Values,* ed. Paula M. Cooey, Sharon A. Framer, and Mary Ellen Ross (San Francisco: Harper & Row, 1987).

5. Judith Plaskow, "Toward a New Theology of Sexuality," chap. 5 in *Standing Again at Sinai: Judaism from a Feminist Perspective* (San Francisco: Harper & Row, 1990); Carter Heyward, *Touching Our Strength: The Erotic Power and the Love of God* (San Francisco: Harper & Row, 1989); Audre Lorde, "Uses of the Erotic: The Erotic as Power," in *Weaving the Visions: New Patterns in Feminist Spirituality,* ed. Judith Plaskow and Carol P. Christ (San Francisco: Harper & Row, 1989); Rita Nakashima Brock, *Journeys by Heart: A Christology of Erotic Power* (New York: Crossroad, 1988); as well as James B. Nelson, *Embodiment: An Approach to Sexuality and Christian Theology* (Minneapolis: Augsburg Publishing House, 1978), are only a few of the examples of contemporary embodied theologies of sexuality.

6. Sallie McFague, *The Body of God: An Ecological Theology* (Minneapolis: Fortress Press, 1993), is a case in point.

7. Catherine Keller, *From a Broken Web: Separation, Sexism, and Self* (Boston: Beacon Press, 1986), is a fine example of feminist process theology. Marjorie Hewitt Suchocki, *The Fall to Violence: Original Sin and Relational Theology* (New York: Continuum, 1995), is a vivid, feminist process theodicy in which sin is defined as "first and foremost a rebellion against creation" (16). As such, sin is "not a contained act, but an extended event in an interdependent world" (45).

8. The black woman's embodied experience is of central concern to womanist thought. Delores S. Williams, for example, in *Sisters in the Wilderness: The Challenge of Womanist God-Talk* (Maryknoll, N.Y.: Orbis Books, 1993), develops her theology of the wilderness experience as a response to her "encounter with Hagar again and again in African-American sources." Williams notes that black American women "had emerged from a slave heritage and still lived in light of it." Thus they were like Hagar, who "had no control over her body. It belonged to her slave owner, whose husband, Abraham, ravished Hagar" (93). Katie Geneva Cannon suggests that the title of her essay, "Katie's Canon," which is also the title of her book, identifies "the critical contestable issues at the center of Black life—issues inscribed on the bodies of Black People" (*Katie's Canon: Womanism and the Soul of the Black Community* [New York: Continuum, 1995], 70); see also Toni Morrison, introduction to *Race-ing Justice, En-gendering Power: Essays on Anita Hill, Clarence Thomas, and the Construction of Social Reality* (New York: Pantheon, 1992), x. Jacquelyn Grant, in *White Women's Christ and Black Women's Jesus: Feminist Christology and Womanist Response* (Atlanta: Scholars Press, 1989), argues that "the significance of Christ [for black women] is not his maleness, but his humanity. The most significant events of Jesus Christ were the life and ministry, the crucifixion, and the resurrection. The significance of these events, in one sense, is that in them the absolute becomes concrete" (220). According to Grant, black women, in this way, are the concrete: They represent the "embodiment" of racism, sexism, and classism and, as such,

"their very embodiment represents a challenge to White women" whose gender-based focus on oppression lacks "a holistic analysis" (221).

9. See notes 2 and 3 for a discussion of this perspective as well as my definition and discussion, immediately below, of the embodied self as an intersubjective description of the self. For a rigorous account of the human body from a Jungian perspective, see Ulanov, *Transforming Sexuality.*

10. See Margaret R. Miles, *Carnal Knowing: Female Nakedness and Religious Meaning in the West* (Boston: Beacon Press, 1989), 185.

11. The theme of the "ambiguity of the body" as both site and sign for human knowledge is developed in Paula M. Cooey, *Religious Imagination and the Body: A Feminist Analysis* (New York: Oxford University Press, 1994). I have replaced the term *body* with *embodiment* to emphasize that body and mind, self and other, are always co-related and thus correlated in every moment of human knowledge and experience.

12. In this regard, my theory is in basic agreement with the positive assessment and emendations of standpoint epistemologies by Lorraine Code in her essay, "Taking Subjectivity into Account," in *Feminist Epistemologies,* ed. L. Alcoff and E. Potter (New York: Routledge, 1993).

13. As intersubjective psychoanalytic theorists Stolorow and Atwood have suggested, an intersubjective perspective on human experience entails the "concept of an intersubjective system [which] brings to focus *both* the individual's world of inner experience *and* its embeddedness with other such worlds in a continual flow of reciprocal mutual influence. From this perspective, the gap between the intrapsychic and interpersonal realms is closed, and indeed, the old dichotomy between them is rendered obsolete" (*Contexts of Being,* 18).

14. "Any system," as intersubjectivist psychoanalytic theorist Maxwell S. Sucharov notes, "that is characterized by the indivisibility of observer and observed is a quantum system and is part of a quantum domain of investigation." See "Psychoanalysis, Self Psychology, and Intersubjectivity," in *The Intersubjective Perspective,* ed. Robert D. Stolorow, George E. Atwood, and Bernard Brandchaft (London: Janson Aronson, 1994), 193.

15. See Heinz Kohut, *Restoration of the Self* (Madison, Wis.: International Universities Press, 1977), 31–32.

16. For a recent discussion of John 1:14 in the context of embodiment theologies, see Sallie McFague, "Christology: The Body of God," in *The Body of God;* and James B. Nelson, preface and chap. 2, "Embodiment in Sexual Theology," in *Embodiment: An Approach to Sexuality and Christian Theology* (Minneapolis: Augsburg Publishing House, 1978).

17. G. W. F. Hegel, *Lectures on the Philosophy of World History: Introduction,* trans. B. Nisbet (Cambridge: Cambridge University Press, 1975), 51. Robert R. Williams, in *Recognition: Fichte and Hegel on the Other* (Albany: State University of New York Press, 1992), analyzes Hegel's "triadic-trinitarian" language in an admirable attempt to make a clear distinction between Hegel's logical, transcendental philosophy and his socially embedded intersubjective, phenomenological standpoint. Williams rightly argues that "Hegel's self-differentiating holism must include both identity and difference. As such, difference and the other cannot be eliminated, because these are the ordering and structuring principles of the whole" (270). Williams acknowledges, however, that Hegel's sys-

tem requires a "threefold mediation." The use of a mediating third to express both identity and difference, as we shall see, is the problem that a Hegelian dialectic cannot resolve.

18. Hegel, *Lectures,* 51.

19. G. W. F. Hegel, *Hegel's Science of Logic,* trans. A. V. Miller (Atlantic Highlands, N.J.: Humanities Press International, 1969), 50.

20. See my book *The Embodied Self: Friedrich Schleiermacher's Solution to Kant's Problem of the Empirical Self* (Albany: State University of New York Press, 1995), 112.

21. See, for instance, Alexandre Kojève, *Introduction to the Reading of Hegel: Lectures on the Phenomenology of Spirit,* ed. Allan Bloom, assembled by Raymond Queneau, trans. James H. Nichols Jr. (New York: Basic Books, 1969). For a discussion of the ambiguous nature of Hegel's success, see Williams, *Recognition.*

22. See Dieter Henrich's essay, "Fichtes ursprüngliche Einsicht," for a discussion and analysis of Fichte's discovery and attempt to resolve this problematic gap in Kant's work. English translation by David R. Lachterman, "Fichte's Original Insight," in *Contemporary German Philosophy I* (University Park: Pennsylvania State University Press, 1982). For a vivid delineation of the nature and structure of the gap in Kant's critical theory, see Eckart Förster, "Is There a 'Gap' in Kant's Critical System?" *Journal of the History of Philosophy* 25 (October 1987).

23. See Mark C. Taylor, *Erring: A Postmodern A/theology* (Chicago: University of Chicago Press, 1984), 15.

24. Jacques Derrida's claim that "we will never be finished with the reading and rereading of Hegel, and, in a certain way, I do nothing other than attempt to explain myself on this point" is very much on target. (Quoted in Taylor, *Errings,* 5. See Jacques Derrida, *Positions,* trans. A. Bass [Chicago: University of Chicago Press, 1981], 77.) Taylor suggests that nowhere have the insights of Hegel, along with Kierkegaard and Nietzsche, been more thoroughly absorbed and reworked than in deconstruction (5).

25. Taylor, *Erring,* 15.

26. See Richard Crouter, "Hegel and Schleiermacher at Berlin: A Many-Sided Debate," in *Journal of the American Academy of Religion* 48 (1980), for an apt summary of this controversy.

27. Thandeka, *The Embodied Self.*

28. As Richard R. Niebuhr notes, feeling, from Schleiermacher's standpoint, "is the medium through which life communicates itself to each person" ("Christ, Nature, and Consciousness: Reflections on Schleiermacher in Light of Barth's Early Criticisms," in *Barth and Schleiermacher: Beyond the Impasse?* ed. James O. Duke and Robert F. Streetman [Philadelphia: Fortress Press, 1988], 39).

29. Karl Barth, *Protestant Thought: From Rousseau to Ritschl* (New York: Harper, 1959), 341–54.

30. See Karl Barth, "The Christian Faith," in *The Theology of Schleiermacher: Lectures at Göttingen, Winter Semester of 1923–24,* ed. Dietrich Ritschl, trans. Geoffrey W. Bromiley (Grands Rapids, Mich.: Eerdmans, 1982).

31. Ibid.

32. Barth, *Protestant Thought,* 340. For an extended discussion of this position, see Barth, *Theology of Schleiermacher.*

33. Barth, *Protestant Thought,* 339–40.

34. Barth, of course, did not accuse Schleiermacher of heresy. Quite the contrary. As Barth said in discussions with Terrence N. Tice from 1959 to 1965, "More and more I tried to be a loving student and not an enemy [of Schleiermacher]. I always accepted him within the *communio sanctorum,* not as a heretic. True there is more formal than material agreement. . . . My own theology may be looked upon as a complete reversal of his" ("Interviews with Karl Barth and Reflections on His Interpretations of Schleiermacher," interview by Terrence N. Tice, in Duke and Streetman, *Barth and Schleiermacher*). According to Barth, there is "no true theology of the Holy Spirit" in Schleiermacher's work (Barth, *Protestant Thought,* 352). Schleiermacher's "good will" (352) prevented his work from dissolving the Word. Accordingly, I use the term *heresy* to refer to Barth's assessment, not of *Schleiermacher,* but of the implications implicit in Schleiermacher's theology of human awareness, which Barth felt "in all seriousness threatened . . . this dissolution [of the Word]" (353).

35. Peter Dews, in *Logics of Disintegration: Post-structuralist Thought and the Claims of Critical Theory* (London: Vesco, 1987), for instance, suggests that "the problem becomes one of explaining why Derrida remains so determined to prevent any contamination between the empirical and the transcendental" (18).

36. See Dews, *Logics of Disintegration,* for a fine analysis of the hidden assumptions that continue speculative philosophical traditions that the work of such thinkers as Derrida, Lacan, and Foucault are ostensibly designed to critique.

37. As a/theologian Mark C. Taylor says in describing his own predicament as a postmodernist:

> Postmodernism opens with the sense of *irrevocable* loss and *incurable* fault. This wound is inflicted by the overwhelming awareness of death—a death that "begins" with the death of God and "ends" with the death of our selves. We are in a time between times and a place which is no place. Here our reflection must "begin." In this liminal time and space, deconstructive philosophy and criticism offer rich, though still largely untapped, resources for religious reflection. One of the distinct features of deconstruction is its willingness to confront the problem of the death of God squarely even if not always directly. (*Erring,* 6)

38. As Freud once wrote: "However philosophy may bridge the gap between physical and mental, it still exists for practical purposes, and our practice on each side of it must differ accordingly." This citation (without reference) was used by Richard A. Shweder, professor of human development at the University of Chicago, in his op-ed article, "It's Time to Reinvent Freud," *New York Times,* 15 December 1995, sec. A, p. 43.

39. The work of the psychoanalytic theoretician Luce Irigaray is a case in point. Irigaray theorizes our identity as sexual from the position of the source of our exploitation: sexual difference. As a philosopher, she marks this identity in the history of human consciousness as the postmodern woman's self-induced French kiss. Difference rather than unity is affirmed. Writes Irigaray in her book, *je, tu, nous: Toward a Culture of Difference* (New York: Routledge, 1993): "Equality between men and women cannot be achieved without a theory of gender as sexed and a rewriting of the rights and obligations of each sex, qua different, in social rights and obligations" (13).

40. Cooey, *Religious Imagination,* 45.

41. Jonathan Z. Smith, *Map Is Not Territory: Studies in the History of Religions* (Leiden: E. J. Brill, 1978), 291.

42. D. W. Winnicott, *Playing and Reality* (London: Tavistock/Routledge, 1971), 2.

43. Marion Milner, "The Role of Illusion in Symbol Formation," in *Transitional Objects and Potential Spaces: Literary Uses of D. W. Winnicott* (New York: Columbia University Press, 1993), 24.

44. Winnicott, *Playing and Reality,* 11.

45. Jessica Benjamin, "Recognition and Destruction: An Outline of Intersubjectivity," in *Relational Perspectives in Psychoanalysis,* ed. Neil J. Skolnick and Susan C. Warshaw (Hillsdale, N.J.: Analytic Press, 1992), 51.

46. Thomas H. Ogden, *The Matrix of the Mind: Object Relations and the Psychoanalytic Dialogue* (Northvale, N.J.: Jason Aronson, 1986).

47. Benjamin, "Recognition and Destruction," 56–57.

48. D. W. Winnicott, *Home Is Where We Start From: Essays by a Psychoanalyst,* ed. Clare Winnicott, Ray Shepherd, and Madeleine Davis (New York: W. W. Norton, 1986), 92.

49. Dilthey, *Selected Works,* 282.

50. Ibid.

51. Ibid.

52. Ulanov, *Transforming Sexuality,* 224–25.

53. Winnicott, *Playing and Reality,* 13.

54. Robert Jay Lifton, *The Protean Self: Human Resilience in an Age of Fragmentation* (New York: Basic Books, 1993), 26.

55. To emphasize the mutuality and reciprocal nature of this relationship, Stolorow and Atwood refer to this unit as a "self-selfobject/selfobject-self relationship" in *Contexts of Being* (4).

56. Daniel N. Stern, *The Interpersonal World of the Infant: A View from Psychoanalysis and Developmental Psychology* (New York: Basic Books, 1985), 145.

57. Ibid., 26–27.

58. Ibid., 27.

59. Benjamin, "Recognition and Destruction," 48.

60. Ibid., 186.

61. Ibid.

62. Ibid., 188.

63. Stern, *Interpersonal World,* 145.

64. Heinz Kohut, *How Does Psychoanalysis Cure?* (Chicago: University of Chicago Press, 1984), 37.

65. Stolorow and Atwood, *Contexts of Being,* 30.

66. Friedrich Schleiermacher, *On Religion: Speeches to Its Cultured Despisers,* trans. John Oman (Louisville: Westminster/John Knox Press, 1994), 43.

67. Summarizing this standpoint, Richard R. Niebuhr has suggested that, for Schleiermacher, "Consciousness has no life of its own apart from the larger whole in which it exists" ("Christ, Nature, and Consciousness," 39).

68. Thandeka, "Schleiermacher's *Dialektik:* The Discovery of the Self That Kant Lost," *Harvard Theological Review* 85 (1992): 439–40.

69. Friedrich Schleiermacher, *Dialektik*, in *Schleiermachers sämmtliche Werke*, 3,1.29, ed. Ludwig Jonas (Berlin: Georg Reimer, 1839).

70. Psychoanalytic theorist Jean Sanville has referred to this feeling of relatedness as the "we-go" in contrast to the ego. See *The Playground of Psychoanalytic Theory* (Hillsdale, N.J.: Analytic Press, 1991).

71. Schleiermacher, *On Religion*, 113.

72. Concerning this moment, Martin Redeker, in *Schleiermacher: Life and Thought* (trans. John Wallhausser [Philadelphia: Fortress Press, 1973]), notes that Schleiermacher "himself referred to the center of his religion as mysticism. In romanticism the concept of 'mysticism' still had a broad and, one may say, 'pre-religious' meaning. Mysticism seeks to exclude sense perceptions in order to partake of the more mysterious internal inspirations and intuitions. It means above all the sphere of intuition in which the epistemological division of subject from object has not yet occurred or has been deliberately avoided. In a pre-religious sense it could mean participation in the ultimate depths of life through existential encounter" (40). See also my discussion of the meaning of Schleiermacher's mysticism (*The Embodied Self*, 13).

73. Barth, *The Theology of Schleiermacher*, 236.

74. Barth, "Interviews with Karl Barth," 56.

75. Barth, *Protestant Thought*, 341.

76. Ibid., 353–54.

77. Ulanov, *Transforming Sexuality*, 79.

78. Psychoanalytic theorist Judith Lewis Herman refers to this "undestroyed capacity for love" as "the extraordinary human capacity for renewal" in persons who have suffered extraordinary, profound, and repeated abuse (*Trauma and Recovery* [New York: Basic Books, 1992]). Concerning this capacity and the restorative power of mourning, Herman writes: "What sustains the patient through this descent into despair is the smallest evidence of an ability to form loving connections. Clues to the undestroyed capacity for love can often be found through the evocation of soothing imagery. Almost invariably it is possible to find some image of attachment that has been salvaged from the wreckage. One positive memory of a caring, comforting person may be a lifeline during the descent into mourning. The patient's own capacity to feel compassion for animals or children, even at a distance, may be the fragile beginning of compassion for herself" (194).

79. Here Schleiermacher and process theology meet. As John B. Cobb Jr., one of the founders of process theology, stated in private correspondence with me about the embodied self: "What strikes me most is how, coming from an entirely different point, Whitehead ended up so close to Schleiermacher with regard to the self. Schleiermacher's *Gefühl* seems to be almost identical with Whitehead's physical feeling. An occasion originates as the outgrowth of its 'actual world.' This largely pre-conscious feeling of what-is fits well with what Schleiermacher says. The two mesh also in locating this in the between" (29 July 1993).

80. Susannah Heschel, "Anti-Judaism in Christian Feminist Theology," *Tikkun* 5 (May/June 1990): 25–28, 95–97.

81. Cannon, *Katie's Canon*, 131.

82. Martin Luther King Jr., "Loving Your Enemies," in *Strength to Love* (Philadelphia: Fortress Press, 1981), 41–50.

83. Audre Lorde, "Outlines," in *Our Dead behind Us* (New York: W. W. Norton, 1986).

Chapter 6

1. Donna Haraway, "'Gender' for a Marxist Dictionary: The Sexual Politics of a Word," in *Simians, Cyborgs, and Women: The Reinvention of Nature* (New York: Routledge, 1992), 131.

2. Alison Jaggar, *Feminist Politics and Human Nature* (Totowa, N.J.: Rowman & Allanheld, 1983), 46–47.

3. Linda Nicholson, "Interpreting Gender," *Signs: Journal of Women in Culture and Society* 20 (autumn 1994): 80.

4. Haraway, "'Gender,'" 132–34.

5. Ibid., 131.

6. Marxist feminists include Frederick Engels, Heidi Hartmann, Paddy Quick, and Juliet Mitchell. See Jaggar, *Feminist Politics,* 51–82, 207–47. Socialist feminists are too numerous to name. See, in the same volume, pp. 123–71, 302–50.

7. Also called or linked with "cultural feminism." Jaggar, Hester Eisenstein, Josephine Donovan, and Rosemarie Tong have typologies that treat this subject with more nuance.

8. Elizabeth V. Spelman, *Inessential Woman: Problems of Exclusion in Feminist Thought* (Boston: Beacon Press, 1988).

9. C. Bally and A. Sechehaye, eds., in collaboration with A. Reidlinger, *Ferdinand de Saussure: A Course in General Linguistics,* trans. Wad Baskin (New York: Philosophical Library, 1959).

10. Poststructuralist feminism includes much variety: French feminists, Catherine Belsey, Chris Weedon, and Rosalind Coward. For background to my argument, see Philip Lewis, "The Poststructuralist Condition," *Diacritics* 12 (spring 1982): 2–22.

11. Jane Tompkins, "A Short Course in Poststructuralism," *College English* 50 (November 1988): 740.

12. Derrida is the best known for his elaboration of the *outside* and its inextricable link to meaning (indicated by his pseudoterm, *différance,* which cannot be aurally distinguished from the real word, *différence*). However, the fundamental insight is found in Saussure.

13. Tompkins, "A Short Course," 743.

14. Ibid., 739.

15. Thus I disagree with some feminist categorizations of this as only "negativism and nominalism." By doing so I am closer to Foucault's take on the outside as image of the Other. See Linda Nicholson, "Feminism and the Politics of Postmodernism," in *Feminism and Postmodernism,* ed. Margaret Ferguson and Jennifer Wicke (Durham, N.C.: Duke University Press, 1994), 77–84.

16. I am grateful to Ellen Armour for her application of this critique to race/gender in feminist theology and theory via Derrida and Irigaray. See her "Deconstruction and Feminist Theology: Toward Forging an Alliance with Derrida and Irigaray" (Ph.D. diss., Vanderbilt University, 1993).

17. In what follows I summarize Judith Butler, *Gender Trouble: Feminism and the Subversion of Identity* (New York and London: Routledge, 1990). Butler assesses the degree to which a figure like Monique Wittig asks the question.

18. Jeffrey Weeks, *Sex, Politics, and Society: The Regulation of Sexuality since 1800* (London and New York: Longman Group Limited, 1981), 12.

19. Thus, the lesbian will always be a lesser copy of a "real woman." See my "Gender: Being It or Doing It? The Church, Homosexuality, and the Politics of Identity," *Union Seminary Quarterly Review* 47 (1993): 29–46. See Romand Coles for a discussion of the contrast between the Western notion of "difference," displayed in social constructionism, and Foucault's (*Self/Power/Other: Political Theory and Dialogical Ethics* [Ithaca, N.Y.: Cornell University Press, 1992], 76–82).

20. Rosemary Radford Ruether, *Sexism and God-Talk: Toward a Feminist Theology* (Boston: Beacon Press, 1983), 18–19.

21. Since it is new, the implications of this affirmation extend to all theological doctrine.

22. One need only look at her definition of revelation to see how important the sociology of knowledge approach is (Ruether, *Sexism*, 12–18, 93–115).

23. Ibid., 20. Ruether insists this is not a matter of "sameness." My argument questions that.

24. I thank Meg Gandy for this observation.

25. See Roman Jakobson, "Two Aspects of Language and Two Types of Aphasic Disturbances," in *On Language*, ed. Linda R. Waugh and Monique Monville-Burston (Cambridge: Harvard University Press, 1990; original, 1956), 120–25.

26. Ibid., 120.

27. The standard question of its effects on signifying God is not unimportant, but beyond the bounds of this article.

28. I show I am not finally a poststructuralist here. Fredric Jameson, "The Vanishing Mediator; or, Max Weber as Storyteller," in *The Ideologies of Theory: Essays, 1971–1986*, vol. 2, *Syntax of History* (Minneapolis: University of Minnesota Press, 1988), 3–34.

29. I thank Gil Greggs for conversations on this topic. See Fredric Jameson, *The Political Unconscious: Narrative as a Socially Symbolic Act* (Ithaca, N.Y.: Cornell University Press, 1981).

30. Tompkins, "A Short Course," 746–47.

31. Donna Haraway, "Ecce Homo, Ain't (Ar'n't) I a Woman, and Inappropriate/d Others: The Human in a Post-humanist Landscape," in *Feminists Theorize the Political*, ed. Judith Butler and Joan W. Scott (New York: Routledge, 1992), 96.

32. Armour, "Deconstruction, Feminist Theology."

33. Donna Haraway, "Ecce Homo," 96. For work on this see Elisabeth Schüssler Fiorenza, *Prophet: Critical Issues in Feminist Christology* (New York: Continuum, 1995).

Chapter 7

1. Elizabeth Grosz, *Sexual Subversions* (St. Leonards, Australia: Allen and Unwin, 1989); Marilyn Frye, "A Response to Lesbian Ethics," *Hypatia* 5 (fall 1990): 133–37;

and Drucilla Cornell, "What Is Ethical Feminism?" in *Feminist Contentions,* ed. Seyla Benhabib et al. (New York: Routledge, 1995).

2. Sarah Schulman, *My American History: Lesbian and Gay Life during the Reagan/Bush Years* (New York: Routledge, 1994), 269. Schulman states, "According to the United States General Accounting Office Congressional Report on homosexuality in the military, white men are the group least affected by the anti-gay ban. For example, in the Marine Corps, black females were discharged for homosexuality at twice the rate of white males" (269).

3. Katie King, *Theory in Its Feminist Travels: Conversations in U.S. Women's Movement* (Bloomington: Indiana University Press, 1994). King delineates how "unmarked" as opposed to "marked" social status contributes to the construction of privilege.

4. Judith Butler, *Bodies That Matter: On the Discursive Limits of "Sex"* (New York: Routledge, 1993), 1–2. Butler's full description of the materialization of "sex" is:

"[S]ex" not only functions as a norm, but is part of a regulatory practice that produces the bodies it governs, that is, whose regulatory force is made clear as a kind of productive power, the power to produce—demarcate, circulate, differentiate—the bodies it controls. Thus, "sex" is a regulatory ideal whose materialization is compelled, and this materialization takes place (or fails to take place) through certain highly regulated practices. In other words, "sex" is an ideal construct which is forcibly materialized through time. It is not a simple fact or static condition of a body, but a process whereby regulatory norms materialize "sex" and achieve this materialization through forcible reiteration of those norms. That this reiteration is necessary is a sign that materialization is never quite complete, that bodies never comply with the norms by which their materialization is impelled. Indeed, it is the instabilities, the possibilities for rematerialization, opened up by this process that mark one domain in which the force of the regulatory law can be turned against itself to spawn rearticulations that call into question the hegemonic force of that very regulatory law. . . . "Sex" is thus, not simply what one has, or a static description of what one is: it will be one of the norms by which the "one" becomes viable at all, that which qualifies a body for life within the domain of cultural intelligibility.

5. Paul Schaper, "The Social Construction of AIDS" (senior honor's thesis, Emory University, 1991).

6. I use the conjunction between lesbian, feminist, queer, and antiracist in order to indicate multiple and complex communities that may overlap but that are not coextensive. Thus, there is slippage in the set of relations among communities, indicating, for example, communities that are lesbian, feminist, queer, and antiracist as well as lesbian communities that may not, for example, intersect with queer communities.

7. For a discussion of the Meese Commission in relation to feminist and lesbian and queer politics, see Janet Jakobsen, "Agency and Alliance in Public Discourses about Sexualities," *Hypatia* 10 (winter 1995): 133–54.

8. Marilyn Frye, "A Response." The work she reviews is Sara Lucia Hoagland, *Lesbian Ethics: Toward New Value* (Palo Alto, Calif.: Institute of Lesbian Studies, 1988). Hoagland focuses on the creation of values and avoids discussion of norms in order to resist a dominant ethics of control. Recent politics have demonstrated, however, that

"values," for example, in conjunction with the term *family,* can also be a site of control. Karla F. C. Holloway, in *Codes of Conduct: Race, Ethics, and the Color of Our Character* (New Brunswick, N.J.: Rutgers University Press, 1995), points out that a reduction of "values," similar to the reduction of norms to sites of controlling judgment, can occur when values become simply marketable "goods" controlled by the logic of exchange in the same way that human beings were reduced to marketable "goods" under slavery.

9. Cornell, "What Is Ethical Feminism?" 80.

10. Ibid., 78. Similarly, in defining ethics Elizabeth Grosz states, "Ethics need not imply a moral or normative code, or a series of abstract regulative principles. Rather, it is the working out or negotiation between an other (or others) seen as prior to and pre-given for the subject, or a subject. Ethics is a response to the recognition of the primacy of alterity over identity" (*Sexual Subversions,* xvii). Both Grosz and Drucilla Cornell draw their definitions of ethics from Emmanuel Levinas. They emphasize the distinction between control and "ethics," while simultaneously emphasizing connections between ethics and politics. Both make a distinction between ethics and morality, and Cornell reverses the order of feminist ethics, naming her project "ethical feminism," as a mark to further distinguish her project from the discipline of "ethics."

11. Seyla Benhabib, *Critique, Norm, and Utopia: A Study of the Foundations of Critical Theory* (New York: Columbia University Press, 1986), 15. Schematically, it is the *norm* in her triad critique, norm, and utopia which, as the middle and mediating term, does the work of providing these criteria, while the *critique* is directed toward the dogmatic foundationalism of neo-Kantianism, and *utopia* provides the possibility for extending norms beyond the limits of modern rationalism.

12. In fact, Benhabib, in *Critique, Norm, and Utopia,* argues that through the process of rational interaction and social interpretation our specific needs can be transformed into common needs or generalizable interests.

13. Ibid., 15.

14. Seyla Benhabib, "The Generalized and the Concrete Other: The Kohlberg-Gilligan Controversy and Moral Theory," in *Women and Moral Theory,* ed. Eva Feder Kittay and Diana T. Meyers (Totowa, N.J.: Rowman and Littlefield, 1987), 154–77.

15. Benhabib, *Critique, Norm, and Utopia,* 351.

16. Ibid. Here she fails to acknowledge the complex relationships between the socially structured categories of identity which frequently inform oppression—such as race, ethnicity, and religion—and the communities and movements which resist this oppression.

17. Seyla Benhabib, *Situating the Self: Gender, Community, and Postmodernism in Contemporary Ethics* (New York: Routledge, 1992), 187. Here she is quoting Lawrence Blum.

18. Ibid., 227–28.

19. Benhabib, *Critique, Norm, and Utopia,* 272.

20. Ibid., 274.

21. Minnie Bruce Pratt, "Identity: Skin Blood Heart," in *Yours in Struggle: Three Feminist Perspectives on Anti-Semitism and Racism,* by Elly Bulkin, Minnie Bruce Pratt, and Barbara Smith (Brooklyn: Long Hall Press, 1984).

22. In the same way that *norm* is for Benhabib the mediating term between *critique* and *utopia*, the *public* becomes the mediating term between two opposing counterpublics and ultimately controls the form of each.

23. This interaction works particularly well when the body politic is signified as the disembodied space of rationality. To represent the body politic, then, is to be the voice (but not the body) of reason. Thus, as we see in the video, visible bodies set in opposition establish the voice of reason, a voice which we frequently hear but do not see.

24. Susan Thistlethwaite, *Sex, Race, and God* (New York: Crossroad, 1989).

25. On the exclusion of material concerns associated with diversity, history, and embodiment from the moral point of view, see Janet Jakobsen, "Deconstructing the Paradox of Modernity: Feminism, Enlightenment, and Cross-Cultural Moral Interactions," *Journal of Religious Ethics* 23 (fall 1995). On the constitution of the liberal state and the body politic based on a similar set of exclusions, see Carole Pateman, *The Sexual Contract* (Stanford: Stanford University Press, 1988); idem, *The Disorder of Women: Democracy, Feminism, and Political Theory* (Stanford: Stanford University Press, 1989); Joan Landes, *Women and the Public Sphere in the Age of the French Revolution* (Ithaca, N.Y.: Cornell University Press, 1988); and Zillah Eisenstein, *The Color of Gender: Reimaging Democracy* (Berkeley: University of California Press, 1994).

26. This line of reasoning was suggested to me by Bruce Robbins, ed., introduction to *The Phantom Public Sphere* (Minneapolis: University of Minnesota Press, 1993). Robbins is concerned that the contemporary leftist critique may have uncritically accepted much of Walter Lippmann's conservative claim in *The Phantom Public* (New York: Macmillan, 1925) that the public is phantom. Robbins argues that "leftists of the 1990s do not know how to argue for the democracy we want without mobilizing an image of the public so hazy, idealized, and distant from the actual people, places, and institutions around us that it can as easily serve purposes that are anything but democratic" (xi–xii).

27. I would like to thank Laura Levitt and Mary Hunt for pointing out the importance of this use of Kramer's body.

28. The multicultural alliance is interesting, because the videotape later attacks multicultural curricula and because homophobia has been used, for example, in New York State, to derail an entire multicultural curriculum.

29. This motif is shown perhaps most poignantly at the very end of the film when a black child apparently is carried away by a white gay person.

30. Schulman, *My American History*, 269.

31. This embrace of dominant public norms of visibility, which also embody racism, seems particularly dangerous given the history of previous attempts by homosexual leaders and movements to accede to dominant norms in bids for mainstream acceptance. See, for example, George Mosse's study of early German homosexual movements in *Nationalism and Sexuality: Middle-Class Morality and Sexual Norms in Modern Europe* (Madison: University of Wisconsin Press, 1985).

32. Kramer's use of this particular politics may be tied to his own distrust of (homo)sexual desire as displayed in his novel *Faggots* (New York: Plume Books, 1987).

33. For example, Kramer's identification with King appears also to be based on his status as a slain leader who died because the American public didn't care to protect his body, just as Kramer, a leader who has made visible his body as a carrier of HIV, is fac-

ing the possibility of death from AIDS because the American public has not cared to act more effectively in response to the pandemic.

34. For example, Michael Warner, ed., *Fear of a Queer Planet: Queer Politics and Social Theory* (Minneapolis: University of Minnesota Press, 1993), suggests, "Organizing a movement around queerness also allows it to draw on dissatisfaction with the regime of the normal in general. . . . Can we not hear in the resonances of queer protest an objection to the normalization of behavior in this broad sense . . . ?" (xxvii).

35. For a brief history of the beginning of Queer Nation, New York, see Michelango Signorile, *Queer in America: Sex, the Media, and the Closets of Power* (New York: Anchor Books, 1994).

36. For a full explanation of how Benhabib's configuration of universality grants recognition to non-Western "others" while simultaneously effacing them, see Jakobsen, "Deconstructing the Paradox of Modernity."

37. I discuss the naturalization of the Western "we" as a universal "we" in Benhabib's texts at length (ibid.). This naturalization depends on a naturalization of historical processes of modernization and rationalization, which assumes that because these historical processes have become "global" processes they form the context for cross-cultural interaction. See Inderpal Grewal and Caren Kaplan, eds., *Scattered Hegemonies: Postmodernity and Transnational Feminist Practices* (Minneapolis: University of Minnesota Press, 1994), for analysis of the unevenness of these "global processes."

38. Benhabib, *Situating the Self,* 228.

39. Benhabib, *Critique, Norm, and Utopia,* 351.

40. For an explanation of cross-cultural moral interaction that does require a mutual entering into each "other's" "worlds" see María Lugones, "Playfulness, 'World'–Travelling, and Loving Perception," in *Making Face, Making Soul, Haciendo Caras: Creative and Critical Perspectives by Women of Color,* ed. Gloria Anzaldúa (San Francisco: Aunt Lute Foundation, 1990), 390–402.

41. Perhaps most tellingly, Benhabib never engages with the question of universals that exceed this modern frame, such as Katie Cannon's *Black Womanist Ethics* (Atlanta: Scholars Press, 1988), which offers an alternative universalism to modern rationalism. For example, at the end of the essay "Feminism and the Question of Postmodernism" (*Situating the Self,* 203–41), Benhabib states, "The fact that the views of Gilligan or Chodorow or Sarah [*sic*] Ruddick (or for that matter Julia Kristeva) only articulate the sensitivities of white, middle-class, affluent, first world, heterosexual women may be true (although I even have empirical doubts about this). Yet what are we ready to offer in their place: as a project of an ethics which should guide us in the future are we able to offer a better vision than the synthesis of autonomous justice thinking and empathetic care?" (230). In order to answer this question, Benhabib's task would be to engage authors like Cannon and Sara Hoagland, *Lesbian Ethics,* who have offered alternatives.

42. Janet Jakobsen, "Agency and Alliance in Public Discourses about Sexualities," *Hypatia* 10 (winter 1995): 133–54.

43. On the practice of articulations, see Ernesto Laclau and Chantal Mouffe, *Hegemony and Socialist Strategy: Towards a Radical Democratic Politics* (London: Verso, 1985).

44. For example, the contemporary turn to mediation rather than adjudication in civil disagreements indicates an alternative form of conflict resolution. Competitive struggle within the singular framework of "the law" does not provide the only means of resolving disputes, and may not even provide the most nonviolent means of so doing. In particular, mediation is a methodology that does not necessarily place the various "sides" to a given conflict within a singular overarching framework that provides for a single set of adjudicative criteria. Rather, mediation works in between the various sides of conflict, and agreement or acceptance is built in this space rather than enforced through the ordering power of the frame.

45. On the necessity of conflict to democracy, see Chantal Mouffe, "Democratic Politics and the Question of Identity," in *The Identity Question,* ed. John Rajchman (New York: Routledge, 1995), 33–46.

46. Craig Calhoun, "Introduction," in *Habermas and the Public Sphere,* ed. Craig Calhoun (Cambridge: MIT Press, 1993), 37.

47. For some initial suggestions on the interrelations of "strong" and "weak" publics, see Nancy Fraser, "Rethinking the Public Sphere: A Contribution to the Critique of Actually Existing Democracy," *Social Text* 25/26 (1990): 56–80. Reprinted in Calhoun, *Habermas and the Public Sphere.*

48. Benedict Anderson, in *Imagined Communities* (London: Verso, 1991), has suggested that certain shifts in social relations and their accompanying technologies of imagination, such as the development of print capitalism, created the possibilities for the imagination of community that became the modern nation-state. One question for the current moment is whether shifts to the conditions of postmodernity, such as those analyzed by David Harvey in *The Condition of Postmodernity* (Cambridge, Mass.: Blackwell, 1990), create similar openings for imagining community. If so, the particular form of that imagination will only be "fixed" in the terms suggested by Laclau and Mouffe, through political struggle.

Chapter 8

1. When not quoting another person directly or punctuating titles, I intend the use of quotation marks, as distinguished from the use of italics in regard to concepts, to convey irony.

2. See Judith Plaskow, *Sex, Sin, and Grace: Women's Experience and the Theologies of Reinhold Niebuhr and Paul Tillich* (New York: American University Press, 1980).

3. A cautionary note is in order here regarding actual bad mothers and daughters. Their actuality is interpreted every step of the way, by their defenders and their detractors, indeed, even as they speak with their own voices.

4. I use the term *prostitute* advisedly here in preference to *sex worker* simply because the latter marks the beginning of the deconstruction of the "badness" or evil attributed to women who provide sex in exchange for material gain; *sex worker* does not sufficiently connote the violation of cultural expectations of women that *prostitute* connotes.

5. See Euripides, *Medea,* in *Three Great Plays of Euripides,* trans. Rex Warner (New York: New American Library, 1958), 21–71; and *The Bacchae,* in *The Bacchae and Other Plays,* trans. Philip Vellacott (Middlesex: Penguin Classics, 1972), 191–244.

6. See Jan Hoffman, "Pregnant, Addicted—and Guilty?" *New York Times Magazine,* 19 August 1990, 6.

7. Reported on *NBC Nightly News with Tom Brokaw,* 28 June 1994.

8. See Linda Gordon, *Heroes of Their Own Lives: The Politics and History of Family Violence, Boston, 1880–1960* (New York: Viking, 1988), 9, 23, 116–67, 176.

9. Ibid., 173; see also 149–50.

10. Ibid., 175.

11. Marie Ashe and Naomi Cahn, "Child Abuse: A Problem for Feminist Theory," *Texas Journal of Women and the Law* 2, no. 1 (1993): 112.

12. See Judith Lewis Herman, M.D., *Trauma and Recovery: The Aftermath of Violence from Domestic Abuse to Political Terror* (New York: Basic Books, 1992), 134; for a debunking to the so-called cycle of violence, see Gordon, *Heroes,* 172–73, 346.

13. Nevertheless, race and ethnicity also play a role. One need only reflect upon the use by white politicians of *welfare queen* as code for black single mother as an instance of racializing poverty. For a fuller treatment of the role played by race in the demonization of welfare mothers, see Patricia J. Williams, *The Rooster's Egg: On the Persistence of Prejudice* (Cambridge: Harvard University Press, 1995).

14. Ashe and Cahn, "Child Abuse," 110.

15. Gordon, *Heroes.*

16. This is no less true in the case of object-relations theory than in the case of previous analytic thought. See Janice Doane and Devon Hodges, *From Klein to Kristeva: Psychoanalytic Feminism and the Search for the "Good Enough" Mother* (Ann Arbor: University of Michigan Press, 1992).

17. Ashe and Cahn, "Child Abuse," 91–92. See Sigmund Freud, "Female Sexuality," in *The Standard Edition of the Complete Psychological Works,* ed. James Strachey, vol. 21 (New York: Norton, 1976), 223–43; and D. W. Winnicott, *The Maturational Process and the Facilitating Environment* 49 (New York: International Universities Press, 1965).

18. Melanie Klein was the first to suggest that children fantasize "good" and "bad" mothers (initially as good and bad body parts, particularly as breasts) and the first to distinguish such representations from actual mothers; see especially "The Oedipus Complex in the Light of Early Anxieties," in *Love, Guilt, and Reparation and Other Works, 1921–1945,* vol. 1 of *The Writings of Melanie Klein,* ed. R. E. Money-Kyrle et al. (London: Hogarth Press and the Institute of Psychoanalysis, 1975), 370–419. See also Susan Suleiman, "Writing and Motherhood," in *The (M)other Tongue: Essays in Feminist Psychoanalytic Interpretation,* ed. Shirley N. Garner, Claire Kohane, and Madelon Springnether (Ithaca, N.Y.: Cornell University Press, 1985), 352, 358; Ashe and Cahn, "Child Abuse," 92ff.; Dorothy Dinnerstein, *The Mermaid and the Minotaur* (New York: Harper & Row, 1977); and Nancy Chodorow, *The Reproduction of Mothering: Psychoanalysis and the Sociology of Gender* (Berkeley: University of California Press, 1978).

19. The most extreme example Ashe and Cahn give is that of the writings of Alice Miller. *See Thou Shalt Not Be Aware: Society's Betrayal of the Child,* trans. Hildegaard Hannum and Hunter Hannum (New York: NAL-Dutton, 1986). There are nevertheless a growing number of exceptions. See Diane E. Eyer, *Mother-Infant Bonding: A Scientific Fiction* (New Haven: Yale University Press, 1993); Sara Ruddick, *Maternal Thinking: Toward a Politics of Peace* (Boston: Beacon Press, 1989); and Jane Swigart, *The Myth of*

the Bad Mother: The Emotional Realities of Mothering (New York: Doubleday, 1991), among others. These works and others of their genre nevertheless do not include the voices or the concerns of actual bad mothers.

20. Many of the early cases that Gordon analyzes in *Heroes* represent immigrants; in the period she examines race later becomes more of an issue.

21. Judith Plaskow makes a similar point in *Sex, Sin, and Grace*, 12–29.

22. Ashe and Cahn, "Child Abuse," 91–92.

23. See, for example, Rita Nakashima Brock, "The Feminist Redemption of Christ," in *Christian Feminism: Visions of a New Humanity,* ed. Judith L. Weidman (San Francisco: Harper & Row, 1984), 55–74; and Paula M. Cooey, "Re-membering the Body: A Theological Resource for Resisting Violence against a People Called Feminine," *Journal of Theology and Sexuality* 3 (1995). Feminist theologians have addressed mothering, though not in terms of abusing mothers. For one of the most recent examples, see Bonnie Miller-McLemore, *Also a Mother: Parenting and Work as Theological Dilemma* (Nashville: Abingdon, 1994).

24. I do not mean to imply that damage exists outside discursive practices; rather, particular kinds of discursive practices ignore or erase the voices of women who damage, from any account of the damage done.

25. Reported in the *San Antonio Express-News,* 23 July 1994, sec. A, 15.

26. Gordon, *Heroes,* 172–73, 346.

27. Toni Morrison, *The Bluest Eye* (New York: Pocket Books, 1970).

28. Toni Morrison, *Beloved* (New York: Alfred A. Knopf, 1987).

29. Gloria Naylor, *The Women of Brewster Place* (New York: Penguin Books, 1983).

30. Jane Smiley, *A Thousand Acres* (New York: Fawcett Columbine, 1991).

31. Joyce Carol Oates, *Foxfire: Confessions of a Girl Gang* (New York: Feminist Press, 1993); and Agnes Smedley, *Daughter of Earth* (New York: Dutton, 1993).

32. I wish to thank Benjamin Charles Cooey-Nichols for his aid in cleaning up my sometimes tortured prose.

Chapter 9

Acknowledgement. I want to thank Miriam Peskowitz, David Watt, Susan Shapiro, and Rebecca Chopp for their careful readings of earlier drafts of this article and for their important editorial suggestions. This article is taken, in part, from the introduction and first chapter of my book, *Jews and Feminism: The Ambivalent Search for Home* (New York: Routledge, 1997).

1. For more theoretical feminist critiques of the unified liberal self, see Alison Jaggar, *Feminist Politics and Human Nature* (Totowa, N.J.: Rowman & Allanheld, 1983); Iris Marion Young, *Throwing like a Girl and Other Essays in Feminist Philosophy and Social Theory* (Bloomington: Indiana University Press, 1990); and Carole Pateman, *The Disorder of Women* (Stanford: Stanford University Press, 1989).

2. For a listing of many of these Jewish feminist works, see note 8 in Miriam Peskowitz and Laura Levitt, "Editor's Introduction: 'A Way In,'" in *Judaism since Gender* (New York: Routledge, 1997). For a more extensive critique of Jewish liberalism, see

Laura Levitt, *Jews and Feminism: The Ambivalent Search for Home* (New York: Routledge, 1997).

3. Teresa de Lauretis, "Feminist Studies, Critical Studies: Issues, Terms, Contexts," in *Feminist Studies/Critical Studies,* ed. Teresa de Lauretis (Bloomington: Indiana University Press, 1986), 8.

4. Minnie Bruce Pratt, "Identity: Skin Blood Heart," in *Yours in Struggle: Three Feminist Perspectives on Anti-Semitism and Racism,* by Elly Bulkin, Minnie Bruce Pratt, and Barbara Smith (Brooklyn: Long Haul Press, 1984), 11–63.

5. Biddy Martin and Chandra Mohanty, "Feminist Politics: What's Home Got to Do with It?" in de Lauretis, *Feminist Studies/Critical Studies,* 191–212.

6. It is these beliefs in America that brought generations of immigrant European Jews to this country to make a new home at the beginning of the twentieth century. The dream of America for Jews was the promise and possibility of a future. Jews would be liberated and safe. This dream has kept Jews loyal to the liberal state. It has also come to shape our understanding of ourselves. At the heart of my larger project is a disruption of these kinds of embraces (see Levitt, *Jews and Feminism*). In this brief article, I offer one such critique, a pointed Jewish feminist critique of being at home in America.

7. In many ways this paper attempts to fill a gap in the discourse at the conference in Denver, out of which this volume has emerged. It tries to make clear that speaking about Jewishness is not just a matter of theology, particularly in relation to issues of Jewish identity. As the only Jew in attendance at that conference in the fall of 1994, it seemed important to make explicit my own assumptions about why a critique of liberalism from a Jewish feminist perspective was necessary. This paper builds on that assumption in order to make clearer how a Jewish faith in liberalism has come to shape my understanding of what it means for Jews to be at home in America at the end of the twentieth century.

8. For a more extensive critique of this scholarship, see Peskowitz and Levitt, *Judaism since Gender.*

9. Gayatri Chakravorty Spivak, "French Feminism Revisited," in *Outside in the Teaching Machine* (New York: Routledge, 1993), 141. Other works of postcolonial criticism that have been particularly helpful to me include: Rajeswari Sunder Rajan, *Real and Imagined Women: Gender, Culture, and Postcolonialism* (New York: Routledge, 1993); and Homi Bhabha, "Of Mimicry and Man: The Ambivalence of Colonial Discourse," *October* 28 (1984): 125–33. On Jewishness and these questions, see Jonathan Boyarin, "The Other Within, the Other Without," in *Storm from Paradise: The Politics of Jewish Memory* (Minneapolis: University of Minnesota Press, 1992), 77–98. For a more extensive critique of liberalism in relation to colonialism, see Levitt, *Jews and Feminism.*

10. It took me a while to recall the exact address. I kept writing down the wrong numbers. Is it Ninth Street or East Ninth? Does the *east* come later as in the northeast (NE) section of the city?

11. "Feminist Theory and Literary Criticism" (taught by Angelika Bammer, Emory University, spring 1988). I am making a distinction here between *thinking* and *writing* since, as I have already noted, I began writing about these issues in 1990.

12. After reading Martin and Mohanty's essay, I went out and bought Bulkin, Pratt, and Smith, *Yours in Struggle.* Moreover, it was in the context of this course that I

was first introduced to many of the other contemporary feminist texts that figure promi-
nently in my *Jews and Feminism,* including Jewish feminist works by Irena Klepfisz and
Melanie Kaye/Kantrowitz.

13. Martin and Mohanty, "Feminist Politics," 210.

14. See Laura Levitt, "Speaking Out of the Silence around Rape: A Personal
Account," *Fireweed* 41 (fall 1993): 20–31.

15. Pratt, "Identity," 33.

16. Referring to my rape is difficult. For the first few years I spoke about it in
terms of *the rape.* I have since worked against reifying this experience while also claiming it as my own. The next permutation was *my rape.* This construction *my being raped*
is new. I thank David Watt for pushing me to reconsider once again how I refer to having been raped. For more on this question of the difficulty of speaking about rape, see
Levitt, "Speaking Out."

17. Pratt, "Identity," 33–34.

18. On this point see, for example, Susan Estrich, *Real Rape: How the Legal System Victimizes Women Who Say No* (Cambridge: Harvard University Press, 1987). For
more on the problematics of rape and marriage, see Laura Levitt, "Reconfiguring Home:
Jewish Feminist Identity/ies" (Ph.D. diss., Emory University, 1993), chap. 2.

19. Although recent efforts to take more seriously the threat to women and children in their homes have resulted in new legislation, allowing police to intervene more
easily in domestic disputes, these remain thorny issues. The propriety of government or
legal intervention into domestic affairs remains heavily skewed in favor of husbands and
fathers. Prosecution of husbands who beat or rape their wives remains difficult.

20. See Levitt, "Reconfiguring Home," chap. 2.

21. Martin and Mohanty, "Feminist Politics," 201.

22. Ibid., 204.

23. For this reading, see Levitt, "Reconfiguring Home," introduction and chaps.
1–3.

24. Pratt lost custody of her two sons in a bitter divorce after she came out as a lesbian. See references in "Identity," her recent collection of essays, *Rebellion: Essays,
1980–1991* (Ithaca, N.Y.: Firebrand Books, 1991), and most especially her award-win-
ning book of poetry about what it means to be a lesbian mother in America, *Crimes
against Nature* (Ithaca, N.Y.: Firebrand Books, 1990).

25. Pratt, "Identity," 35–36.

26. Ibid., 36.

27. In addition to Pratt, recent scholarship on Poe has raised similar issues about
the complicated relationship between the legacy of slavery and issues of gender in Poe's
work, especially the work of Joan Dayan. For example, Dayan writes:

> For Poe the cultivation of romance and the facts of slavery are inextricably
> linked. . . . It is perhaps not surprising that some of Poe's critics—the found-
> ing fathers of the Poe Society, for example—sound rather like the proslavery
> ideologues who promoted the ideal of the lady as elegant, white, and delicate.
> Poe's ladies, those dream-dimmed, ethereal living dead of his poems, have
> been taken as exemplars of what Poe called "supernal Beauty"—an entitle-
> ment that he would degrade again and again. Think about Lady Madeline
> Usher returning from the grave as a brute and bloodied thing, reduced from

a woman of beauty to the frenzied iterated "*it*" of her brother Roderick. Many of the dissolutions and decays so marked in Poe's tales about women subvert the status of the women as a saving ideal, thus undermining his own "Philosophy of Composition": the "death of a beautiful woman is, unquestionably, the most poetic topic in the world." No longer pure or passive, she returns as an earthy—and very unpoetical—subject. ("Amorous Bondage: Poe, Ladies, and Slaves," *American Literature* 66 [June 1994]: 240)

See also Joan Dayan, "Romance and Race," in *The Columbia History of The American Novel,* ed. Emory Elliot (New York: Columbia University Press, 1991), 94–102. I thank Janet Jakobsen for calling my attention to Dayan's work.

28. Pratt, "Identity," 36. In fact, in "Amorous Bondage," Dayan makes a strong case for "a rereading of Poe that depends absolutely on what has so often been cut out of his work: the institution of slavery." She also refers to

Poe's troubled sense of himself as a southern aristocrat, and, finally the precise and methodical transactions in which he revealed the threshold separating humanity from animality. . . . [H]is most unnatural fictions are bound to the works of natural history that are so much a part of their origination. Read in this way, Poe's sometimes inexplicable fantasies become intelligible. Poe's gothic is crucial to our understanding of the entangled metaphysics of romance and servitude. What might have remained local historiography becomes a harrowing myth of the Americas. (241)

29. Martin and Mohanty, "Feminist Politics," 201.

30. Spivak, "French Feminism Revisited," 141.

Chapter 10

1. Sharon D. Welch, *A Feminist Ethic of Risk* (Minneapolis: Augsburg Fortress, 1990), 150–51. Seyla Benhabib, with different emphases and concerns, engages in a similar strategy of combining modern (Habermas's critical theory) and postmodern insights in a feminist ethic. See her *Situating the Self: Gender, Community, and Postmodernism in Contemporary Ethics* (New York: Routledge, 1992).

2. Alice A. Jardine, *Gynesis: Configurations of Woman and Modernity* (Ithaca, N.Y.: Cornell University Press, 1985), 154–55.

3. Joan Scott, *Gender and the Politics of History* (New York: Columbia University Press, 1988), 46.

4. Ibid., 46–50.

5. Ibid., 48.

6. Translated in J. Stevenson, ed., *Creeds, Councils and Controversies,* revised edition with additional documents by W. H. C. Frend (London: SPCK, 1989), 337.

7. See the essays collected in Frieda Johles Forman, ed., with Caoran Sowton, *Taking Our Time: Feminist Perspectives on Temporality* (Oxford: Pergamon Press, 1989).

8. See the essays by Maïr Verthuy, Heide Göttner-Abendroth, and Margaret Davis in Forman, *Taking Our Time.*

9. Immanuel Kant, *Critique of Pure Reason,* translated and with an introduction by Norman Kemp Smith, abridged ed. (New York: Modern Library, 1958), A33, B49.

Chapter 11

1. See Raymond Williams, *Marxism and Literature* (Oxford and New York: Oxford University Press, 1977); Stuart Hall, "Cultural Studies and the Center," in *Culture, Media, Language,* ed. S. Hall et al. (London: Hutchinson, 1980), 15–47; idem, "Notes on Deconstructing the 'Popular,'" in *People's History and Socialist Theory,* ed. R. Samuel (London: Routledge and Kegan Paul, 1981), 227–40; idem, "The Toad in the Garden," in *Marxism and the Interpretation of Culture,* ed. C. Nelson and L. Grossberg (Urbana and Chicago: University of Illinois Press, 1988), 35–58; and Ernesto Laclau and Chantal Mouffe, *Hegemony and Socialist Strategy: Towards a Radical Democratic Politics* (London: Verso, 1985).

2. Roberto Unger, *Social Theory: Its Situation and Tasks* (Cambridge: Cambridge University Press, 1987), 10.

3. Joan Cocks, *The Oppositional Imagination* (London and New York: Routledge, 1989), 30.

4. Williams, *Marxism and Literature,* 108.

5. See, for example, James Boon, *Other Tribes, Other Scribes* (New York: Cambridge University Press, 1982); James Clifford, *The Predicament of Culture* (Cambridge: Harvard University Press, 1988); and George Marcus and James Fischer, *Anthropology as Cultural Critique* (Chicago and London: University of Chicago Press, 1986).

6. See, for example, Cocks, *Oppositional Imagination;* Hall, "Cultural Studies," "Notes on Deconstructing," and "Toad"; Ernesto Laclau, *Politics and Ideology in Marxist Theory* (London: NLB, 1977); Laclau and Mouffe, *Hegemony and Socialist Strategy;* Chantal Mouffe, "Hegemony and Ideology in Gramsci," in *Gramsci and Marxist Theory,* ed. C. Mouffe (London: Routledge and Kegan Paul, 1979), 170–201; and Barry Smart, "The Politics of Truth and the Problem of Hegemony," in *Foucault: A Critical Reader,* ed. D. Hoy (Oxford: Basil Blackwell, 1986), 157–73.

7. Williams, *Marxism and Literature,* chap. 6.

8. See Paul Hirst, *On Law and Ideology* (Atlantic Highlands, N.J.: Humanities Press, 1979).

9. Smart, "Politics of Truth," 158–59.

10. Michel Foucault, *The Order of Things* (New York: Vintage Books, 1973).

11. See Laclau and Mouffe, *Hegemony and Socialist Strategy,* chap. 3.

12. See Iris Marion Young, *Justice and the Politics of Difference* (Princeton: Princeton University Press, 1990), 41–42, 86–90.

13. Hall, "Toad."

14. Laclau, *Politics and Ideology.*

15. See Alain Touraine, *The Self-Production of Society* (Chicago: University of Chicago Press, 1977); and idem, *The Return of the Actor* (Minneapolis: University of Minnesota Press, 1988).

16. See Chantal Mouffe, *The Return of the Political* (London: Verso, 1993); Chris Weedon, *Feminist Practice and Poststructuralist Theory* (Oxford: Basil Blackwell, 1987); and Paul Smith, *Discerning the Subject* (Minneapolis: University of Minnesota Press, 1988).

17. Laclau, *Politics and Ideology.*

18. See Sabina Lovibond, *Realism and Imagination in Ethics* (Minneapolis: University of Minnesota Press, 1983), 185.

19. See Mouffe, "Hegemony and Ideology," 197.

20. Ibid., 182–83.

21. See Williams, *Marxism and Literature,* 51–52, 115–17; and Hall, "Notes on Deconstructing," 236–37.

22. Williams, *Marxism and Literature,* 116.

Chapter 12

The first part of the title of this article is a paraphrase from a children's story by Berkeley Breathed, *Goodnight Opus* (Boston: Little, Brown, and Co., 1993).

1. Not all feminist theologies gave expression to all four of these elements. Some thinkers emphasized one or another, while others explicitly repudiated certain points. Nonetheless, I think it is accurate to say that these four claims were widespread and that they functioned together to give feminist theology its critical and compelling edge.

2. See Mary Daly, *Gyn/Ecology* (Boston: Beacon Press, 1978); Elisabeth Schüssler Fiorenza, "The Will to Choose or to Reject: Continuing Our Critical Work," in *Feminist Interpretation of the Bible,* ed. Letty M. Russell (Philadelphia: Westminster Press, 1985); idem, *Bread Not Stone* (Boston: Beacon Press, 1984); and Rosemary Radford Ruether, "Feminist Interpretation: A Method of Correlation," in Russell, *Feminist Interpretation of the Bible.*

3. See Rosemary Radford Ruether, *Sexism and God-Talk: Toward a Feminist Theology* (Boston: Beacon Press, 1983), 18; and Schüssler Fiorenza, "The Will to Choose," 128.

4. Daly, *Gyn/Ecology,* and idem, *Pure Lust: Elemental Feminist Philosophy* (Boston: Beacon Press, 1984). See especially Daly's discussion of deep memory.

5. The stance of Evangelicals for Biblical Equality is an example of this approach.

6. See Ruether, "Feminist Interpretation," 117f.; Letty M. Russell, *Household of Freedom: Authority in Feminist Theology* (Philadelphia: Westminster Press, 1987), 71; Sallie McFague, *Models of God: Theology for an Ecological Nuclear Age* (Philadelphia: Fortress Press, 1987), 27. On this issue of the liberating core of the tradition, Schüssler Fiorenza has taken a far more skeptical stance.

7. Schüssler Fiorenza, "The Will to Choose," 129; Ruether, "Feminist Interpretation," 115.

8. Elsa Tamez, "Women's Rereading of the Bible," in *With Passion and Compassion: Third World Women Doing Theology,* ed. Virginia Fabella and Mercy Amba Oduyoye (Maryknoll, N.Y.: Orbis Books, 1988), 179.

9. Jacquelyn Grant, *White Women's Christ and Black Women's Jesus: Feminist Christology and Womanist Response* (Atlanta: Scholars Press, 1989), 195.

10. Katie Geneva Cannon, *Black Womanist Ethics* (Atlanta: Scholars Press, 1988); Delores S. Williams, *Sisters in the Wilderness: The Challenge of Womanist God-Talk* (Maryknoll, N.Y.: Orbis Books, 1993); Kwok Pui-lan, "Mothers and Daughters, Writers and Fighters," in *Inheriting Our Mothers' Gardens: Feminist Theology in Third World Perspective,* ed. Letty M. Russell et al. (Philadelphia: Westminster Press, 1988); Chung Hyun Kyung, "Following Naked Dancing and Long Dreaming," in Russell, *Inheriting*

Our Mothers' Gardens; Ada María Isasi-Díaz, *En la Lucha: A Hispanic Women's Libera-tion Theology* (Minneapolis: Fortress Press, 1993).

11. See especially Mary McClintock Fulkerson, *Changing the Subject: Women's Discourses and Feminist Theology* (Minneapolis: Fortress Press, 1994).

12. Kwok Pui-lan, "Mothers and Daughters," 31; and Chung Hyun Kyung, "Fol-lowing Naked Dancing," 68.

13. Aurora Levins Morales and Rosario Morales, *Getting Home Alive* (Ithaca, N.Y.: Firebrand Books, 1986), 212, quoted in Lourdes Torres, "The Construction of the Self in U.S. Latina Autobiographies," in *Third World Women and the Politics of Femi-nism,* ed. Chandra Talpade Mohanty, Ann Russo, and Lourdes Torres (Bloomington: Indiana University Press, 1991), 284.

14. Linda Alcoff, "Cultural Feminism versus Post-structuralism: The Identity Crisis in Feminist Theory," *Signs* 13, no. 3 (spring 1988): 434.

15. Teresa de Lauretis, "Feminist Studies/Critical Studies: Issues, Terms, and Contexts," in *Feminist Studies/Critical Studies,* ed. Teresa de Lauretis (Bloomington: Indiana University Press, 1986), 9.

16. bell hooks, *Yearning: Race, Gender, and Cultural Politics* (Boston: South End Press, 1990), is a sustained discussion of counterhegemonic practices.

17. Ibid., 28. hooks makes this point when she states, "Should we not be suspi-cious of postmodern critiques of the 'subject' when they surface at a historical moment when many subjugated people feel themselves coming to voice for the first time?"

18. Richard Rorty, *contingency, irony, and solidarity* (Cambridge: Cambridge Uni-versity Press, 1989), 91.

19. For feminists in other disciplines attempting to link historicism and pragma-tism, see Nancy Fraser, *Unruly Practices, Power, Discourse, and Gender in Contemporary Social Theory* (Minneapolis: University of Minnesota Press, 1989); and Charlene Had-dock Seigfried, *Pragmatism and Feminism: Reweaving the Social Fabric* (Chicago: Uni-versity of Chicago Press, 1996).

20. I am indebted to the nonessentialist theory of tradition articulated in Delwin Brown, *Boundaries of Our Habitations: Tradition and Theological Construction* (Albany: State University of New York Press, 1994).

Chapter 13

1. Seyla Benhabib et al., *Feminist Contentions: A Philosophical Exchange,* with an introduction by Linda Nicholson (New York and London: Routledge, 1995).

2. The recent anthology *Feminism beside Itself,* edited by Diane Elam and Robyn Wiegman (New York and London: Routledge, 1995), questions the history and identity of feminism. Judith Evans, in her *Feminist Theory Today: An Introduction to Second-Wave Feminism* (London: Sage, 1995), attempts a kind of history of feminism, identify-ing early liberalism, liberalism's second stage, cultural feminism (stages one and two), socialist feminism, and the postmodern and legalist challenges.

3. See Jane Flax, "Postmodernism and Gender Relations in Feminist Theory," in *Feminism/Postmodernism,* edited and with an introduction by Linda J. Nicholson (New York: Routledge, 1990), 41–42.

4. Jane Flax, *Thinking Fragments: Psychoanalysis, Feminism, and Postmodernism in the Contemporary West* (Berkeley: University of California Press, 1990), 32ff.; Ben-

habib, *Feminist Contentions,* 10. For a theological yet decidedly nonfeminist account of the death knell for modern warrants, see Mark C. Taylor, *Erring: A Postmodern A/theology* (Chicago: University of Chicago Press, 1984). It is extremely difficult to have any univocal or essential definition for *postmodernism.* A term originating in architecture, *postmodernism* is, as much as anything else, the attempt to render problematic the basic contours of modernity. Feminist theorists have given a great deal of attention to the alliance of feminism and postmodernism, not only in *Feminist Contentions,* but in a great many texts. For one excellent survey, see Nicholson, *Feminism/Postmodernism.*

5. Julia Kristeva, *In the Beginning Was Love: Psychoanalysis and Faith* (New York: Columbia University Press, 1987). For a feminist theological appropriation of Kristeva's notion, see Rebecca S. Chopp, *The Power to Speak: Feminism, Language, God* (New York: Crossroad, 1989).

6. Judith Butler, *Bodies That Matter: On the Discursive Limits of "Sex"* (New York: Routledge, 1993).

7. Joan Scott, "Experience," in *Feminists Theorize the Political,* ed. Judith Butler and Joan W. Scott (New York and London: Routledge, 1992), 26.

8. Nancy Hartsock, "Foucault on Power," in Nicholson, *Feminism/Postmodernism,* 163.

9. Such a position, drawing heavily on linguistic theory, is open to the criticism of privileging linguistic metaphors over understanding the subject. Such privileging can overlook the other structures that constitute the subject. In feminist theory, Seyla Benhabib makes this criticism of Judith Butler's work. See Benhabib, *Feminist Contentions,* 109.

10. Seyla Benhabib, *Situating the Self: Gender, Community, and Postmodernism in Contemporary Ethics* (New York: Routledge, 1992).

11. Butler, *Bodies That Matter.*

12. Chandra Talpade Mohanty, "Feminist Encounters: Locating the Politics of Experience," in *Destabilizing Theory: Contemporary Feminist Debates,* ed. Michele Barrett and Anne Phillips (Stanford: Stanford University Press, 1992).

13. Nancy Fraser, "False Antitheses" and "Pragmatism, Feminism, and the Linguistic Turn," in Benhabib, *Feminist Contentions,* 59–74, 157–71. See also Anne Phillips, "Universal Pretensions in Feminist Thought," in Barrett and Phillips, *Destabilizing Theory,* 10–30.

14. Why do theologians (including Jakobsen for the moment, on the basis of this issue) seem to have more consensus than feminist theorists? I can only render a hypothesis. My hunch is that feminist theologians tend to be carried, implicitly if not explicitly, by a narrative of the Christian story. This narrative is, of course, always a site of conflict and contestation, but it has basic symbols within which to employ human action. As foundationalism is banished, so to speak, the narrative begins to establish the emplotment, and the pragmatic criteria grow out of the story as it is being transformed. See the articles by Fulkerson and Tanner for supporting evidence.

15. Rebecca S. Chopp, "Feminism's Theological Pragmatics," *Journal of Religion* 67 (1987): 239; idem, "From Patriarchy into Freedom: A Conversation between American Feminist Theology and French Feminism," in *Transfigurations,* ed. C. W. Maggie Kim, Susan M. St. Ville, and Susan Simonaitis (Minneapolis: Fortress Press, 1993); and idem, *Saving Work: Feminist Practices of Theological Education* (Louisville: Westminster/John Knox Press, 1995).

Index

Abjection, 68, 74, 76
Agency, 8, 11, 205, 210, 218, 220, 221. *See also* Women as agents/victims
Alcoff, Linda, 18, 23, 24, 204
Anderson, Benedict, 249-50 n.48
Androgyny, 56-57
Anti-Semitism, 126, 128, 130
Armour, Ellen, 115
Articulation, 179-80, 188-90, 192, 196-97, 249 n.43
Ashe, Marie, 141, 143, 144

Barth, Karl, 82, 94, 95-96, 240-41 n.34
Beauvoir, Simone de, 61, 100, 101, 177
Benhabib, Seyla, 31, 63, 120-26, 134, 135, 218, 221, 223, 225, 247 n.11, 247 n.12, 247 n.22, 248 n.36, 248 n.37, 249 n.41, 254-55 n.1, 258 n.9
Benjamin, Jessica, 87, 88, 90, 91
Binarism, 9, 11, 70, 71, 72, 75, 78, 170, 218; and gender, 105-6, 109, 160, 219, 222
Bodies, lesbian/gay, 10, 116-36, 225; racial/ethnic, 127, 129, 133
Body, 9, 59, 79-98, 220, 229-30, 231, 238 n.8, 239 n.11
Body politic, 10, 118-36, 225, 231, 247 n.23, 247 n.25
Bordo, Susan, 23, 60, 62
Briggs, Sheila, 7, 13, 230-31
Brock, Rita Nakashima, 34, 39-42, 61, 69, 71, 72, 259 n.18
Brown, Delwin, 30, 209

Butler, Judith, 24, 58, 105-6, 113, 118, 219, 224, 258 n.9

Cady, Linell, 1, 7, 11-12, 15-16, 221, 228, 229
Cahn, Naomi, 141, 143, 144
Cannon, Katie Geneva, 98, 203, 238 n.8, 249 n.41
Capitalism, 12, 22-23, 25, 180, 182
Chodorow, Nancy, 41, 61, 62, 143
Chopp, Rebecca, 1, 3, 15, 34, 50-52, 221
Christian Right, 125-32, 149
Christology, 56, 73, 81-82, 173-75, 230, 235 n.4; feminist, 69-71, 73, 230-31
Chung Hyun Kyung, 203, 204
Civil rights movement, 20, 126-30, 132, 180
Class, 4, 11, 12, 44, 97, 99, 102, 108, 118, 119, 138-42, 144, 146, 149, 151, 178, 182, 203, 209, 219
Clement of Alexandria, 54, 77
Cocks, Joan, 180
Common sense, 106, 180, 189, 219, 224
Community, 12-13, 31-32, 62-63, 120-22, 134, 135, 231, 249-50 n.48
Cooey, Paula E., 1, 6, 11, 83-84, 222, 224, 228, 229, 239 n.11
Cornell, Drucilla, 120, 246 n.10
Counterhegemonic, 109-11, 194, 205
Counterpublic(s), 10-11, 119-22, 126-33, 247 n.22
Culpepper, Emily, 60

Culture, 6, 14, 42, 45, 48, 49, 59-60, 215. *See also* Politics, cultural

Daly, Mary, 56, 62, 67, 111, 200, 218
Davaney, Sheila Greeve, 7, 11, 12, 15-16, 80, 83, 217, 224, 225, 228
Derrida, Jacques, 60, 62, 63
Difference, 4, 8, 9, 10, 11, 13, 48, 61-64, 67, 99, 102, 103, 105, 109-13, 121, 132, 152, 161, 164, 170, 199, 204-5, 214, 222, 224, 226, 227, 229, 231, 244 n.12, 244 n.19
Dinnerstein, Dorothy, 143
Dualism. *See* Binarism

Edwin Meese, 119, 126, 128-30
Epistemology, and the body, 9, 80; feminist, 2, 60, 73, 74, 77, 223, 229
Essentialism, 8, 12, 18, 20-22, 33-34, 36-38, 40, 43, 45-50, 62, 67, 75-76, 97, 99, 101, 111, 143, 177, 200-3, 205, 208, 210, 211, 213, 216-21, 231, 236 n.23, 236 n.25; and antiessentialism, 12, 62, 64, 67, 68, 69, 70, 229, 236 n.23, 236 n.25; and antirelationalism, 12, 62, 68, 75, 236 n.25
Ethics, 116, 120, 136, 138, 216, 225, 246 n.10
Exclusion, 9-11, 13, 48, 71, 104-5, 111, 115, 124, 125, 133, 134, 170, 173, 211-13, 222, 224, 225, 227
Experience, 33-34, 37, 84, 170, 176, 199, 203. *See also* Women's experience

Feminism, 4, 20, 109, 111, 215-16, 219-20, 226-27, 229, 232 n.2, 258 n.2; cultural, 18, 244 n.7; essentialist, 20-22, 67; French, 51, 60, 68, 244 n.10; Jewish, 12, 154-55, 157, 164, 222, 252 n.2, 252 n.7; liberal, 18-20, 61, 100, 101; Marxist, 100-1, 101-2, 244 n.6; radical, 101, 102
Feminist Contentions, 215
Feminist theology, 54-56, 66, 72, 75-76, 79-80, 83, 97-98, 99, 103, 107-8, 111-15, 137-38, 141, 145, 150, 165-68, 176, 178, 183, 188, 198-214, 215-31, 256 n.1, 259 n.14; and feminist theory, 1-16, 40, 68, 83, 96, 99, 113, 165-67, 183, 198-99, 202, 205, 207-8, 215-31, 232 n.3; and historicism, 23, 208-14,

225, 257 n.19; and history, 13, 165-78, 206, 231; and Jewish/Christian relations, 97-98, 216, 252 n.7; and liberation, 69, 71, 74, 75, 99, 198, 201-2, 206; and process theology, 39-42, 61; Roman Catholic, 35-39; task of, 14, 150, 179, 184, 186-97, 211, 214. *See also* Mujerista theology; Theology, task of; Womanist theology
Feminist theory, 17-26, 57, 97, 99, 112-13, 116, 120, 136, 137, 167, 170, 203, 204, 206, 215-31, 259 n.14; and poststructuralism, 18, 50-52, 60, 68, 76, 77, 99-115, 224, 226, 236 n.23, 244 n.10; and postmodernism, 7-8, 9, 22-23, 55, 73, 166-67, 218, 258 n.4; and women of color, 4, 21-22, 70-71, 99, 202-4. *See also* Theory, role of
Flax, Jane, 23, 218
Foucault, Michel, 60, 63, 65, 106, 169, 177, 179, 181, 224, 227, 244 n.19
Foundationalism, 8, 216-19, 223, 224, 259 n.14
Fraser, Nancy, 224, 226
Freud, Sigmund, 83-84, 85, 90, 223
Frye, Marilyn, 120
Fulkerson, Mary McClintock, 9-10, 11, 50, 222, 224, 229, 231, 259 n.14

Gay rights movement, 127, 128, 131, 180
Gay Rights, Special Rights, 119, 126, 136
Gender, 13, 54, 56-63, 66-72, 74-78, 97, 99-101, 105-7, 109, 114, 118, 119, 129, 144, 146, 165, 167, 169-75, 177-78, 182, 198, 202, 203, 219-20, 221, 226, 227, 231
Gilligan, Carol, 61, 62, 218
Global accountability and interdependence, 9, 63-66, 68, 73-74, 209, 212, 213
God, 35-39, 43-45, 57, 78, 81-83, 93-96, 107-9, 110, 112, 114-15, 186, 189, 202, 206, 208, 210, 230
God's purpose, 201-2, 206, 207, 217
Gordon, Linda, 140, 141, 144
Grace, 80, 96, 138, 152
Grant, Jacquelyn, 203, 238 n.8
Grant, Judith, 20-21
Grosz, Elizabeth, 246 n.10

Habermas, Jürgen, 169, 223, 254-55 n.1
Hagar, 43, 203, 238 n.8

Haraway, Donna, 100, 114, 115

Hartsock, Nancy, 220

Hegel, Georg Wilhelm Friedrich, 74, 81, 82, 239 n.17, 240 n.24

Hegemony/hegemonic, 43, 99, 101-3, 106-8, 112-15, 180, 187, 190-91, 193, 194, 209, 220, 227. See also Counter-hegemonic

Heschel, Susannah, 98

Heterosexism, 106, 138, 160, 219. See also Binarism, gender

Heyward, Carter, 69

Historicism, 45, 199, 207, 221, 224, 225, 226, 257 n.19. See also Feminist theology and historicism; Subjectivity, historicist conception

History, 13, 51, 171, 176, 226, 227, 228, 259 n.16. See also Feminist theology and history

Hoagland, Sara Lucia, 246 n.8, 249 n.41

Holy Spirit, 81-82, 88, 89-90, 94

Home, 12-13, 154-64, 215, 227, 252 n.6, 252 n.7

Homophobia, 130, 132

hooks, bell, 21-22, 23, 205

Human nature, 100-1, 107, 137-38, 141, 153

Humanism, 59, 102, 103, 114

Identity (Similarity), 109-11, 161, 164. See also Difference

Identity (Subjectivity). See Subjectivity

Identity politics, 70, 99, 106

Imago Dei, 99, 107-9, 110-11, 113-15, 222, 231

Intersubjectivity, 80, 87, 91, 93, 95-98, 223, 237 n.2

Irigaray, Luce, 75, 77, 241 n.39

Isasi-Díaz, Ada María, 34, 47, 49-50, 51, 203, 221

Jakobsen, Janet, 10-11, 216, 224, 225, 229

Jardine, Alice, 64, 169, 170

Johnson, Elizabeth, 34, 35, 36-37, 221

Jones, Serene, 8, 220-21

Jung, C. G., 41, 42, 89, 237 n.2

Kant, Immanuel, 81, 82, 83-84, 85, 93, 178, 240 n.22

Kaplan, Ann, 23

Keller, Catherine, 7, 8-9, 34, 39-42, 46, 221, 229, 238 n.7, 259 n.18

Kierkegaard, Soren, 81, 82

King, Martin Luther, Jr., 98, 127, 128, 132, 136, 162-63

Knowledge. See Epistemology

Kohut, Heinz, 84, 85, 90-93, 230

Kramer, Larry, 127, 128, 132, 136, 248 n.32, 248 n.33

Kristeva, Julia, 55, 64-65, 68, 73, 74, 75, 76, 219, 230, 258 n.5

Kwok Pui-lan, 203, 204

Kyriarchy, 71, 72, 76

Lacan, Jacques, 60, 83, 90

LaCugna, Catherine, 34, 35, 37-39, 46, 221

Language, 36, 42, 48-49, 51, 72, 169, 216, 218, 221, 223, 229. See also Linguisticism

Lauretis, Teresa de, 23-24, 57, 67, 205

Lesbian theory, 99, 101, 116, 120, 136, 229, 246 n.8

Levitt, Laura, 11, 12-13, 15, 215, 216, 220, 221, 224, 227

Liberalism, 12, 19-20, 63, 125, 128, 154, 155, 160-62, 180, 216, 222, 226, 227, 232-33 n.3, 233 n.4, 247 n.25, 252 n.1, 252 n.7. See also Feminism, liberal; Humanism

Liberation, 14-15, 101-2, 111, 113, 181, 182, 189, 218, 220, 223. See also Feminist theology and liberation

Lindbeck, George, 27-29

Linguisticism, 9, 72, 73, 74, 169, 218, 258 n.9

Local knowledge, 63-64, 65, 203, 207, 209, 212. See also Global accountability and interdependence

Lorde, Audre, 67, 98

Marxism, 14, 179, 181, 182-83, 223, 224, 226

Matriphobia, 68, 74, 76, 77

McFague, Sallie, 34, 42, 44-46, 51, 201, 217, 221

Miller, Jean Baker, 61

Modernism, 7-8, 17, 120, 167, 169, 170, 216-19, 221-22, 258 n.4. See also Postmodernism

Mohanty, Chandra Talpade, 154, 158, 161-62, 224

Morales, Aurora Levins, 204
Morales, Rosario, 204
Morrison, Toni, 151
Motherhood, 139, 140-45, 251 n.23
Mujerista theology, 49-50, 189, 203

National Gay and Lesbian Task Force, 132
Naylor, Gloria, 151
New social movements, 121, 179, 182-84, 187, 227. *See also* Counterpublic(s)
Norms, 3, 5, 10, 11, 23, 48, 50, 116-36, 200-14, 215, 221, 223-26, 227, 246 n.8, 247 n.11, 247 n.22; criteria for, 7, 15, 116-36, 198-202, 207, 215, 217, 220, 223-26, 227, 259 n.14

Oates, Joyce Carol, 151
Other, 101, 105-7, 115, 120, 124, 125, 134, 153, 155, 218, 248 n.36. *See also* Difference; Exclusion

Particularity, 5, 8, 12, 97, 102-4, 109, 114, 119, 122-25, 133-36, 203-5, 207, 226
Past, nature and status of, 14-16, 166, 179, 192-97, 202, 210-12, 214, 215, 217, 226-29. *See also* Religious traditions
Patriarchy, 18, 21, 54, 56-58, 61, 69, 76, 149, 187-94, 226, 228
Plaskow, Judith, 217
Poe, Edgar Allen, 162, 162-63, 154 n.27, 254 n.28
Politics, 4, 14, 20, 23, 26, 47-48, 51, 117, 121, 132, 134, 151, 154, 158, 166, 167-69, 171-73, 177, 215, 198, 219, 225, 226; cultural, 14-15, 179-97, 209, 227-28. *See also* Identity politics
Post-structuralism, 10, 14, 34, 70, 72, 75, 179, 181, 185, 199, 218, 220, 222, 227. *See also* Feminist theory and post-structuralism
Postmodernism, 7-8, 9, 12, 17, 64, 65, 66, 72, 75, 81, 103, 120, 169, 170, 175, 177, 199, 203, 205, 218, 221-22, 250 n.48, 258 n.4. *See also* Feminist theory and postmodernism; Modernism
Power, 4, 34, 46, 47, 48, 51-52, 57, 73, 75-6, 84, 86, 105-6, 118, 124-25, 144, 150, 157, 165, 166, 171-72, 173, 179-83, 186, 189, 190-91, 193, 205, 209, 211, 214, 218, 219, 220, 224, 226, 227

Pragmatism, 15, 208, 210, 212, 214, 224-26, 227, 257 n.19, 259 n.14
Pratt, Minnie Bruce, 24, 124, 154-55, 157-59, 161-64, 254 n.24
Process metaphysics, 34, 40-42, 67, 71, 243 n.79. *See also* Feminist theology and process theology
Protection, 116, 124-26, 132-33, 155, 157, 159-63
Public, 10, 19, 116-36, 160, 223, 233 n.4, 247 n.22, 248 n.26

Race/ethnicity, 1, 44, 71, 97, 102, 108, 115, 118, 119, 127, 128, 129, 132, 133, 139, 144, 146, 148, 151, 158, 178, 182, 202, 203, 209, 219, 250 n.13. *See also* Feminist theory and women of color
Racism, 12, 126, 130, 132, 158-59
Rape, 12, 156-60, 162, 215, 220, 222, 253 n.16
Relationality, 8-9, 37-39, 42, 46, 54-78, 155, 236 n.25. *See also* Essentialism and antirelationalism
Relativism, 23, 218-19, 221-24
Religious tradition(s), nature and status of, 7, 13-15, 32, 200-1, 203-4, 206, 209, 210, 213, 217; and theological task, 14-16, 29-30, 48-49, 192-97, 202, 207, 208, 212, 226-29. *See also* Past, nature and status of
Rich, Adrienne, 67
Rorty, Richard, 72, 207, 214, 225-26
Ruether, Rosemary Radford, 107-9, 111, 200-1, 217
Russell, Letty, 201, 217

Saussure, Ferdinand de, 103-4, 109, 111, 223
Schleiermacher, Friedrich, 82, 84-85, 93-96, 167, 230, 240-41 n.34, 242-43 n.72, 243 n.79
Schüssler Fiorenza, Elisabeth, 55, 69-73, 74, 76, 200-1, 217, 259 n.18
Scott, Joan, 171-73, 219, 226
Sex, 118, 119, 225, 245-46 n.4. *See also* Gender
Sexual orientation, 1, 108, 130-33, 203
Sin, 80, 96, 98, 138, 152
Smedley, Agnes, 151
Smiley, Jane, 151

Social constructionism, 101-8, 113, 175-76, 178, 220, 244 n.19

Solidarity, 4, 8, 9, 200, 202, 205, 207, 209, 213, 214, 217

Sophia, 36, 69, 77, 78

Spelman, Elizabeth, 102

Spirit, 80, 81-83. *See also* Holy Spirit

Spivak, Gayatri Chakravorty, 67, 155, 163

State, 124-25, 160-61, 171-72, 180, 182, 185, 222

Stern, Daniel, 91, 93

Story, 45, 111-15, 227, 229, 259 n.14

Subjectivity, 4, 6, 7-13, 14, 17-26, 32, 51, 55, 57, 67, 79-81, 99-103, 106-7, 108, 113, 137, 138, 141-45, 148-50, 153, 154, 155, 157, 158, 161, 166, 174-75, 193, 199-209, 213, 215, 218, 219-23; historicist conception, 8, 12, 15, 23-26, 202, 208, 210, 220, 221; modernist conception, 7-8, 25, 154, 216, 220, 221; as multiple, 12, 22-23, 59, 154, 161, 204-6, 209, 221, 231; postmodernist conception, 7-8, 25, 58-59, 77, 221

Suchocki, Marjorie Hewitt, 238 n.7

Suleiman, Susan, 143

Symbolism, 14, 36-37, 179-83, 185-86, 192-93; Christian, 185-86, 202, 227-31, 259 n.21

Tamez, Elsa, 201-2

Tanner, Kathryn, 3, 13-15, 16, 34, 47-49, 51, 221, 224, 227-28, 229, 259 n.14

Thandeka, 8-9, 229-30, 259 n.19

Theological anthropology, 137-38, 148, 152. *See also* Human nature

Theology, task of, 14-16, 26-27, 29-32, 184-87

Theory, role of, 2-3, 75, 165-66, 183-84, 187, 205, 215, 224

Thistlethwaite, Susan, 50, 71, 124

Time, 176-78

Tompkins, Jane, 104

Townes, Emilie, 50

Tradition(s). *See* Religious tradition(s)

Traditional Values Coalition, 119, 126

Trinity, 38, 81-83, 89-90

Ulanov, Ann and Barry, 89, 95, 237 n.2, 238 n.9

Universalism/universalizing, 3, 36-37, 39, 45-46, 49, 75, 99, 108, 113, 121, 122, 125, 134, 167, 170, 203-4, 206-8, 212, 217-21, 223-25, 248 n.36, 248 n.37, 249 n.41. *See also* Essentialism; Particularity

Victimization. *See* Women, as agents/victims

Violence, 124-25; against women, 159-63, 253 n.19; by women, 137, 138, 139, 145, 148, 150, 152. *See also* Rape

Visibility, 117-19, 128, 132, 134, 218, 248 n.31

Welch, Sharon, 169

West, Cornel, 25

Williams, Delores, 34, 42, 43-44, 45, 51, 203, 221, 238 n.8

Winnicott, D. W., 84-90, 93, 230

Woman/women, 4, 21, 74, 97, 99-103, 104, 105, 106, 111, 114, 167; moral ambiguity of, 11, 138, 141, 143, 145, 222, 228; nature of, 2, 11, 33, 137, 140-41, 148-50, 202, 204, 205, 208, 211, 213, 219

Womanist theology, 43-44, 98, 203, 238 n.8

Women, as agents/victims, 11, 137-53, 222

Women's experience, 2, 6, 8, 13, 21, 33-53, 83, 167-71, 199-200, 203-4, 206, 208, 210, 213, 217, 220, 221; African-American, 42, 43-44; appeal to, 4, 7, 198, 200-2, 204, 207-8, 212, 214, 225; cultural-anthropological accounts, 47-50; literary/textual accounts, 42-46; phenomenological accounts, 35-39; post-structuralist accounts, 50-52; and process metaphysics, 40-42; psychoanalytic accounts, 39-42, 84-93. *See also* Experience

Young, Iris Marion, 19, 55, 62, 63, 65